C. K. Law
Yu Cheung Wong
John Yat Chu Fung
Editors

HUSITA7–The 7th International Conference of Human Services Information Technology Applications: Digital Inclusion– Building a Digital Inclusive Society

HUSITA7–The 7th International Conference of Human Services Information Technology Applications: Digital Inclusion– Building a Digital Inclusive Society has been co-published simultaneously as *Journal of Technology in Human Services,* Volume 25, Numbers 1/2 2007.

Pre-publication
REVIEWS,
COMMENTARIES,
EVALUATIONS . . .

"**A**s someone who has been interested in and researching both the Information Society and the Digital Divide for over 20 years this was always going to be a title that WAS HARD TO RESIST. Having worked at the general level of the application of Information Society and digital exclusion theories and in the domain of organisational knowledge management, this volume offered a number of specific attractions. In the first place, it is located in the domain of social work/social welfare, with contributions from a mix of educators and practitioners in the field. It was STIMULATING to read accounts of research and practice that addressed the relationship between society, technology and the digital divide that were at once familiar, and unfamiliar, the latter owing to domain-specific perceptions. . . . STRONG MEDICINE, but it is relevant to other countries with indigenous populations and to anyone interested in any form of social inclusion. I look forward to seeing this volume in our own university library and would certainly recommend it to others."

Bill Martin, PhD
Research Director
School of Business
Information Technology
RMIT University, Melbourne, Australia

The Haworth Press, Inc.

www.HaworthPress.com

HUSITA7–
The 7th International Conference of Human Services Information Technology Applications: Digital Inclusion–Building a Digital Inclusive Society

HUSITA7–The 7th International Conference of Human Services Information Technology Applications: Digital Inclusion–Building a Digital Inclusive Society has been co-published simultaneously as *Journal of Technology in Human Services,* Volume 25, Numbers 1/2 2007.

Monographic Separates from the *Journal of Technology in Human Services*®

For additional information on these and other Haworth Press titles, including descriptions, tables of contents, reviews, and prices, use the QuickSearch catalog at http://www.HaworthPress.com.

The *Journal of Technology in Human Services*®, Volume 16 started in Spring 1999. Subscribers should note that Volume 1-Volume 15 were published under the title of *Computers in Human Services.*

HUSITA7–The 7th International Conference of Human Services Information Technology Applications: Digital Inclusion–Building a Digital Inclusive Society, edited by C. K. Law, DSW, Yu Cheung Wong, PhD, and John Yat Chu Fung, PhD (Vol. 25, No. 1/2, 2007). *A compelling selection of conference proceedings from HUSITA7, The 7th International Conference of Human Services Information Technology Applications that focuses on ways to facilitate a digital inclusive society.*

Web-Based Education in the Human Services: Models, Methods, and Best Practices, edited by Robert J. MacFadden, PhD, Brenda Moore, PhD, Marilyn Herie, PhD, and Dick Schoech, PhD (Vol. 23, No. 1/2/3/4, 2005). *"This information-rich book reflects the vitality and diversity of WBE in human services and invites instructors to move beyond conversion of their courses to re-examine the educational process of their curriculum." (Julie Birkenmaier, Associate Clinical Professor, Saint Louis University School of Social Work.)*

Technology-Assisted Delivery of School Based Mental Health Services: Defining School Social Work for the 21st Century, edited by Bhavana A. Pahwa, MA, LMSW (Vol. 21, No. 1/2, 2003). *"A MUST for any school social worker trying to incorporate technology into practice. The online resource guide is extensive and the chapter on technology assisted program evaluation will help any school social worker." (Vaughn Morrison, MSEd, MSW, Executive Director, Illinois Association of School Social Workers)*

Human Services Technology: Innovations in Practice and Education, edited by Hy Resnick, PhD, and Phoebe Sade Anderson, MSW (Vol. 20, No. 1/2/3/4, 2002). *"This book provides you with a full manual in each of the specific spheres of the various human relation professions, as well as the technical specificity required within each sphere of practice. In reality, this book is an updated manual of contemporary practice with a full and clear review of competence requirements and the empirical research evaluation of each practice endeavor." (Henry W. Maier, PhD, DShc, Professor Emeritus, University of Washington)*

Using the Internet as a Research Tool for Social Work and Human Services, edited by Goutham M. Menon, PhD (Vol. 19, No. 2/3, 2002). *Explores ways to use the Internet in many aspects of social work research, including the development of online studies and psychological testing.*

New Advances in Technology for Social Work Education and Practice, edited by Julie Miller-Cribbs, PhD (Vol. 18, No. 3/4, 2001). *"A valuable tool for educators who want to introduce students of social work to the numerous applications of technology within the field. . . . Goes a long way toward helping social work become proactive in its approach to technology integration within the field." (Sharon D. Johnson, PhD, Assistant Professor, Department of Social Work, University of Missouri, St. Louis)*

Using Technology in Human Services Education: Going the Distance, edited by Goutham M. Menon, PhD, and Nancy K. Brown, PhD (Vol. 18, No. 1/2, 2001). *"A refreshingly realistic and balanced collection. . . . Highlights many innovative eforts in both education and practice. Will be extremely valuable in courses on technology in social work, or for courses examining emerging trends in social work practice." (Paul P. Freddolino, PhD, Professor and Coordinator of Distance Education, School of Social Work, Michigan State University, East Lansing)*

Human Services Online: A New Arena for Service Delivery, edited by Jerry Finn, PhD, and Gary Holden, DSW (Vol. 17, No. 1/2/3, 2000). *Focuses on the ways that human services are using the Internet for service delivery, social change, and resource development as more and more agencies can be found on the Internet.*

Computers and Information Technology in Social Work: Education, Training, and Practice, edited by Jo Ann R. Coe, PhD, and Goutham M. Menon, PhD (Vol. 16, No. 2/3, 1999). *Discusses the impact that recent technological advances have had on social work practice and education. Social workers and educators will discover ideas and projects that were presented at a week long conference presented at the University of South Carolina College of Social Work. This unique book covers a wide range of topics, such as different aspects of technology applied to assist those in helping professions, how computers can be used in child protective cases in order to practice more effectively, social services via videoconferencing, and much more.*

Information Technologies: Teaching to Use–Using to Teach, edited by Frank B. Raymond III, DSW, Leon Ginsberg, PhD, and Debra Gohagan, MSW, ACSW, LISW* (Vol. 15, No. 2/3, 1998). *Explores examples of the use of technology to teach social work knowledge, values, and skills across the curriculum.*

The History and Function of the Target Cities Management Information Systems, edited by Matthew G. Hile, PhD* (Vol. 14, No. 3/4, 1998). *"Essential reading for anyone invested in improving the coordination and delivery of substance abuse services in large metropolitan areas." (Albert D. Farrell, PhD, Professor of Psychology, Virginia Commonwealth University, Richmond)*

Human Services in the Information Age, edited by Jackie Rafferty, MS, Jan Steyaert, and David Colombi* (Vol. 12, No. 1/2/3/4, 1996). *"Anyone interested in the current state of the development of human service information systems of all types needs to read this book." (Walter F. LaMendola, PhD, Consultant, Wheat Ridge, CO)*

Electronic Tools for Social Work Practice and Education, edited by Hy Resnick, PhD* (Vol. 11, No. 1/2/3/4, 1994). *"Opens a new world of opportunities for readers by introducing a variety of electronic tools available when working with various clients." (Ram A. Cnaan, PhD, Associate Professor, School of Social Work, University of Pennsylvania)*

Technology in People Services: Research, Theory, and Applications, edited by Marcos Leiderman, MSW, Charles Guzzetta, EdD, Leny Struminger, PhD, and Menachem Monnickendam, PhD, MSW* (Vol. 9, No. 1/2/3/4, 1993). *"Honest reporting and inquiry into the opportunities and limitations for administrators, managers, supervisors, clinicians, service providers, consumers, and clients. . . . A well-integrated and in-depth examination." (John P. Flynn, PhD, Associate Director for Instructional Computing, University Computing Services and Professor of Social Work, Western Michigan University)*

Computer Applications in Mental Health: Education and Evaluation, edited by Marvin J. Miller, MD* (Vol. 8, No. 3/4, 1992). *"Describes computer programs designed specifically for mental health clinicians and their work in both private practice and institutional treatment settings." (SciTech Book News)*

Computers for Social Change and Community Organizing, edited by John Downing, PhD, Robert Fasano, MSW, Patricia Friedland, MLS, Michael McCullough, AM, Terry Mizrahi, PhD, and Jeremy Shapiro, PhD* (Vol. 8, No. 1, 1991). *This landmark volume presents an original and–until now–unavailable perspective on the uses of computers for community- and social-change-based organizations.*

Computer Literacy in Human Services Education, edited by Richard L. Reinoehl and B. Jeanne Mueller* (Vol. 7, No. 1/2/3/4, 1990). *This volume provides a unique and notable contribution to the investigation and exemplification of computer literacy in human services education.*

Computer Literacy in Human Services, edited by Richard L. Reinoehl and Thomas Hanna* (Vol. 6, No. 1/2/3/4, 1990). *"Includes a diversity of articles on many of the most important practical and conceptual issues associated with the use of computer technology in the human services." (Adult Residential Care)*

The Impact of Information Technology on Social Work Practice, edited by Ram A. Cnaan, PhD, and Phyllida Parsloe, PhD* (Vol. 5, No. 1/2, 1989). *International experts confront the urgent need for social work practice to move into the computer age.*

HUSITA7–
The 7th International Conference of Human Services Information Technology Applications: Digital Inclusion– Building a Digital Inclusive Society

C. K. Law, DSW
Yu Cheung Wong, PhD
John Yat Chu Fung, PhD
Editors

HUSITA7–The 7th International Conference of Human Services Information Technology Applications: Digital Inclusion–Building a Digital Inclusive Society has been co-published simultaneously as *Journal of Technology in Human Services,* Volume 25, Numbers 1/2 2007.

The Haworth Press, Inc.

www.HaworthPress.com

HUSITA7–The 7th International Conference of Human Services Information Technology Applications: Digital Inclusion–Building a Digital Inclusive Society has been co-published simultaneously as *Journal of Technology in Human Services*®, Volume 25, Numbers 1/2 2007.

The development, preparation, and publication of this work has been undertaken with great care. However, the publisher, employees, editors, and agents of The Haworth Press and all imprints of The Haworth Press, Inc., including The Haworth Medical Press® and Pharmaceutical Products Press®, are not responsible for any errors contained herein or for consequences that may ensue from use of materials or information contained in this work. With regard to case studies, identities and circumstances of individuals discussed herein have been changed to protect confidentiality. Any resemblance to actual persons, living or dead, is entirely coincidental.

The Haworth Press is committed to the dissemination of ideas and information according to the highest standards of intellectual freedom and the free exchange of ideas. Statements made and opinions expressed in this publication do not necessarily reflect the views of the Publisher, Directors, management, or staff of The Haworth Press, Inc., or an endorsement by them.

Library of Congress Cataloging-in-Publication Data

International Conference for Human Service Information Technology Applications (7th : 2004 : Hong Kong, China)
HUSITA7– the 7th International Conference of Human Services Information Technology Applications : digital inclusion–building a digital inclusive society / C.K. Law, Yu Cheung Wong, John Yat Chu Fung, Editors.
     p. cm.
"Co-published simultaneously as Journal of Technology in Human Services, volume 25, numbers 1/2 2007."
Includes bibliographical references and index.
ISBN-13: 978-0-7890-3371-0 (hard cover : alk. paper)
ISBN-10: 0-7890-3371-2 (hard cover : alk. paper)
ISBN-13: 978-0-7890-3372-7 (soft cover : alk. paper)
ISBN-10: 0-7890-3372-0 (soft cover : alk. paper)
1. Social work education–Data processing–Congresses. 2. Human services–Data processing –Congresses. 3. Computers and people with disabilities–Congresses. I. Law, C. K., 1953- . II. Wong, Yu Cheung. III. Fung, John Yat Chu. IV. Journal of technology in human services. V. Title. VI. Title: HUSITA7. VII. Title: 7th International Conference of Human Services Information Technology Applications. VIII. Title: Seventh International Conference of Human Services Information Technology Applications. IX. Title: Digital inclusion–building a digital inclusive society.
HV11.I53 2007
361.3078'5–dc22

2006013907

This section provides you with a list of major indexing & abstracting services and other tools for bibliographic access. That is to say, each service began covering this periodical during the the year noted in the right column. Most Websites which are listed below have indicated that they will either post, disseminate, compile, archive, cite or alert their own Website users with research-based content from this work. (This list is as current as the copyright date of this publication.)

Abstracting, Website/Indexing Coverage . . . . Year When Coverage Began

- ****Academic Search Premier (EBSCO)****
    <http://search.ebscohost.com>. 2006
- ****Applied Social Sciences Index & Abstracts (ASSIA)
    (Cambridge Scientific Abstracts)**** <http://www.csa.com> 1993
- ****CINAHL (Cumulative Index to Nursing & Allied Health
    Literature) (EBSCO)**** <http://www.cinahl.com> 2006
- ****CINAHL Plus (EBSCO)**** <http://search.ebscohost.com> 2006
- ****INSPEC (The Institution of Engineering and Technology)****
    <http://www.iee.org.uk/publish/>. 1999
- ****LISA: Library and Information Science Abstracts
    (Cambridge Scientific Abstracts)****
    <http://www.csa.com/factsheets/list-set-c.php>. 2006
- ****Psychological Abstracts (PsycINFO)****
    <http://www.apa.org>. 1985
- ****Social Services Abstracts (Cambridge Scientific Abstracts)****
    <http://www.csa.com> 2000
- ****Social Work Abstracts (NASW)****
    <http://www.silverplatter.com/catalog/swab.htm> 1989
- ****Sociological Abstracts (Cambridge Scientific Abstracts)****
    <http://www.csa.com> 2000

(continued)

(continued)

(continued)

(continued)

- *Physics Abstracts (INSPEC–The Institution of Engineering and Technology) <http://www.iee.org.uk/publish/>* 2006

- *PSYCLINE <http://www.psycline.org>* 2006

- *Referativnyi Zhurnal (Abstracts Journal of the All-Russian Institute of Scientific and Technical Information–in Russian) <http://www.viniti.ru>* 1985

- *ScienceDirect Navigator (Elsevier) <http://www.info.sciencedirect.com>*. 2003

- *Scopus (See instead Elsevier Scopus) <http://www.info.scopus.com>*. 2003

- *Social Care Online (formerly CareData) <http://www.elsc.org.uk>* 1987

- *Solid State and Superconductivity Abstracts (Cambridge Scientific Abstracts) <http://www.csa.com/factsheets/solid-state-set-c.php>* 2006

- *Subject Index to Literature on Electronic Sources of Information <http://library2.usask.ca/~dworacze/SUB_INT.HTM>* 2004

- *SwetsWise <http://www.swets.com>* 2001

- *TOC Premier (EBSCO) <http://search.ebscohost.com>* 2007

- *zetoc (The British Library) <http://www.bl.uk>*. 2004

Bibliographic Access

- *Cabell's Directory of Publishing Opportunities in Educational Technology & Library Science <http://www.cabells.com>*

- *Magazines for Libraries (Katz)*

- *MedBioWorld <http://www.medbioworld.com>*

- *MediaFinder <http://www.mediafinder.com/>*

- *Ulrich's Periodicals Directory: The Global Source for Periodicals Information Since 1932 <http://www. bowkerlink.com>*

Special Bibliographic Notes related to special journal issues (separates) and indexing/abstracting:

- indexing/abstracting services in this list will also cover material in any "separate" that is co-published simultaneously with Haworth's special thematic journal issue or DocuSerial. Indexing/abstracting usually covers material at the article/chapter level.
- monographic co-editions are intended for either non-subscribers or libraries which intend to purchase a second copy for their circulating collections.
- monographic co-editions are reported to all jobbers/wholesalers/approval plans. The source journal is listed as the "series" to assist the prevention of duplicate purchasing in the same manner utilized for books-in-series.
- to facilitate user/access services all indexing/abstracting services are encouraged to utilize the co-indexing entry note indicated at the bottom of the first page of each article/chapter/contribution.
- this is intended to assist a library user of any reference tool (whether print, electronic, online, or CD-ROM) to locate the monographic version if the library has purchased this version but not a subscription to the source journal.
- individual articles/chapters in any Haworth publication are also available through the Haworth Document Delivery Service (HDDS).

As part of Haworth's continuing committment to better serve our library patrons, we are proud to be working with the following electronic services:

AGGREGATOR SERVICES

EBSCOhost

Ingenta

J-Gate

Minerva

OCLC FirstSearch

Oxmill

SwetsWise

FirstSearch

Oxmill Publishing

SwetsWise

LINK RESOLVER SERVICES

1Cate (Openly Informatics)

CrossRef

Gold Rush (Coalliance)

LinkOut (PubMed)

LINKplus (Atypon)

LinkSolver (Ovid)

LinkSource with A-to-Z (EBSCO)

Resource Linker (Ulrich)

SerialsSolutions (ProQuest)

SFX (Ex Libris)

Sirsi Resolver (SirsiDynix)

Tour (TDnet)

Vlink (Extensity, *formerly Geac*)

WebBridge (Innovative Interfaces)

LinkSolver

SerialsSolutions

SirsiDynix

TOUR

extensity

WebBridge

HUSITA7–
The 7th International
Conference of Human Services
Information Technology Applications:
Digital Inclusion–
Building a Digital Inclusive Society

CONTENTS

ICT IN SOCIAL WORK EDUCATION APPLICATIONS

SOCIAL INCLUSION

SOCIAL INCLUSION APPLICATIONS

KNOWLEDGE MANAGEMENT IN HUMAN SERVICES

KNOWLEDGE MANAGEMENT IN HUMAN SERVICES APPLICATIONS

ABOUT THE EDITORS

C. K. Law, PhD, was a graduate of the University of Hong Kong (1976 B.Soc.Sc, 1981 M.S.W.), the Chinese University of Hong Kong (1986 M.B.A.), and the University of California, Los Angeles (1988 D.S.W.). He is currently Associate Professor at the Department of Social Work and Social Administration, University of Hong Kong. He had served as the Head of Department from 1993-1997. His current researches are related to digital inclusion, management in human services, welfare reform, and community building and planning. He served as chairperson/treasurer/member of the executive/management committees of several welfare agencies. He had also served as a member of Legislative Council of Hong Kong, in 1995-97 and 1998-2004. In environment protection issues, he is currently a member of the Environment Campaign Committee and the Country and Marine Parks Board of the HKSAR government. He is also a member of the Commission on Poverty and the Commission on Strategic Development of the HKSAR government.

Yu Cheung Wong, PhD, is currently Assistant Professor in the Department of Social Work and Social Administration at the University of Hong Kong. He serves as a consultant for Fu Hong Society to develop and evaluate e-training modules for persons with mental disabilities. He is also a committee member in the Central & Western District Young Service District Committee, and a member of the Caritas Community Centre Advisory Committee–Mok Cheung Sui Kun. Dr. Wong has published research papers in areas such as ICT in Education and ICT in Human Services.

John Yat Chu Fung, PhD, is currently Director in the Information Technology Resource Centre at the Hong Kong Council of Social Service. He serves as a member of the Community Research Sub-Committee in ICAC, and a member in the Management Committee of the Hong Kong Cybersenior Network Development Association Ltd. He is a co-opt member in the Community Service Committee of the Hong Kong Computer Society as well as a member in the IT Easy Link Project Steering Committee of the Office of Government Chief Information Officer, SAR Government. Dr. Fung has been involved in numerous ICT in Human Services research and IT projects.

Preface

Colleagues in Hong Kong hosted the Seventh International Conference of Human Services Information Technology Applications (HUSITA7) in the summer of 2004. After one year of hard work of the contributors and the editors, this volume, incorporating several important contributions to the conference, was at last completed.

Information technology, being the crux of the Information Society, helps to keep information and knowledge flowing among individuals and organizations. Applications of information technology are efforts to actualize this connectivity among entities aiming at the enhancement of human welfare. HUSITA serves as the catalyst to this process and the efforts made by the contributors to this collection are supports to this mission.

This volume focuses on papers and applications relating to:

- ICT in social work education
- Social inclusion
- Knowledge management in human services

No matter if it was in attending HUSITA7, reviewing the articles, or preparing for this Preface, I found myself picking up new knowledge. I am pleased to present papers and applications from Hong Kong, India, Japan, as well as North America, Europe and New Zealand.

ICT IN SOCIAL WORK EDUCATION

Being a social work educator, I found very informative the articles on the learning object approach of e-learning for social work education (by

[Haworth co-indexing entry note]: "Preface." Law, C. K. Co-published simultaneously in *Journal of Technology in Human Services* (The Haworth Press, Inc.) Vol. 25, No. 1/2, 2007, pp. xxv-xxvi; and: *HUSITA7– The 7th International Conference of Human Services Information Technology Applications: Digital Inclusion–Building a Digital Inclusive Society* (eds: C. K. Law, Yu Cheung Wong, and John Yat Chu Fung) The Haworth Press, Inc., 2007, pp. xix-xx. Single or multiple copies of this article are available for a fee from The Haworth Document Delivery Service [1-800-HAWORTH, 9:00 a.m. - 5:00 p.m. (EST). E-mail address: docdelivery@haworthpress.com].

N. Ballantyne), the pedagogical and policy challenges in implementing e-learning in social work education (by A. Knowles), the relationship between technological content in social work education and the use of technology in social work practice (by E. Youn), and international collaboration in offering web-based teaching (by Y. C. Wong and D. Schoech). These articles provided new insights to the development and the use of information technology in professional training. Two other articles are related to the content of web-based learning, namely the incorporation of emotion (by R. J. MacFadden) and the inclusion of indigenous knowledge (by G. C. Dumbrill and J. R. Green). The adoption of Web CT for improving issues, such as intradepartmental communication and quality of teaching, is also discussed in application descriptions provided by B. D. Friedman and by T. Y. Lee.

SOCIAL INCLUSION

Digital inclusion is currently the key issue of discussion in international platforms as exemplified by the agenda of the World Summit on the Information Society held at Tunis, November 2005. In this volume, we have three articles addressing the relevant issues, namely, the effectiveness of digital government in bringing about social inclusion (by M. Asgarkhani), the impact of technical advances on assistive technology (by G. C. Vanderheiden), and the effect of self-efficacy of older persons in picking up ICT skills (by J. Lam and M. K. O. Lee). The implementation of a communication tool for the speech impaired and for people with multiple disorders which benefits children with cerebral palsy at schools is discussed in an application description by S. Bhattacharya, S. Sarkar, and A. Basu.

KNOWLEDGE MANAGEMENT IN HUMAN SERVICES

Managing knowledge in a human service organization is challenging and yet important to its ability to deliver quality services. Z. C. S. Leung in his paper proposes a "knowledge-as-process" perspective in knowledge management in social work. In addition, I. Kobayashi reports in an applications description on "SenSui" which serves as an information exchange platform of disability-related resources.

C. K. Law, DSW
Co-Editor

Object Lessons:
A "Learning Object" Approach
to E-Learning for Social Work Education

Neil Ballantyne

SUMMARY. Learning objects are bite-sized digital learning resources designed to tackle the e-learning adoption problem by virtue of their scale, adaptability, and interoperability. The learning object approach advocates the creation of small e-learning resources rather than whole courses: resources that can be mixed and matched; used in a traditional

Neil Ballantyne, BSc (Hons), is Learning Technology Manager, Scottish Institute for Excellence in Social Work Education, Room D001, David Stow Building, University of Strathclyde, 76 Southbrae Drive, Glasgow G13 1PP, Scotland, UK (E-mail: neil.ballantyne@strath.ac.uk.) (Project Website: http://www.storcuram.ac.uk).

The project described in this article is funded by the Scottish Institute for Excellence in Social Work Education: http://www.sieswe.org/.

[Haworth co-indexing entry note]: "Object Lessons: A 'Learning Object' Approach to E-Learning for Social Work Education." Ballantyne, Neil. Co-published simultaneously in *Journal of Technology in Human Services* (The Haworth Press, Inc.) Vol. 25, No. 1/2, 2007, pp. 1-16; and: *HUSITA7–The 7th International Conference of Human Services Information Technology Applications: Digital Inclusion–Building a Digital Inclusive Society* (eds: C. K. Law, Yu Cheung Wong, and John Yat Chu Fung) The Haworth Press, Inc., 2007, pp. 1-16. Single or multiple copies of this article are available for a fee from The Haworth Document Delivery Service [1-800-HAWORTH, 9:00 a.m. - 5:00 p.m. (EST). E-mail address: docdelivery@haworthpress.com].

1

or online learning environment; and adapted for reuse in other discipline areas and in other countries. Storing learning objects within a subject specific digital repository to enable search, discovery, sharing and use adds considerable value to the model. This paper explores the rationale for a learning object approach to e-learning and reflects on early experiences in developing a national learning object repository for social work education in Scotland. *doi:10.1300/J017v25n01_01 [Article copies available for a fee from The Haworth Document Delivery Service: 1-800-HAWORTH. E-mail address: <docdelivery@haworthpress.com> Website: <http://www.HaworthPress.com> © 2007 by The Haworth Press, Inc. All rights reserved.]*

KEYWORDS. E-learning, learning objects, digital repositories, web-based learning

INTRODUCTION

The emergence of the World Wide Web and web-based applications, the development of international interoperability standards and specifications, the widespread adoption within universities of virtual learning environments (VLEs)–such as WebCT and Blackboard, and the slow but steady diffusion of broadband access on campus and at home are creating the conditions for a significant step-change in the use of e-learning within higher education. The term e-learning is used here as a generic term, defined by the UK Joint Information Systems Committee (JISC) as "*. . . learning facilitated and supported through the use of information and communications technology*" (JISC, 2004). A recent JISC good practice guide stated that "e-learning can cover a spectrum of activities from supporting learning, to blended learning (the combination of traditional and e-learning practices), to learning that is delivered entirely online. Whatever the technology, however, learning is the vital element."

E-learning is not new to social work education and, despite concerns expressed by some commentators (Hick, 1999; Kreuger & Stretch, 2000), contemporary literature includes many case studies describing the successful integration of learning technology into social work curricula: notably through the use of computer-mediated discussions (for example: Bertera & Littlefield, 2003; Cooper, 2001; Hodge, 2004; Knowles, 2001; Massimo, 2003; Schoech, 2000) and multimedia case material (for example: Evans, Petrakis, & Swain, 2001; Seabury, 2003). However, growing evidence of the value of e-learning, and improvements in the technological infrastructure have not yet led to the widespread adoption of e-learning in social work education. In a recent audit of e-learning resources for social work education, commissioned by the UK Department of Health, Rafferty and Waldman (2003) reported that:

> The list of the range of available resources indicates that learners and educators are well-supported in the provision of resources related to knowledge management and research skills, although many of these are generic rather than social work orientated. However, in terms of content rich, interactive resources to support theory and practice related to different areas of social work, the resources available are very limited. (pp. 10-11)

Building e-learning capacity for social work education is problematic. The production of high quality e-learning resources is a skilled task, and digital resources can be very expensive to produce: a fact that, as Littlejohn (2003) points out ". . . *makes resource development only viable for courses with large student numbers or a sizeable budget.*" This is not a description of most schools of social work. Equally, although some publishers are venturing into the creation of digital learning resources, social work is not a market segment that will warrant significant investment–except where there is a crossover with mass-market subject areas (such as psychology or sociology).

In this context the idea of joint investment by schools of social work in the centralized production of e-learning content is a strategy that might seem to recommend itself. However, centralising content production may solve one problem only to create another: heavy investment in expensive content that is not widely adopted by educators. The history of educational technology is littered with examples of costly initiatives where the learning resources produced failed to diffuse beyond the initial sites of development. Several reasons have been identified for this problem including: problems with technical interoperability; the resistance and/or lack of skills and confidence of educators; and the "*not invented here syndrome*" (i.e., the alleged reluctance of educators to adopt a learning resource they were not involved in developing).

The problems of e-learning content creation and adoption are driving new developments in the field of learning technology that offer innovative ways of creating learning resources with a much higher degree of adaptability by educators and interoperability with systems. These developments include the emergence of a learning object approach to learning resource design and development (Littlejohn, 2003; McGreal, 2004; Wiley, 2000a); the arrival of learning object repositories for managing and sharing digital learning resources (Duncan & Ekmekcioglu, 2003); and the adoption of internationally agreed standards and specifications for learning object interoperability (Olivier & Liber, 2003).

This article will, firstly, discuss the rationale for a learning object approach and the role of learning object repositories; secondly, describe the way in which a collaboration between nine universities in Scotland is attempting to implement a learning object approach for social work education; and finally, explore some pedagogical issues and issues for the development of a learning object economy.

LEARNING OBJECTS
AND LEARNING OBJECT REPOSITORIES

Wiley (2000b) captured the essence of the learning object approach when he observed that ". . . *the fundamental idea behind learning objects is that instructional designers can build small (relative to the size of the entire course) instructional components that can be reused a number of times in different learning contexts.*" This idea of small, self-contained, reusable components that can be aggregated and disaggregated with other components has been borrowed from object orientated programming, though applied in the very different context of instructional design (Sosteric & Hesemeier, 2004).

Developing an understanding of the learning object approach is not helped by the many different definitions of learning objects within the literature: definitions that range from the very general to the highly specific (McGreal, 2004). One of the most widely cited definitions is that offered by Wiley (2003a): "*Any digital resource that can be reused to support learning.*" Downes (2004, p. 28-29) elucidates the approach by defining five key characteristics of learning objects. He argues that learning objects are, or ought to be:

- shareable–may be produced centrally but used in many different courses;
- digital–can be distributed using the Internet;
- modular–freestanding, non-sequential, coherent, unitary and capable of being combined with other resources;

- interoperable–capable of being used by different institutions using different tools and systems; and
- discoverable–users can easily locate useful educational resources.

It's an unfortunate fact–and a significant weakness–that the language and concepts associated with the learning object approach can seem clumsy, unfamiliar, and off-putting to most educators (Friesen, 2004). However, one of the main strengths of the approach is that it has a good fit with the way educators actually go about the business of course construction in the non-digital world. During a single lesson within a course on stress management a social work educator might use the following resources: an image of the endocrine system to illustrate the physical effects of stress; a diagram of a theoretical model of stressors in the environment; a table with reported research findings of stress levels amongst social workers; a learning activity where students self-assess their own stress levels. Each of these elements can be considered as separate assets used in the production of the course session, aggregated together for a particular educational purpose and combined with a narrative exposition offered by the educator. Each time the educator presents the lesson he or she might add new or updated content, or might recombine the assets and use them slightly differently for a class working at a different educational level, or for a different professional context such as school-based social workers. The resources described above, including the narrative exposition, could equally be made available as digital assets combined and recombined by educators in different ways to produce learning objects and delivered in the classroom or online.

This perspective on the way educators use learning resources calls into question the idea of the "not invented here syndrome." If the above characterisation is correct, then educators constantly reuse resources they did not invent, but want to be able to adapt them to the local context. The harder it is to adapt a resource, the less likely it is to be reused. In other words, the "not invented here syndrome" may actually be a "not adapted here syndrome." So, if educational content is wrapped up in a technology that makes it difficult to adapt–in large, integrated, monolithic slabs–it may not be easily adopted. Cuban (2001) notes that while few schoolteachers have readily adopted film, radio or television as routine classroom technologies, most have adopted overhead projectors, mimeographs and photocopy machines. The former are effectively content broadcast technologies with little scope for teacher control; the latter are all technologies that allow teachers to disaggregate content and present it in a manner and at a pace selected by them. The learning object approach offers a way of accessing digital learning resources that are adaptable, and that can be combined with other digital and traditional resources as the educator sees fit.

The degree of reusability of a learning object is a function of its "size" or scope, often described as the granularity of a learning object (Duncan, 2003a; South & Monson, 2000). Although there is a broad consensus that it is useful to think about the different degrees of granularity a learning object possesses, and that the degree of granularity has implications for the reusability of a learning object, there is no agreement in the literature on how best to describe these different degrees of granularity. The IEEE Learning Technology Standards Committee (2002) identifies four different levels of learning object aggregation or "functional granularity" of learning objects from the finest grained, such as a single image or other digital asset, through to the largest level of a complete certificated course:

- Level 1: The smallest level of aggregation, e.g., raw media data or fragments;
- Level 2: A collection of level 1 learning objects, e.g., a lesson.
- Level 3: A collection of level 2 learning objects, e.g., a course.
- Level 4: The largest level of granularity, e.g., a set of courses that lead to a certificate.

Others argue that the term learning object ought to be reserved for a collection of digital assets linked to a specific learning objective (Wagner, 2002) and would describe the lower levels of granularity–such as a single image or text fragment–as information objects and/or content objects.

Leaving aside these efforts to precisely define levels of granularity, the important point is that the more decontextualised and granular a learning object is, the more reusable it will be across a range of different contexts (South & Monson, 2000). But at the same time, the more granular a learning object is, the less educationally useful it will be: this has become known as the "reusability paradox" (Wiley, 2003b). For example, a graphical representation of a family in the form of a genogram may be a useful asset for an educator but will not, of itself, have much educational value. If we add a learning objective such as *"To enable students to appreciate the value of genograms for recording and analysing family relationships"*; a narrative description of the family over three generations; and a question such as *"In what ways might the historical relationship between Mrs. Green and her father be influencing her approach to managing her daughter's sexual behaviour?*"; then, by providing a specific context and focus, we will have created an educationally useful learning experience. The same image of the genogram, contextualised in a different way, could equally be used with student nurses studying genetic inheritance. South and Monson (2000) argue that, "*For our instructional needs, objects have the greatest potential for reuse when they center on a single, core concept. At this level, they can easily slip into another context while still retaining significant instructional utility.*"

Since collections of learning objects are designed to be used independently, and/or in combination with each other, the objects are of most value when stored in a database or repository with descriptions of their characteristics that are sufficiently rich to allow instructors to search for and find the resources they require. If the learning objects are to be shared by a large community of users and be capable of being exchanged with other repositories, then both the repositories and the descriptions of the learning objects need to be interoperable. Several international learning technology bodies–including major proprietary vendors–have been working together for several years to produce just such a set of international standards and specifications (Olivier & Liber, 2003) including standards for descriptions of learning objects, otherwise known as learning object metadata (IEEE Learning Technology Standards Committee, 2002).

Learning object repositories are special databases for sharing, storing, and searching for learning objects; they make learning objects discoverable and do so by using metadata. Metadata is commonly described as data about data and usually compared to the kind of information a library catalogue would hold about a book: typically cataloguing the book by author, date, title, place and date of publication, etc. Learning object metadata can include a number of different categories of metadata. The IEEE Learning Object Metadata specification (IEEE Learning Technology Standards Committee, 2002) includes: *technical metadata* describing the technical requirements and characteristics of the learning object; *educational metadata* that describes the educational and pedagogic characteristics of the learning object; and *rights metadata* describing the intellectual property rights and conditions of use for the learning object. Some repositories contain only metadata records of learning objects that are themselves stored at remote locations–the MERLOT repository *http://www.merlot.org* is a good example of this type. Other learning object repositories contain both learning objects and metadata and so are used to *locate* and *deliver* the learning object (Downes, 2004).

A learning object repository is not to be confused with a virtual learning environment (VLE) like WebCT or Blackboard–though it may store content that can be deployed within a VLE. A repository is more like a library containing digital resources where instructors can search, view and download educational content they will then use in the classroom, or upload into a VLE, or embed into the teaching and learning environment in some other way. Since a learning object could be a text-based file describing a learning activity–for example, an exercise designed to illustrate some issues about the different roles people take in group settings–the instructor may simply download the file, print, copy and distribute it by hand for use in a face-to-face class. Equally, an instructor could use a learning object repository to discover a multimedia case study of a family struggling to come to terms with a grandparent's Alzheimer's disease that she could download for presentation in the classroom using a data projector, and/or place on her school VLE for groups of students to review and discuss during an online discussion. So, in this sense, the learning object repository provides the infrastructure, and the learning object approach gives the design principles, that enable the sharing and discovery of educational resources that may be used to support learning in a traditional classroom and/or an online learning environment (Duncan, 2003b). The repository is neutral with regard to pedagogy, but the learning object will carry with it a greater or lesser degree of pedagogical specificity depending on its design and level of granularity.

THE LEARNING EXCHANGE

The Learning Exchange is a Scottish social work e-learning intiative funded by the Scottish Institute for Excellence in Social Work Education (a collaboration of all nine Scottish universities offering qualifying social work courses). The initiative was funded to achieve three aims: establish a national digital learning object repository for social work education; create high-quality, multimedia "learning objects," and collect and repurpose other content; and develop the skills and understanding of social work educators and trainers in embedding digital learning resources. This section will focus on the first two of these aims and the staff development element of the project will be discussed in a future article.

The initiative is using the Intralibrary learning object repository *http://www.intrallect.com/* as the storehouse for our content. Although this is a proprietary product it was selected because of the vendor's strong commitment to open standards and maximum interoperability with other systems. Since the repository was released–in late 2006–social work educators and learners who are authorised users have been able to gain authenticated access from their desktop using a normal web browser (Figure 1). They are able to search for resources by key word or phrase, or browse the repository using a specially designed social work education taxonomy. Once a suitable learning object is located it can be viewed within the repository and downloaded into the user's own system. Users are also be able to add Amazon style comments on individual learning objects they have used, and award a learning object a "star-rating" introducing a degree of user-contributed quality assurance. We intend developing this "recommender system" to enable users to share ideas and experiences about different ways of embedding the learning objects.

The initiative is commissioned to populate the learning object repository with learning objects from three different sources: new multimedia learning objects created from scratch; learning objects re-purposed from existing published learning materials–with the agreement of rights

FIGURE 1. Learning Object Repository Screenshot

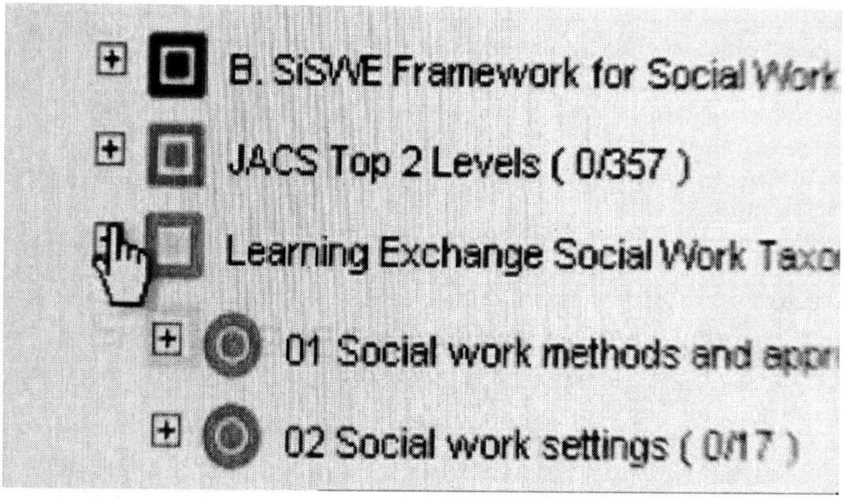

holders; and learning objects from educators, materials "as is" (i.e., material created by educators whether in the form of PowerPoint slides, text-based learning activities, handouts or other content deemed to be educationally useful). Our content is therefore likely to include everything from a short text-based learning activity on risk assessment, through an audio clip from a radio programme on autism, to an interactive multimedia case study highlighting attachment issues in child development. The remainder of this section will focus on our plans for the development of multimedia learning objects created from scratch.

The initiative is funded to create multimedia learning objects, and to assist in this process we have developed a set of priority areas and a learning object production process including: a content specification template (one for conceptual learning objects; and another for case-based learning objects); a two-stage peer review process to assure quality; and a Macromedia Flash-based software template for the actual learning objects (further information available from the Learning Exchange website *http://www.sieswe.org/learnx*). The content specification template and the peer review process have been adapted from the UCeL project: a medical education learning object project based at the University of Cambridge (Leeder & Morales, 2004; see *http://www.ucel.ac.uk/* for further information).

During the earlier start-up phase of the initiative the project team were acutely conscious that their success would be highly contingent on the extent to which the learning objects produced were actually used by educators. Every effort was made to ensure maximum consultation, collaboration, and buy-in from our user community. A project advisory group was established including one social work educator from each of the nine Scottish universities offering social work education in Scotland, plus other key stakeholders from employer groups and agency-based practice teachers. In addition, project staff held workshops at each of the partner universities–and at other conferences. The learning object specification template to capture the ideas of workshop participants, many of whom have been subsequently recruited as content providers for the learning objects. This was an arduous process and one that involved project staff in many hours of planning and negotiation. However, it is a process that has a good fit with the values of social work and should ensure a stronger sense of ownership of the learning objects created.

Our learning technology team developed a Flash template for the creation of learning objects with Macromedia Flash MX. Initial concerns about possible accessibility issues with Flash were assuaged by accessibility improvements in the latest version of Flash and a positive review of the new version published by the UK Royal National Institute for the Blind, *http://www.rnib.org.uk.*

This template–shown in Figure 2–has been designed to conform to accessibility standards; has a user-friendly standard approach to navigation; and includes other standard features such as a glossary, copyright information, references, information about the authors, etc. It is in itself designed to be a reusable shell for multimedia content and can incorporate text from an external XML file, making textual content easy to update and revise. Flash learning objects have the added advantage of being very scalable, so their size can easily be increased or decreased to be presented on a web page, or projected in a large lecture theatre, making them ideal for blending online and face-to-face learning.

At the same time as developing the learning object repository, developing multimedia content, and repurposing other material, project staff

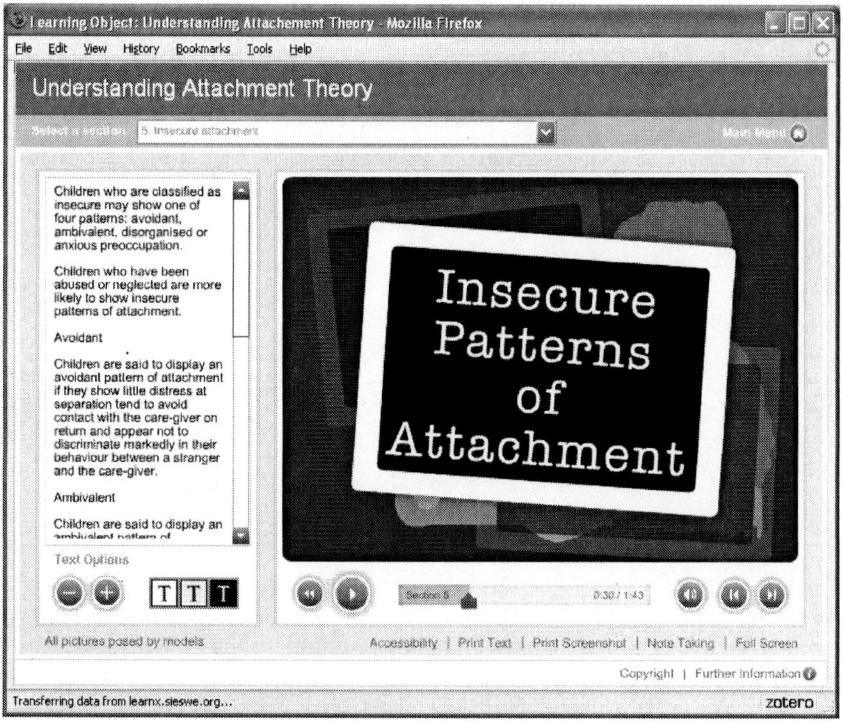

FIGURE 2. The Flash Template for the Multimedia Learning Objects

offered a national staff development programme to support social work educators in embedding the new materials imaginatively into the curriculum. At this early stage in the development of the project we cannot yet report on outcomes, but plans are in hand to evaluate two aspects of the project: the usability and accessibility of our learning objects; and the overall impact of the project on teaching and learning.

CONCLUDING ISSUES

The Learning Object Economy

One of the most promising aspects of a learning object approach to e-learning is the idea that widespread adoption of this approach may lead to the emergence of a learning object economy. This vision of a learning object economy has been described by some commentators as a new educational marketplace staked out by commercial content providers, with learning objects as educational commodities circulating in the new market (Purcel, 2003). However, just as there are different perspectives and approaches to engaging with the economics of the marketplace, so learning object economies may also be constituted in different ways. For example, Campbell (2003) argues that ". . . *within public sector education, we are more likely to see the emergence of micro-trading economies where resources are exchanged within and between recognised communities of practice.*" The idea of the "learning commons" is another perspective, with members of a particular community of practice sharing resources for the benefit of the wider community, underpinned by some agreed rules for exchange and the protection of intellectual property rights. The Creative Commons initiative in the U.S., *http://creativecommons.org/* is one approach to safeguarding the rights of authors whilst facilitating not-for-profit sharing within the wider community.

The products of the Learning Exchange initiative have been funded to benefit social work educators in Scotland; however, we have already started negotiations with colleagues in other educational sectors, different professional groupings, and other countries to collaborate and share content. Rather than make our content available on the open Internet for the consumption of all, we believe we are more likely to maintain incentives to develop new content, and build joint capacity, by reaching agreements with other agencies and institutions on resource exchange.

This approach is also necessary if we are to protect the intellectual property rights of content providers (a mix of university academics, commercial publishers, not-for-profit organisations, and governmental bodies) and at the same time capitalize on the capacity of Web-based delivery and international standards to make possible the trans-global exchange of learning objects for social work education. Resolving issues around intellectual property rights, and the more human and cultural dimensions of learning object use and exchange may, however, prove to be less tractable than the creation of content.

Pedagogical Issues

While the learning object approach offers great potential to create a pool of adaptable learning resources accessible by social work educators globally, the mere fact of accessing learning resources, however compelling, will not of itself necessarily lead to effective educational outcomes. Indeed, some commentators have become concerned that an undue emphasis on learning objects within the learning technology literature carries with it the risk of an inappropriate accent on content, and on individualised, information-transmission approaches to learning, rather than more constructivist and collaborative approaches. There are, however, three responses to this critique.

Firstly, if learning objects were designed only for individual users and consisted only of mini-multimedia lectures, concerns about information-transmission would be well-founded. However, a learning object might be a learning activity or a case study used as the focus for collaborative problem-based learning. And even the most conceptual and information-based learning object will only achieve its educational value if embedded in some kind of student learning activity that promotes internal dialogue for the learner and/or external dialogue with other learners and tutors: a fact that is recognised inside the project and forms the rationale for our staff development programme.

Secondly, and related to the first point, so long as learning objects are viewed as resources for educators to select and embed within the curriculum, then the instructor remains in charge of the learning design. The approach is designed to empower educators to embed materials in a range of ways but it will be the skill of the educators embedding learning resources in pedagogically sound learning designs that leads to effective learning, not the learning objects themselves. As Duncan (2003) argues, *"It is not the objects that form a coherent course but the skill of*

*the teacher in supplying a structure, a set of activities and occasional
course-specific material that act as the 'glue' to tie together the entire
course"* (p. 18).

Thirdly, within the learning technology community there is growing
interest in emerging standards for learning design (see, for example,
Koper & Tattersall, 2005). Learning design is about standardised ways
of describing learning activities and learning processes that could themselves be captured and shared inside a repository–a welcome emphasis
that does not contradict the learning objects approach but could work effectively alongside learning objects. E-learning is not all that there is to
learning for social work, and the learning object approach is not all that
there is to e-learning. It may help us to build a valuable and necessary
infrastructure for social work education in the 21st century, but is no
more likely to replace the need for intelligent educational design than libraries are likely to replace universities.

REFERENCES

Bertera, E.M., & Littlefield, M. (2003). Evaluation of electronic discussion forums in
    social work diversity education: A comparison of anonymous and identified partici-
    pation. *Journal of Technology in Human Services, 21*(4), 53-71.
Campbell, L. (2003). Engaging with the learning object economy. In A. Littlejohn
    (Ed.), *Reusing online learning resources: A sustainable approach to e-learning* (pp.
    35-45). London: Kogan Page.
Cooper, L. (2001). Using on-line technology to teach controversial issues. *New Tech-
    nology in the Human Services, 13*(3-4), 11-21.
Cuban, L. (2001). *Oversold and underused: Computers in the classroom.* Cambridge,
    MA: Harvard University Press.
Downes, S. (2004). Learning objects: Resources for learning worldwide. In R. McGreal
    (Ed.), *Online education using learning objects* (pp. 21-31). London: Routledge
    Falmer.
Duncan, C. (2003a). Granularization. In A. Littlejohn (Ed.), *Reusing online learning
    resources: A sustainable approach to e-learning* (pp. 12-19). London: Kogan Page.
Duncan, C. (2003b). Digital repositories: E-learning for everyone. Retrieved 17th January,
    2005, from http://www.intrallect.com/products/intralibrary/papers/elearninternational_
    edin_feb2003.pdf.
Duncan, C., & Ekmekcioglu, C. (2003). Digital libraries and repositories. In A.
    Littlejohn (Ed.), *Reusing online learning resources: A sustainable approach to
    e-learning.* London: Kogan Page.
Evans, S., Petrakis, M., & Swain, P. (2001). Experiencing practice complexities via
    computer: Multimedia innovation in social work education. *New Technology in the
    Human Services, 13*(3-4), 31-42.

Friesen, N. (2004). Three objections to learning objects. In R. McGreal (Ed.), *Online education using learning objects* (pp. 59-70). London: Routledge Falmer.

Hick, S. (1999). Rethinking the debate: Social work education on the internet. *New Technology in the Human Services, 12*(3-4), 65-74.

Hodge, D. (2004). Creating a virtual community of learners using WebCT: Lessons learned. *Journal of Technology in Human Services, 22*(3), 69-78.

IEEE Learning Technology Standards Committee (2002). Draft standard for learning object metadata. Retrieved 15th January, 2005, from http://ltsc.ieee.org/wg12/20020612-Final-LOM-Draft.html.

JISC (2004). Effective practice with e-learning: A good practice guide in designing for e-learning. Retrieved 15th January, 2005, from http://www.jisc.ac.uk/uploaded_documents/ACF5D0.pdf.

Knowles, A.J. (2001). Implementing web-based learning: Evaluation results from a mental health course. *Journal of Technology in Human Services, 18*(3/4), 171-187.

Koper, R., & Tattersall, C. (Eds.) (2005). *Learning design: A handbook on modelling and delivering networked education and training.* London: Springer Verlag.

Kreuger, L., & Stretch, J. J. (2000). How hypermodern technology in social work education bites back. *Journal of Social Work Education, 36*(1), 103-115.

Leeder, D., & Morales, R. (2004). Universities collaboration in elearning (ucel): Post-fordism in action. Retrieved 20th December, 2004, from http://www.ucel.ac.uk/documents/docs/LEEDERMORALES.pdf.

Littlejohn, A. (Ed.) (2003). *Reusing online learning resources.* London: Kogan Page.

Massimo, V.S. (2003). Integrating the webct discussion feature into social work courses: An assessment focused on pedagogy and practicality. *Journal of Technology in Human Services, 22*(1), 49-65.

McGreal, R. (Ed.) (2004). *Online education using learning objects.* London: Routledge Falmer.

Olivier, B., & Liber, O. (2003). Learning content interoperability standards. In A. Littlejohn (Ed.), *Reusing online learning resources: A sustainable approach to e-learning.* London: Kogan Page.

Purcel, J. (2003). Capitalizing on the learning object economy: The strategic benefits of standard learning objects. Retrieved 20th December, 2004, from http://www.learningobjectsnetwork.com/resources/LONWhitePaper_StrategicBenefits OfStandardLearningObjects.pdf.

Rafferty, J., & Waldman, J. (2003). *Building capacity to support the social work degree: A scoping study for the department of health e-learning steering group.* Southampton: University of Southampton.

Schoech, D. (2000). Teaching over the internet: Results of one doctoral course. *Research on Social Work Practice, 10*(4), 467-486.

Seabury, B. (2003). On-line, computer-based, interactive simulations: Bridging classroom and field. *Journal of Technology in Human Services, 22*(1), 29-48.

Sosteric, M., & Hesemeier, S. (2004). A first step towards a theory of learning objects. In R. McGreal (Ed.), *Online education using learning objects.* London: Routledge Falmer.

South, J.B., & Monson, D.W. (2000). A university-wide system for creating, capturing, and delivering learning objects. In D.A. Wiley (Ed.), *The instructional use of learning objects: Online version.*

Wagner, E.D. (2002). Steps to creating a content strategy for your organization. *eLearning Developers' Journal.* Retrieved 21st January, 2005, from http://www.elearningguild.com/pdf/2/102902MGT-H.pdf.

Wiley, D.A. (2000a). *The instructional use of learning objects.* Bloomington, IN: AECT.

Wiley, D.A. (2000b). Connecting learning objects to instructional design theory. *The instructional use of learning objects.* Retrieved 20th December, 2004, from http://www.reusability.org/read/chapters/wiley.pdf.

Wiley, D. (2003a). Learning objects–a definition. In A. Kovalchick & K. Dawson (Eds.), *Educational technology: An encyclopedia.* Santa Barbara CA: ABC-CLIO.

Wiley, D. (2003b). Learning objects: Difficulties and opportunities. Retrieved 20th December, 2004, from http://wiley.ed.usu.edu/docs/lo_do.pdf.

doi:10.1300/J017v25n01_01

Pedagogical and Policy Challenges in Implementing E-Learning in Social Work Education

Alan J. Knowles

SUMMARY. This paper provides a summary of the findings from in-depth interviews with thirty social work educators and administrators involved in developing and offering e-learning in their programs in Canada. Using qualitative data analysis, four interrelated categories were developed: Professional Challenges, Pedagogical Challenges, Faculty Challenges and Administrative Challenges. A large number of issues were identified in each of these categories. Six themes emerged from the study. These themes form a two-part framework for examining policy issues and implementation tasks. The findings have pedagogical and policy implications for social work educators who are implementing e-learning in their programs. doi:10.1300/J017v25n01_02 *[Article copies available for a fee from The Haworth Document Delivery Service: 1-800-HAWORTH. E-mail address: <docdelivery@haworthpress.com> Website: <http://www.HaworthPress.com> © 2007 by The Haworth Press, Inc. All rights reserved.]*

Alan J. Knowles, MSW, PhD, is a full-time instructor and former Chair, Social Work Program, Grant MacEwan College, 165 South Campus, 7319 29 Avenue, Edmonton, Alberta, Canada, T6K 2P1 (E-mail: knowlesa@macewan.ca).

[Haworth co-indexing entry note]: "Pedagogical and Policy Challenges in Implementing E-Learning in Social Work Education." Knowles, Alan J. Co-published simultaneously in *Journal of Technology in Human Services* (The Haworth Press, Inc.) Vol. 25, No. 1/2, 2007, pp. 17-44; and: *HUSITA7–The 7th International Conference of Human Services Information Technology Applications: Digital Inclusion–Building a Digital Inclusive Society* (eds: C. K. Law, Yu Cheung Wong, and John Yat Chu Fung) The Haworth Press, Inc., 2007, pp. 17-44. Single or multiple copies of this article are available for a fee from The Haworth Document Delivery Service [1-800-HAWORTH, 9:00 a.m. - 5:00 p.m. (EST). E-mail address: docdelivery@haworthpress. com].

KEYWORDS. Online learning, social work education, technology integration, implementation framework, program and policy development

Over the past six-to-seven years social work educators in Canada
have begun to offer online learning in their programs as a result of the
availability of new learning technologies, policy initiatives of the Federal and provincial governments, and a perceived need to incorporate
e-learning into curricula. Over the next few years, it is expected that
programs will continue to integrate e-learning as a way of responding to
learner needs and a rapidly changing higher education environment.

The purpose of this study was to identify and develop in-depth understanding of the issues and concerns of social work educators who were
implementing e-learning in their programs in Canada and provide recommendations for policy development. The primary research questions
that guided this study were "What are the challenges in implementing
e-learning in social work education?" and, "What are the implications
for policy development?" This paper will focus on the themes that
emerged from the study and summarize a two-part framework for examining pedagogical and policy issues in implementing e-learning in
social work education.

METHODOLOGY

In-depth interviews were conducted with 30 social work educators
and administrators who were implementing e-learning in their programs (Johnson, 2002; Tierney & Dilley, 2002). Participants were purposefully selected based on their involvement in online learning,
interest and willingness to participate in the study, and on the author's
perception of their ability to contribute to the study (Creswell, 1998;
Silverman, 2000b). Many of the participants were interested in the
study as an opportunity to engage in dialogue about their work and contribute to emerging knowledge of e-learning in social work education.
The participants were from 12 university social work programs from
western, central, and eastern Canada. Twenty-five participants were
faculty directly involved in teaching and developing online learning;
five were involved in program coordination, distance delivery, and instructional design consultation. The interviews were conducted between December 2001 and April 2002.

These educators had a broad range of experience and involvement in online learning and the use of other learning technologies. The majority of the faculty participants were between the ages of 40 and 60, had been teaching between 10 and 20 years and were assistant or associate professors in their respective programs. Ten were men and 15 were women. Two held non-tenure track teaching positions. Participants had multiple roles including teaching, the development of online learning, field education, administration of programs, technology leadership, program planning, and policy development.

Participants were involved in teaching a wide range of social work content, including practice skills courses. Of 44 courses taught by participants, 21 were offered in a fully online format, 11 were offered in a hybrid format (where some face-to-face class contact was replaced with online learning), and 12 were offered in a web-enhanced format (online learning activities and resources added to face-to-face classes). Eighteen of the fully online courses were offered to both distance and local students. Eight courses were offered to distance students only (three fully online and five hybrid courses). Six courses were offered to local students only (two hybrid courses and four in a web-enhanced format). Where distance students were involved in hybrid courses, students travelled to the university or regional sites for the face-to-face portion of the course.

Qualitative data analysis included coding of interviews and categorizing of segments, and identifying emerging themes. Field notes were kept throughout the data collection phase to reflect on emerging issues, questions, and themes. All participants were provided with a copy of their transcript for review, correction and comment, and were provided with the opportunity to review a draft of the findings. Four participants with several years experience in the use of learning technologies, online teaching, and administration of programs were asked to reflect on the findings and recommendations during the Fall of 2003. Their observations, feedback and recommendations were incorporated into the analysis.

FINDINGS AND THEMATIC ANALYSIS

Through analysis of the data a large number of findings were identified that are relevant for social work educators implementing e-learning in their programs. Initial and evolving coding of interviews led to the development of four interrelated categories: Professional Challenges, Pedagogical Challenges, Faculty Challenges, and Administrative Challenges (Knowles, 2004). Each of these are briefly summarized in Appendix A (Tables A1, A2, A3, A4). Six interrelated themes linked to program and policy development were also identified. These themes form a two-part framework for examining pedagogical and policy issues in implementing e-learning in social work education (see Figure 1). The first set of themes, transformation, alignment, and coherence provide a framework for examining policy issues and program development. The second set, faculty engagement, resources, and leadership provide a framework for examining implementation issues and tasks.

TRANSFORMATION

An overarching theme that emerged from this study was transformation. As a result of the influence of information and communications technologies (ICTs), implementing e-learning was requiring the educators in this study to rethink their goals, approaches to teaching and learning, and academic and administrative policies. Participants identified the need for social work educators to adapt to a rapidly changing, ICT-rich, higher education environment and take advantage of emerging learning technologies. Specific tensions included the need to clarify the motivation for incorporating e-learning, to respond to shifts and disruption to the teaching-learning process, and to carefully evaluate the fit of e-learning with the goals and traditions of social work education. They were also concerned about the effects of commercialization and competition in higher education, a perceived technological imperative, and the effect of e-learning on the quality of professional education.

This theme is also found in the literature on technology integration and higher education. It has been suggested that the integration of new information and communication technologies represents a paradigm shift for higher education, one with as much significance as the introduction of the printing press (Collis, 1996; Hafner & Oblinger, 1998; Van Dusen, 1997). ICTs are disruptive technologies that challenge established disciplinary traditions, introduce new pedagogical models, and require organizational and sociocultural change (Archer, Garrison, & Anderson, 1999; Szabo, 2002). The growing availability of e-learning is requiring programs and institutions to examine their goals, organizational structures and ability to respond to an increasingly wired and competitive higher education environment (Bates, 2000; Duderstadt, 1997, 2000; Graves, 1997; Hanna, 1998, 2003; Turoff, 1997; Van Dusen, 1997). In Canada, the Advisory Committee for Online Learning

FIGURE 1. Framework for Examining Policy Development and Tasks in Implementing E-Learning in Social Work Education

Transformation	• Shifting Context of HE • Influence of ICTs • Philosophical/Ideological Challenges • Pedagogical Challenges • Policies • Program and Organizational Structures
Alignment	• Philosophical Alignment • Pedagogical Alignment • Policy Alignment • Program Structure/Organizational Alignment
Coherence	• Congruence with the Values and Mission of Social Work Education • Professional Development and Socialization • Pedagogical Approach and Organization of Learning • Program Standards and Accreditation • Organizational Goals, Policies, Processes, Culture and Resources

Faculty Engagement	• Workload, Compensation and Recognition
	• Pedagogical Orientation, Interest and Skills
	• Faculty Choice
	• Faculty Dialogue
	  • Philosophical/Professional Dialogue
	  • Pedagogical Dialogue
	  • Policy and Program Development
	• Faculty Development

Resources	• Organizational
	  • Support
	  • Infrastructure
	• Pedagogical
	  • Course Development
	  • E-learning Resources and Learning Objects in Social Work Education
	  • Collaboration

Leadership	• Faculty • Program • Institutional • Profession-wide } Facilitating Dialogue Strategic Planning Securing Resources Policy and Organizational Alignment Sociocultural Change

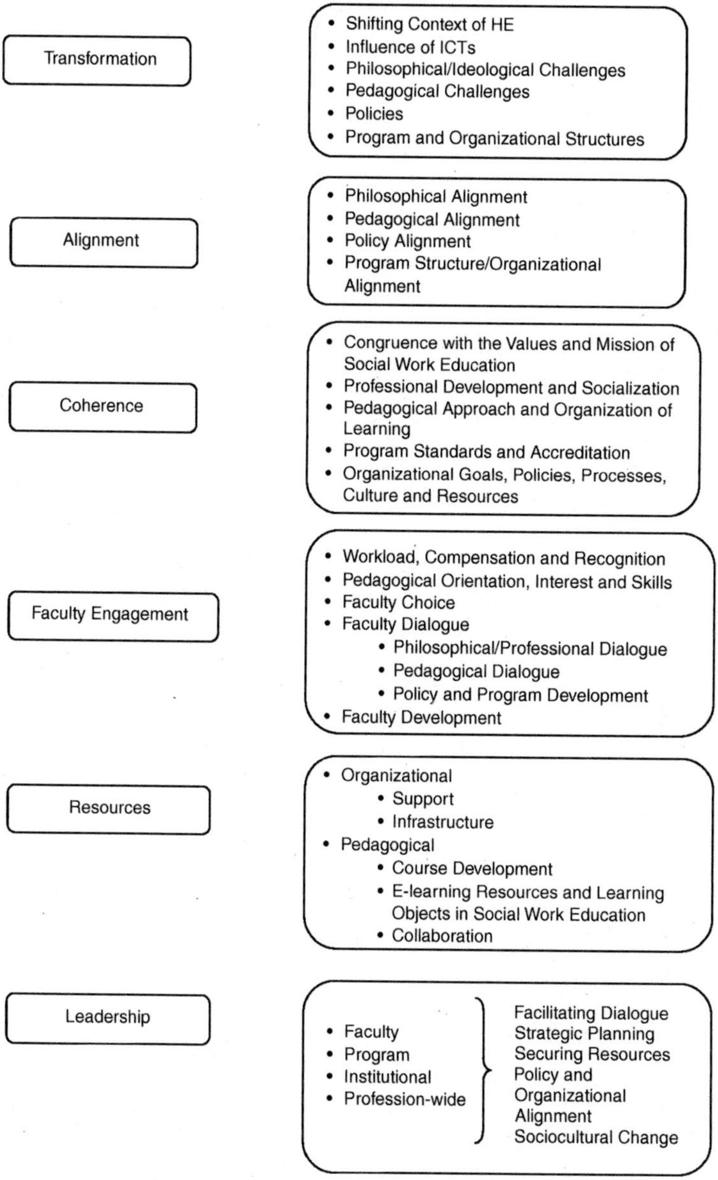

(2001) suggests there is an urgent need to implement a pan-Canadian plan to support the implementation of e-learning in higher education institutions.

Social work programs are not immune from these forces, and are having to incorporate and adapt to the influence of ICTs and e-learning (Freddolino, 2002; Sandell & Hayes, 2002). Implementing e-learning will require that programs transform and adapt a wide range of practices and policies in order for diffusion to expand beyond the initial innovations of individual faculty and programs. Future integration of e-learning will require an expanded and concerted effort if programs are to move e-learning from the initial stages of implementation to an integral part of mainstream social work education.

ALIGNMENT

A second key theme that emerged from this study was the need for alignment: philosophical alignment, pedagogical alignment, policy alignment, and program and organizational alignment.

Philosophical Alignment

On a philosophical level, participants conveyed the need to ensure that their programs and initiatives are congruent with the values and mission of the profession. This included resolution of tensions involving core values such as equity, and ethical principles such as confidentiality, privacy, and the responsibility to educate competent practitioners. On a pragmatic level, participants recognized that programs operate within an institutional environment guided by vision and mission statements, goals, and strategic plans, and within the context of a rapidly changing higher education environment. On a societal level, recent shifts to neo-liberalism and fiscal restraint for social services and higher education in general have had a significant impact on both the social service delivery system and higher education. Professional programs must also meet external accreditation standards which have not kept pace with the rapid evolution of e-learning and other learning technologies. Freddolino (2002) observes that in social work education, there really is no choice. He asserts that social work educators need to recognize that ICTs are here to stay and that they will need to find ways to resolve these tensions. The participants in this study had begun the process of identifying and resolving the professional challenges identified in Table A1, Appendix A.

Pedagogical Alignment

Participants acknowledged that the use of e-learning requires significant shifts in how learning is designed, offered, and evaluated. E-learning required new skill sets for both faculty and students, increased knowledge of pedagogy and instructional design, and major shifts in the role of the instructor. It also meant finding solutions to the professional and pedagogical challenges involved in the loss of face-to-face interaction and immediacy and ensuring opportunities for professional socialization.

Aligning pedagogy is a major challenge and necessary task if social work educators are going to successfully implement and sustain e-learning in their programs. It requires an examination of curricula, integrating learning models that are appropriate for both social work education and online learning environments, balancing asynchronous and synchronous learning, the ability to teach in online environments, developing new approaches to assessment and evaluation, and resources to develop high quality interactive learning experiences that are specifically designed for a broad range of social work content and professional skill development.

Garrison, Anderson and Archer (2000, 2001, 2003) have developed a framework for understanding and researching computer mediated communication in distance education. Based on the assumption that critical thinking is best achieved in a community of inquiry, their model incorporates three overlapping elements: social presence, cognitive presence, and teaching presence (Garrison et al., 2003). The amount of interaction and the level of social, cognitive, and teaching presence integrated into the instructional design of e-learning environments are particularly important for social work and other human service educators, especially as they relate to professional socialization.

Policy Alignment

Participants identified a number of areas for academic and administrative policy development and alignment in their programs and institutions (see Table B1, Appendix B). Academic policies included developing clear expectations and guidelines for students, revision of participation policies, policies that address confidentiality, privacy and security in online learning environments, teaching expectations and guidelines for faculty, faculty development, assessment processes, clarification of the roles of various people involved in developing and managing online learning environments, and accreditation policies and standards.

Administrative policies included workload and compensation policies, recognition and reward processes, policies supporting shifts in faculty roles, faculty knowledge and skill requirements, and intellectual property and ownership. They also included policies governing funding, tuition, and program quality. The alignment of both academic and administrative policies will require a significant commitment on the part of program leaders and their institutions.

Program Structure and Organizational Alignment

Several structural and organizational barriers were identified, including restrictions in the movement of students between distance and on-campus programs. Cost recovery funding and tuition fee structures for distance programming represented an equity concern for participants. Differential funding and tuition fee structures have generally been rationalized with the argument that the increased costs of distance learning are justified by the increased access provided to learners. This was less of an issue when distance education students were separated in their learning by both geography and learning model, typically a self-paced tutor model supplemented with audiovisual materials and occasional contact with other students through audio or video conferencing. Given that e-learning is blurring the boundaries between on-campus and distance programming, integrating the administration and funding of distance and on-campus learning is an important area for program and organizational alignment.

A further area of organizational development is the development of partnerships with other social work programs to share in the cost of development of e-learning. To date, there has been little collaboration between Canadian Social Work programs in developing e-learning. Exploiting the benefits of inter-program collaboration would require that programs align their policies to facilitate collaboration and sharing of e-learning resources.

The literature reflects the need for philosophical, pedagogical, program, and policy alignment in social work education. Social work educators have expressed concerns about professional socialization, the loss of face-to-face interaction and the quality of learning in distance education programs (Siegel, Jennings, Conklin, & Napoletano-Flynn, 1998). Similar concerns have also been identified about the use of e-learning in social work education (Collins, Gabor, Coleman, & Ing,

2002; Kreuger & Stretch, 2000). Butterfield (1998) and Schoech (2002) note that social workers have been slow to adopt technology compared to other sectors of society, however, increasing access to technology and the changing nature of work and service delivery are influencing the profession's need to integrate technology. Developing skills in the use of ICTs in social work is viewed as crucial for the profession, educators, and students (Butterfield, 1998; Cummins & Hamilton, 2000; Freddolino, 2002; Gonchar & Adams, 2000; Grant Thornton & CS/RESORS, 2000; MacFadden, 2002; Lawrence-Web, 2000; Miller-Cribbs & Chadiha, 1998; Sandell & Hayes, 2002).

The need for policy and organizational alignment to integrate e-learning is also identified in the literature (Gellman-Danley & Fetzner, 1998; Olcott, 1996a). A number of authors have suggested that the rapidly evolving context of higher education, including the integration of ICTs, is creating a need for higher education institutions to reexamine their policies, cultures and organizational structures (Bates, 2000; Duderstadt, 1997; Graves, 1997; Hanna, 1998, 2003; Turoff, 1997; Van Dusen, 1997). In social work education, Blakely (1992) identified the need for programs to examine and modify policies before they consider involvement in distance education initiatives. Although Blakely's recommendations predate the use of online learning, many of the issues he identified continue to apply to the implementation of e-learning in social work education. For example, Blakely recommended the need for revised incentives and rewards for faculty involved in distance education, revision of both academic and administrative policies, the importance of preparing faculty to teach in media-rich versus face-to-face environments, and the need to develop adequate teaching resources. Many participants in this study commented on the rapid adoption of e-learning in their programs and felt there had been insufficient planning and policy development. Ashery (2001) found that while many schools were involved in some form of distance education, most did not have a strategic plan for the implementation of technology. When participants were asked about strategic planning, only two programs had developed strategic plans at the time of our interviews.

COHERENCE

The importance of achieving and maintaining coherence emerged as an important underlying theme for the participants. Given that ICTs disrupt and challenge strongly-held beliefs and educational practices, participants were concerned about how social work education hangs together in e-learning environments. Coherence was important for participants on several levels: maintaining high quality educational experiences and program standards, professional accountability, and meeting accreditation standards. Important questions identified included: Is the use of e-learning congruent with the values, beliefs, skill sets, and standards of particular programs? How does e-learning fit with the needs of learners? What is an effective balance between asynchronous and synchronous learning? What strategies can be used to ensure high levels of interaction and enhanced observational opportunities? What resources are required to effectively offer social work curricula in e-learning environments? What aspects of programming and levels course are not suited for e-learning, and what format (fully online, hybrid, supplemental)?

Coherence was also important on a programmatic and organizational level. The participants noted that as social work educators rethink curricula and integrate e-learning, they also need to rethink how program organization and practices support or impede new and flexible approaches to learning. Important questions they identified included: How does e-learning fit with the vision and mission of the program? Does the program have a strategic plan for the integration of e-learning and other learning technologies? How is the learning organized and sequenced? Who should be involved? Does e-learning fit with overall institutional goals? Does the program have the resources to support well designed and high quality e-learning? What new organizational structures are required to create efficiencies, collaborate, and compete in a rapidly changing higher education environment? Has the program and institution realigned academic and administrative policies to support e-learning?

FACULTY ENGAGEMENT

Faculty engagement emerged as a fourth key underlying theme from this study. The metaphor of engagement seems particularly relevant, as it reflects an important concept in social work practice theory. Participants stated that implementing e-learning was contingent on a number of factors including faculty interest and preferred teaching style, having the time to learn new skills, knowledge of instructional design, a shift in teaching role and identity, compensation, and revised faculty evaluation and recognition processes. Without significant effort to engage social work faculty, it is unlikely that the implementation of e-learning will move beyond small scale projects, with the exception of those programs already committed to integrating e-learning in existing distance programming. An important underlying question then is: How will the majority of social work educators who are not yet involved in e-learning get from here to there?

A key aspect of engagement identified was the need for faculty dialogue on a number of levels that include: philosophical dialogue, pedagogical dialogue, and dialogue and input into program planning and policies. Participants felt there had been insufficient dialogue within their programs about these issues and insufficient preparation and planning for the implementation of e-learning. The speed of technology integration and sense of urgency to adopt e-learning in a competitive higher education environment had simply outpaced the opportunity for in-depth dialogue about their questions and concerns.

Participants also identified a need for dialogue with faculty at other social work programs. Most were unaware of initiatives in other social work programs in Canada, or conferences such as the Annual Technology Conference for Social Work Education and Practice hosted by the University of South Carolina or HUSITA (Human Services Information Technology Applications). They expressed high interest in opportunities to learn and consult with other social work educators involved in e-learning. Several commented that they were looking forward to our interview as an opportunity to engage in dialogue about e-learning. Another key aspect to faculty engagement is the need for custom-designed and proactive faculty development. Given the significant pedagogical and faculty challenges identified by participants, faculty development initiatives need to include a range of new technical and pedagogical skills, a focus on issues specific to e-learning in social work courses, access to instructional design consultation, and ongoing support. Faculty development could also involve collaboration, exchange and consultation with faculty in other social work programs as part of the expanded dialogue noted above.

A final key aspect of faculty engagement was that of faculty choice. Several participants emphasized the need for faculty (and student) choice of involvement in e-learning. In this regard, some programs had decided to make involvement in e-learning voluntary. This was both as a matter of principle and a specific implementation strategy to encourage early adopters and intrinsically motivated faculty to experiment, gain success and provide modeling and support to other faculty. In other programs, participants were less clear about whether or not faculty had the option of being involved in e-learning. The issue of voluntary involvement in e-learning will be a difficult and delicate one for program administrators to deal with, given the challenges identified in this study and the strong tradition of academic freedom in higher education. At the same time, faculty who are not involved may find they are unable to fully participate in a technology-rich higher education environment in the not-too-distant future. It is likely that continued integration of learning technologies will require faculty to use e-learning, and in two instances participants commented that their programs had begun to include e-learning skills and knowledge in hiring criteria for new faculty.

Given the magnitude of changes required to implement e-learning, social work programs will need to be proactive in their engagement of faculty. Many of these issues have been identified in the previous literature in both social work and education. For example, Blakely (1992) recommends the development of incentives and rewards and enhanced faculty development for social work faculty involved in distance education. Likewise, Ashery (2001) recommends that social work educators should work with their universities in revising tenure policies to recognize technology integration. Padgett and Conceao-Runlee (2000), in evaluating a technology training program for social work educators, identify the need for faculty development, the need for faculty input into faculty development programming, and recommend that faculty development initiatives be linked to rewards, workload, and promotion and tenure processes.

These barriers are not specific to social work educators and similar recommendations have been made in relation to higher education faculty in general (Olcott, 1996a, 2000; O'Quinn & Corry, 2002; Wolcott, 2003). Olcott (1996b, 2000) emphasizes that faculty involvement is central to adapting to alternate learning environments and that it is "imperative that institutions address faculty policy issues if distance education (is) to become an integral part of the academic culture" (Olcott, 1996b, p. 10). Olcott (2000) suggests there is a need for complete restructuring of compensation and reward structures, a need for enhanced knowledge of instructional design and faculty development, and revised tenure criteria that value innovative teaching and technology integration. Wolcott (2003), in a comprehensive review of the literature on faculty participation in distance education, makes a similar observation: "Accommodating faculty time and effort associated with distance teaching, the creation of online materials, and digital scholarship challenges the existing system for acknowledging and rewarding faculty for their teaching, research, and service" (p. 550). Wolcott identified several key disincentives for faculty participation including demand on faculty time, workload, diversion from research activities, especially for non-tenured faculty, and lack of recognition in promotion and tenure. COHERE (2002), a group of Canadian educators collaborating on issues related to shared learning objects, also identify the need for increased emphasis on the scholarship of teaching as a component of recognition processes.

RESOURCES

The need for resources to develop and implement high quality e-learning in social work education was the fifth key theme. While many participants felt it was possible to achieve high levels of interactivity and positive learning outcomes, they also emphasized that developing effective online learning was contingent on having resources and support. In particular, there is a need for the development of e-learning resources that specifically focus on social work content and skills that are flexible and can be re-purposed. The lack of e-learning resources in social work education is a serious barrier to implementation.

Participants were concerned about e-equity and differential tuition fees for distance students. Olcott (2000) recommends the radical position that universities stop the practice of supporting distance education through cost recovery funding. Given the organization and current funding structures of higher education in Canada, it is unlikely that implementing Olcott's recommendation is realistic without a significant infusion of public resources. At the same time, his point is well taken and helps bring into focus several resource tensions that social work education must deal with: a limited ability to generate revenues, a philosophical commitment to access and equity, expanding mandates and learner driven demand to integrate e-learning, and increasing competition from other Canadian and international universities.

In light of the resource demands of e-learning, programs will need to find ways to access new funding through their university or other sources, generate further efficiencies, or increase revenues through tuition fee increases. The latter is the least palatable of these strategies given social work educators' commitment to equity, publicly funded higher education, and their concerns about the commercialization of higher education. Without securing additional resources, it is unlikely that large scale implementation will be sustainable in the long run, with the exception of programs that are in a position to be able to generate or secure additional funding. Depending on what resources become available, it is possible that programs will become e-learning "haves" and "have nots."

The need for resources is also identified in the literature. Blakely (1992) noted the need for resources to develop learning materials for social work distance education. More recently, as programs adopt e-learning for distance and on-campus programming, this need has intensified. Cummins and Hamilton (2000) note that: "To date, few technology-based products are available for integrating technology and imagery into social work classrooms and social service organizations" (p. 5). Based on a review of the literature, they identify a number of technology gaps including the need for technology-based learning materials for all levels of social work education and technology training resources for social work faculty.

LEADERSHIP

The sixth underlying theme was the importance of strong leadership to initiate, support and sustain the significant pedagogical and administrative shifts required to implement e-learning. Leadership tasks included the need to develop revised vision and mission statements and strategic plans for implementing e-learning in social work education programs. Several participants emphasized the need for strong leadership to transform faculty roles, introduce new approaches to teaching and learning, and revise policies and practices. A need for leadership on four levels was identified: faculty and disciplinary leadership, program administration, institutional leadership, and profession-wide leadership. In reviewing the findings, expert participants (pseudonyms) reemphasized the importance of program and institutional leadership:

> There is a real need for social work deans and directors who have e-learning programs to effectively advocate for resources, research, ethical practice in teaching online, and to be proactive in pursuing partnerships and cooperation, rather than getting into a competitive position with other schools of social work. (Maureen)

> I also agree with your recommendation for reviewing and adjusting a wide range of academic and administrative policies and practices to respond to the challenges of e-learning. This has not been adequately addressed at my institution. (Susan)

Several participants conveyed that their programs had been support-ive and encouraging in their development of e-learning. In two in-stances, social work faculty had been the first to implement online learning in their university. Many of the participants provided informal leadership in their programs as a result of their interest and expertise in e-learning. Some programs had created technology committees to pro-vide direction and leadership to programs. As noted, only two programs had developed strategic plans for the integration of e-learning. Other programs had developed elements of strategic plans, for example, business plans, and a few programs had established technology com-mittees. In some programs, participants were the only faculty involved in e-learning and had forged informal relationships with colleagues from other disciplines in the university with similar interests. In a few examples, programs had created technology leadership or coordination positions.

The need for strong leadership is also identified in the e-learning lit-erature. Implementing ICTs requires significant institutional change, vision, and leadership from senior levels of institutions (D'Antoni, 2003; Mason, 2003). Beaudoin (2003a, 2003b) suggests that while indi-vidual faculty may continue to experiment with learning technologies, wide scale or efficient systematic adoption will not occur without strong leadership, and that there is a need for "new millennium thinking" in or-der to adapt to an information economy in a competitive higher education environment. The importance of strategic planning in implementing e-learning is also identified by Bates (2000), Ashery (2001), and Haché (1998). In this regard, several participants expressed concerns about a lack of planning in the rapid adoption of e-learning in their programs.

DISCUSSION

The challenges and themes identified in this study have important implications for social work educators and administrators who are im-plementing e-learning in their programs. The large number of profes-sional, pedagogical, faculty, and administrative challenges identified by participants is daunting, and addressing these challenges and underly-ing themes will require a substantial commitment of time, leadership and resources. Resolving these challenges will also require substantial shifts in how learning and programs are organized, revised policies and organizational structures. The overall implication is that there is a lot of work to be done, likely in a short period of time, in order for social work educators and programs to integrate e-learning and remain competitive in a rapidly changing higher education environment. A summary of the recommendations generated from this study is in Appendix C.

Given the limited resources available to social work education programs, there are a number of possible strategies that social work educators could consider to support the continued integration of e-learning in their programs. The first is increased lobbying of their universities and respective departments of higher education for additional resources to implement e-learning. Social work programs need to make a strong case for support, given their limited ability to generate revenues and public service mandate. There is a limit to how much tuition fees can continue to rise and continue to attract students into social work and other human services professions. Governments have, or should have, a vested interest in supporting professional programs that provide important public services. The need for technology integration in social work education programs was also identified as a high priority in a recent study of the social work sector in Canada (Grant Thornton & CS/Resors, 2000).

Secondly, social work educators and programs could collaborate with other programs and jurisdictions to develop online learning, and share resources and other initiatives such as faculty development and exchange. None of the participants had been involved in collaborating in the development or exchange of online courses or e-learning resources at the time of our interviews. Some programs had been involved in collaboration in regional initiatives that were non-competitive in nature. Key challenges involved in collaboration include venturing beyond traditional programming, institutional and geographic boundaries, resolving concerns about competition, and realigning policies that impede collaboration.

As e-learning and other forms of distributed learning expand in programs, it will be a challenge for social work educators to find ways to collaborate in an increasingly competitive higher education environment, align their initiatives with the philosophical foundations of the profession, and rethink how their programs are offered. It is likely that a continued demand for flexible access to learning will require programs to become more creative in how courses and programs are offered. Competition is likely to come not only from other Canadian Social Work Programs, but also from programs in other countries, especially for professional degrees at the graduate level. Government departments of higher education are likely to continue to promote the goals of flexible access to higher education through higher education policy and funding initiatives.

A third and related strategy is that programs could advocate with their respective provincial governments and the Federal Government to support the development of a national organization to support innovation in social work education, including the development of e-learning resources. At the present time, there is no learning object repository for social work educators in Canada, and limited resources on an international level. Social work is not listed as a topic area or discipline in repositories such as MERLOT (2005) and CAREO (2005). MERLOT does have some resources such as Chipper Online (2005) accessible through a general search. Commercially funded repositories, such as course resources hosted by WebCT (2005) and Blackboard (2005) are beginning to include a small number of social work e-packs and course cartridges. Although publishing houses are beginning to bundle e-learning resources with commercially available textbooks, there are very few resources focused specifically on social work content. Much of what is available is from related disciplines such as psychology, or marketed under generic topics such as "counselling." While some of these resources may be useful for social work educators, they require extensive time to locate and determine whether particular elements are appropriate for social work courses. Further, the pedagogical approach may not be suited for social work learning, or incorporate relevant local examples. Useful elements may not be accessible without purchasing the entire package and lack a social work orientation.

From a public policy perspective, leveraging collaboration amongst programs could be an effective strategy to assist social work educators to contribute to the vision for a pan-Canadian Learning System as advocated by the Advisory Committee for Online Learning (2001). Two examples from other countries are the Social Policy and Social Work Subject Centre of the Higher Education Academy, a support network for 24 disciplines in the UK, and the Stòr Cùram Learning Object Repository hosted by the Scottish Institute for Excellence in Social Work Education (SIESWE, 2005; Stòr Cùram, 2005; SWAP, 2005). These initiatives have been developed to provide online e-learning resources for social work educators that include information on learning and teaching in e-learning environments, learning object exchange, a discussion forum for social work educators, coordination of funding initiatives, and the development of innovative projects. The development of similar initiatives in Canada would require both funding and willingness for programs to collaborate in the development and exchange of e-learning resources. A fourth strategy is to develop and extend partnerships with commercial publishing houses to develop e-learning resources and integrate these with customized print, video, and other digital resources.

Given the large number of challenges identified by participants in this study, more effort needs to be directed towards faculty engagement. In particular, there is a need for enhanced faculty dialogue about the professional, pedagogical, policy, and program implications in integrating e-learning. In many instances participants felt that their programs had adopted e-learning without sufficient dialogue or planning. The need for enhanced leadership was also a key implementation theme.

CONCLUSION

This paper summarizes the findings, themes, and recommendations from a study of 30 social work educators and administrators who were implementing e-learning in their programs in Canada. A framework for examining policy development and tasks in implementing e-learning in social work education has also been proposed. The findings have implications for social work educators who are implementing, or considering implementing, e-learning in their programs. In particular, there is a need to review and align a wide range of policies and practices, and a need for increased faculty dialogue and engagement, increased resources, and strong leadership in order to address the challenges identified in this study.

REFERENCES

Advisory Committee for Online Learning. (2001). The E-Learning E-Volution in Colleges and universities: A Pan-Canadian Challenge. Retrieved March 30, 2001, from http://www.cmec.ca/postsec/evolution.en.pdf.

Archer, W., Garrison, R., & Anderson, T. (1999). Adopting disruptive technologies in traditional universities: Continuing education as an indicator for innovation. *Canadian Journal of University Continuing Education, 25*(1), 13-30.

Ashery, R. S. (2001). The utilization of technology in graduate schools of social work. *Journal of Technology in Human Services, 18*(1/2), 5-18.

Bates, T. W. (2000). *Managing technological change: Strategies for college and university leaders.* San Francisco: Jossey Bass.

Beaudoin, M. (2003a). Distance education leadership: Appraisal of research and practice. In M. Moore & W. Anderson (Eds.), *Handbook of distance education* (pp. 519-530). Mahwah, NJ: Lawrence Erlbaum Associates, Inc.

Beaudoin, M. (2003b). Distance education leadership for the new century. *Online Journal of Distance Learning Administration, 6*(2). Retrieved July 16, 2003, from http://www.westga.edu/%7Edistance/ojdla/summer62/beaudoin62.html, 1-13.

Blackboard (2005). Blackboard Course Cartridges. Retrieved July 19, 2005, from http://cartridgecatalog.blackboard.com/catelog.

Blakely, T. J. (1992). A model for distance education delivery. *Journal of Social Work Education, 28* (2), 214-221.

Butterfield, W. H. (1998). Human services and the information economy. *Computers in Human Services, 15* (2/3), 121-142.

Campus Alberta Repository of Educational Objects (CAREO) (2005). CAREO Description. Retrieved July 19, 2005, from http://www.careo.org.

Chipper Online (2005). Counselling Simulations and Tutorials. Retrieved July 19, 2005, from http://www.ssw.umich.edu/simulation.

COHERE Group (2002). The learning object economy: Implications for developing faculty expertise. *Canadian Journal of Learning and Technology, 28* (3), 1-10. Retrieved July 13, 2003, from http://www.cjlt.ca/content/vol28.3/cohere.html.

Collins, D., Gabor, P., Coleman, H., & Ing, C. (2002). In love with technology: A critical review of the use of technology in social work education. *Ninth International Literacy and Education Research Network Conference on Learning.* Beijing, China, July 16-20, 2002.

Collis, B. (1996). *Tele-learning in a digital world: The future of distance learning.* London: Thompson Computer Press.

Creswell, J. W. (1998*). Qualitative inquiry and research design: Choosing among the five traditions.* Thousand Oaks: Sage Publications.

Cummins, L., & Hamilton, S. (2000). Promoting the social work mission through technology: A model. *4th Annual Technology Conference for Social Work Education and Practice.* Columbia, SC: College of Social Work, University of South Carolina.

D'Antoni, S. (2003). Messages and lessons learned. In S. Antoni (Ed.), *The virtual university: Models and messages–Lessons from case studies* (pp. 1-9). International Institute for Educational Planning, UNESCO. Retrieved July 13, 2003, from http://www.unesco.org/iiep/eng/focus/elearn/webpub/home.html.

Denzin, N., & Lincoln, Y. (2000). *Handbook of qualitative research* (2nd ed.). Thousand Oaks: Sage Publications, Inc.

Duderstadt, J. J. (1997). The future of the university in an age of knowledge. *Journal of Asynchronous Networks, 1* (2), 78-88.

Duderstadt, J. J. (2000). *A university for the 21st century.* Ann Arbor: The University of Michigan Press.

Freddolino, P. P. (2002). Thinking 'outside the box ' in social work distance education: Not just for distance anymore. *Electronic Journal of Social Work, 1* (1), article 6, 1-13. Retrieved July 10, 2002, from http://www.ejsw.net/.

Garrison, R., & Anderson, T. (2003). *E-learning in the 21st century.* New York: Routledge Falmer.

Garrison, R. D., Anderson, T., & Archer, W. (2000). Critical inquiry in a text-based environment: Computer conferencing in higher education. *The Internet and Higher Education, 2* (2-3), 87-105.

Garrison, R. D., Anderson, T., & Archer, W. (2001). Critical thinking, cognitive presence, and computer conferencing in distance education. *American Journal of Distance Education, 15* (1), 7-23.

Garrison, R. D., Anderson, T., & Archer, W. (2003). A theory of critical inquiry in online distance education. In M. Moore & W. Anderson (Eds.), *Handbook of distance education* (pp. 113-127). Mahwah, NJ: Lawrence Erlbaum Associates.

Gellman-Danley, B., & Fetzner, M. (1998). Asking the really tough questions: Policy issues for distance learning. *Online Journal of Distance Learning Administration, 1* (1). Retrieved July 7, 2003, from http://www.westga.edu/%7Edistance/danley11.html.

Gonchar, N., & Adams, J. R. (2000). Living in cyberspace: Recognizing the importance of the virtual world in social work assessments. *Journal of Social Work Education, 36* (3), 578-596.

Grant Thornton, & CS/RESORS (2000). *In critical demand: Social work in Canada.* Ottawa: Canadian Association of Schools of Social Work.

Graves, W. H. (1997). Free trade in higher education: The meta university. *Journal of Asynchronous Learning Networks, 1* (1), 97-108.

Haché, D. (1998). *Strategic planning of distance education in the age of teleinformatics. Online Journal of Distance Learning Administration, 1* (2). Retrieved July 7, 2003, from http://www.westga.edu/~distance/Hache12.html, 1-17.

Hafner, K., & Oblinger, D. (1998). Transforming the academy. In D. Oblinger, & S. Rush (Eds.), *The future compatible campus: Planning, designing, and implementing information technology in the academy* (pp. 2-23). Bolton, MA: Anker Publishing Co.

Hanna, D. E. (1998). Higher education in an era of digital competition: Emerging organizational models. *Journal of Asynchronous Learning Networks, 2* (1), 66-95.

Hanna, D. E. (2003). Distance education, emerging organizational models, and change. In M. Moore & W. Anderson (Eds.), *Handbook of distance education* (pp. 67-78). Mahwah, NJ: Lawrence Erlbaum Associates, Inc.

Johnson, J. J. (2002). In-depth interviewing. In J. F. Gubrium, & J. A. Holstein. *Handbook of interview research: Context and methods* (pp. 103-119). Thousand Oaks: Sage Publications.

Knowles, A. J. (2002). E-learning in social work education: Emerging pedagogical and policy issues. *Currents: New Scholarship in the Human Services, 1*(1). Available url: http://fsw.ucalgary.ca/currents/.

Knowles, A.J. (2004). *Pedagogical and policy challenges in implementing e-learning in social work education.* Unpublished doctoral dissertation. University of Alberta, Edmonton.

Kreuger, L. W., & Stretch, J. J. (2000). How hypermodern technology in social work education bites back. *Journal of Social Work Education, 36* (1), 103-114.

Lawrence-Webb, C. (2000). Electronic portfolios: A vision for social work education and practice. *4th Annual Technology Conference for Social Work Education and Practice.* Columbia: College of Social Work, University of South Carolina.

MacFadden, Robert J. (2002). Information technology in social work practice. In F. Turner (Ed.) *Social work practice: A Canadian perspective* (2nd ed., pp. 515-530). Toronto: Prentice Hall.

Mason, R. (2003). The university: Current challenges and opportunities. In S. D'Antoni (Ed.), *The virtual university: Models and messages–Lessons from case studies* (pp. 1-19). International Institute for Educational Planning, UNESCO. Retrieved July 13, 2003, from http://www.unesco.org/iiep/eng/focus/elearn/webpub/home.html.

Middlehurst, R. (2003). A world of borderless higher education–impact and implications. In Susan D'Antoni (Ed.), *The virtual university: Models and messages*. International Institute for Educational Planning, UNESCO. Retrieved July 13, 2003, from http://www.unesco.org/iiep/eng/focus/elearn/webpub/home.html.

Miller-Cribbs, J., & Chadiha, L. (1998). Integrating the Internet in a human diversity course. *Computers in Human Services, 15* (2/3), 97-109.

Multimedia Educational Resource for Learning and Online Teaching (MERLOT) (2005). Description of MERLOT. Retrieved July 19, 2005, from http: merlot.org.

Olcott, D. (1996a). Destination 2000: Strategies for managing successful distance education programs. *Journal of Distance Education, 11* (2), 1-11.

Olcott, D. (1996b). Aligning distance education practice and academic policy: A framework for institutional change. *Continuing Higher Education Review, 60* (1). Retrieved July 19, 2003, from: http://busboy.sped.ukans.edu/sped997/unit1/readings/olcott1.html, 10 pages.

Olcott, D. (2000). Redefining faculty policies and practices for the knowledge age. Paper presented at Distance Learning: An Open Question. September 11-13, 2000. Adelaide, South Australia: University of South Australia.

O'Quinn, L., & Corry, M. (2002). Factors that deter faculty from participating in distance education. *Online Journal of Distance Learning Administration, 5* (4) Retrieved July 16, 2003, from http://www.westga.edu/!distance/ojdla/winter54/Quinn54.htm,18 pages.

Padgett, D., & Conceao-Runlee, S. (2000). Designing a faculty development program on technology: If you build it, will they come? *Journal of Social Work Education, 36* (2), 325-335.

Patton, M. Q. (2002). *Qualitative research and evaluation methods* (3rd. ed.). Thousand Oaks, CA: Sage Publications.

Sandell, K. S., & Hayes, S. (2002). The Web's impact on social work education: Opportunities, challenges, and future directions. *Journal of Social Work Education, 38* (1), 85-99.

Schoech, D. (2002). Technology challenges facing social work. *Electronic Journal of Social Work, 1*(1), article 5, 1-11. Retrieved July 10, 2002, from http://www.ejsw.net/.

Scottish Institute for Excellence in Social Work Education (SIESWE) (2005). SIESWE Description. Retrieved July 19, 2005, from http://www.sieswe.org.

Siegel, E., Jennings, J., Conklin, J., & Napoletano-Flynn, S. A. (1998). Distance learning in social work education: Results and implications of a national survey. *Journal of Social Work Education, 34* (1), 71-80.

Silverman, D. (2000). Analyzing talk and text. In N. Denzin & Y. Lincoln (Eds.), *Handbook of qualitative research* (2nd ed., pp. 821-834). Thousand Oaks: Sage Publications, Inc.

Silverman, D. (2000b). *Doing qualitative research.* Thousand Oaks: Sage Publications, Inc.

Stòr Cùram (2005). Stòr Cùram Learning Object Repository. Retrieved July 19, 2005, from http://www. storcuram.ac.uk.

SWAP (2005). Description: Social Policy and Social Work Subject Centre of the Higher Education Academy. Retrieved July 19, 2005, from http://www.swap. ac.uk/default.asp.

Szabo, M. (2002). *Educational reform as innovation diffusion: Development of a theory and a test of a model using continuing professional development and instructional technology.* Paper prepared for Informing Science & IT Education 2002, Cork Ireland. Retrieved October 15, 2002 from http://www.quasar.ualberta.ca/ DRMIKE/ Szabo/Publications_R+NR.pdf.

Tierney, W.G., & Dilley, P. (2002). Interviewing in education. In J. F. Gubrium & J. A. Holstein. *Handbook of interview research: Context and methods* (pp. 453-471). Thousand Oaks: Sage Publications.

Turoff, M. (1997). Alternative futures for distance learning: The force and the darkside. *UNESCO / Open University International Colloquium: Virtual Learning Environments and the Role of the Teacher.* Retrieved December 6, 1999, from http://eies. njit.edu/~turoff.

Van Dusen, G. C. (1997). The virtual campus: Technology and reform in higher education. ASHE-ERIC Higher Education Report Vol. 25, No. 5. Washington: The George Washington University, Graduate School of Education and Human Development.

WebCT (2005). WebCT Digital Content. Retrieved July, 19, 2005, from http://www. webct.com/content.

Wolcott, L. (2003). Dynamics of faculty participation in distance education: Motivations, incentives, and rewards. In M. Moore & W. Anderson (Eds.), *Handbook of distance education* (pp. 549-566). Mahwah, NJ: Lawrence Erlbaum Associates, Inc.

doi: 10.1300/J017v25n01_02

APPENDIX A

TABLE A1. Professional Challenges

Professional Challenges
The Fit of E-learning with Social Work Education
The Importance of Professional Socialization
E-equity
Key Ethical Concerns

TABLE A2. Pedagogical Challenges

Pedagogical Challenges

The Importance of Relationship in Professional Induction
    Loss of Face-to-Face Interaction, Immediacy, and Personal Connection
    Enhanced Interactivity in E-learning

Rethinking Curricula
    Competency in E-communication
    Student Adjustment to E-learning
    The Importance of Student Choice
    Content Areas
    Class Size
    The Need to Support Multiple Approaches and Learning Environments
    Face-to-Face and Observational Contact
    Enhancement to Field Education and the Role of Field Instructor
    The Importance of Student Orientation
    Rethinking Assessment of Learning

Faculty Knowledge
    Pedagogical Knowledge and Approaches to Instructional Design
    Increased Planning and Strategic Teaching
    Shift in Role and Online Teaching Skills
    Instructor Control of the Learning Environment Software

The Need for Pedagogical Dialogue
    Build in a Critique of Technology
    Evaluation of Online Learning

APPENDIX A (continued)

TABLE A3. Faculty Challenges

Faculty Challenges

Time, Workload, and Compensation
  Time Pressures
  Workload
  Differential Compensation: E-equity for Faculty
  Setting Class Size Limits
  Sessional and Pre-Tenure Vulnerability
  Lack of Recognition
  The Question of Faculty Choice

Instructional Concerns
  Pedagogical Orientation, Skills, and Role Shifts
  Need for Teaching Expectations and Guidelines
  Intellectual Property
  Collaboration
  Confidentiality and Privacy in Online Environments

Faculty Development
  Technical Skills: Basic Literacy, Course Management Software
  Technical Support and Interpersonal Skills of Support Person
  Instructional Design Support
  Informal Leadership

Need for Faculty Dialogue and Input into Decision Making

TABLE A4. Administrative Challenges

Administrative Challenges

Program and Institutional Leadership
  Strategic Planning
  Institutional Support: Rhetoric and Resources
  Incremental and Thoughtful Implementation
  Revised Workload and Compensation Practices and Policies
  Revised Recognition and Incentives
  Faculty Demographics
  Student Demographics: Learner Driven Demand

Program Structure and Policies: Integrating On-Campus and Distance Learners

Revision and Alignment of Academic Policies
  Develop Confidentiality and Privacy Policies
  Clear Guidelines and Expectations for Students
  Maintaining Program Quality
  Accreditation Standards
  Need for Research

Collaboration

APPENDIX B

TABLE B1. Areas of Policy Alignment in Implementing E-Learning in Social Work Education

Academic Policies	Administrative Policies	Administrative Policies
• Faculty Development • Develop models and guides for developing e-learning • Develop Online Teaching Guidelines • Clear expectations and guidelines for students • Confidentiality and Privacy Policies • Intellectual Property • Student support • Enhanced role of Field Supervisors and Mentors • Residency requirements • Transfer policies • Class size • Participation policies • Responsibility and control of learning environment • Revised course evaluation procedures • Revised Accreditation Standards	Workload, Compensation, Incentives • Develop workload guidelines that recognize time demands of e-learning development and teaching contingent on model and format • Develop incentive programs to encourage faculty involvement with e-learning • Hiring Policies: E-competency and teaching expectations for faculty • Policy/strategy regarding faculty choice and involvement in e-learning • Review tutor model of compensation for self-paced distance courses converted to online learning. Compensation contingent on pedagogical model Recognition • Revised recognition processes; consider peer review of e-learning projects, learning objects • Increased focus on the scholarship of teaching • Revised course and instructor evaluations and processes • Encourage research focused on teaching	Organizational • Develop Program Strategic Plan for technology integration • Establish Technology Steering Committees • Integrate administrative and support structures for distance and on-campus courses • Decisions and policies regarding the maintenance of multiple learning environments and formats • Student Support • Develop structures and processes to facilitate inter-program collaboration and strategic alliances • Secure resources to support strategic plan, longer term implementation Collaboration • Policies regarding shared resources • Revenue and cost sharing of courses or learning materials • Ownership • Registration of students

APPENDIX C. Recommendations

It is important to note that these recommendations are based on the author's interpretation of the findings and specific program contexts. As a result they are not generalizable to all social work educators and programs. Readers will need to reflect on the findings and recommendations to determine whether or not they fit with their own experience, needs and contexts.

Policy Recommendations

1. Social work programs need to review and align a wide range of academic and administrative policies and practices in order to respond to the challenges identified by participants in this study. These are listed in Appendix B.

2. Social work programs and institutions need to revise workload and compensation policies and practices to recognize the amount of time required to develop high quality e-learning, provide for time for faculty development, and respond to concerns about differential compensation.

3. Class size should be limited to less than thirty students in online social work courses in order to: recognize the nature of intensive online discussions; the need for coherence in professional development and the learning process; the need for high levels of interactivity; the need to build in social, cognitive and teaching presence; and in recognition of the time demands placed on faculty teaching online.

4. Social work programs and institutions need to revise faculty evaluation, reward, recognition processes for both tenure and non-tenure track faculty, and find ways to incorporate faculty involvement in the development of e-learning projects into recognition and promotion processes. Recognition processes are a significant barrier to faculty involvement in e-learning.

5. Social work programs need to review and balance the number of part-time and full-time faculty involved in developing and teaching online courses.

6. Social work programs need to ensure that there is adequate student support including technical support available on weekends, orientation to course management software, orientation to the skills and expectations involved in online learning.

7. Social work programs need to develop guidelines and policies governing online communication, confidentiality and privacy, and the unique qualities of online communications in the context of social work education and practice. They also need to develop policies governing who has access to online courses and course archives, designer access and control of the course management software, the deletion of course discussions, and the archiving of course discussions.

8. Social work programs need to ensure that there is adequate support for faculty, including technical support, instructional design support, resources to develop high quality interactive learning activities, and faculty development. Ideally, individuals providing technical and instructional design consultation should be knowledgeable about the nature of social work education.

9. Social work programs need to develop teaching expectations and guidelines for faculty teaching in online environments. These should include expectations regarding technical skills, pedagogical approaches and strategies to promote high levels of interactivity, and social, cognitive and teaching presence.

10. Social work programs need to develop revised course evaluation instruments and processes that are suited for evaluating online learning. In particular, evaluations need to provide opportunities for student feedback on their experiences, perspectives, and recommendations. They also need to incorporate evaluation of instructor online teaching skills and presence in the online environment.

11. The Canadian Association of Schools of Social Work (CASSW) should consider enhancements to the draft policy recommendations on distance education including statements about: confidentiality and privacy in online environments; skill requirements of faculty; the need for faculty development; further elaboration on instructional design and levels of interactivity; enhancement to field education in distance programs; recognition of the shift in instructional role and time involved in developing online learning for faculty; class size in e-learning environments; recognition and reward processes for innovation and the scholarship of teaching; and, transfer and residency requirements.

12. Programs need to align organizational and administrative structures and processes to integrate distance and on-campus programming. Potential areas of integration include shared course development, student support, faculty support, and instructional design support. Programs should revise policies to allow for student movement between distance and on-campus status and build in the flexibility to mix "distance" and on-campus students in courses.

Implementation Recommendations

1. Social work programs need to develop strategic plans for the implementation of e-learning. Plans should include how programs plan to integrate e-learning, identification of policies and practices that will need revision, resources required to support implementation, how faculty and student support will be provided, the fit of the program's plan with the overall institutional plan, and potential strategic alliances.

2. Integration of e-learning should be incremental and developmental in order to prepare and assist faculty for significant shifts in their role, skills and knowledge and to build experience and confidence in the use of e-learning environments. Ideally, faculty involvement should be voluntary. Programs should establish minimum expectations for faculty skills levels in the use of e-learning that are tied to their mission statements and strategic planning.

3. Social Work Faculty need to be engaged in dialogue in implementing e-learning in social work education. There is a need for faculty dialogue about the fit of e-learning in social work education and for input into strategies to respond to the professional, pedagogical, policy, and resource challenges identified in this study. This dialogue needs to take place at the program level and amongst social work educators as a group. Key areas for dialogue include e-equity for students and faculty, rethinking curricula in the context of rapidly changing higher education environments, maintaining coherence and quality, and realignment of academic and administrative policies.

APPENDIX C (continued)

4. There is a need for social work educators to explore pedagogical models suited for e-learning and to develop interactive online learning resources for social work education. In particular, social work educators need to build in high levels of interactivity and social, cognitive, and teaching presence into the design of online learning and opportunities for direct observation of practice skills.

5. In distance programs, the role of local field instructors should be enhanced to include increased opportunities for direct observation of practice skills. Field instructors could be further involved in online practice discussion seminars. Additional orientation and resources should be available for field instructors that could also be utilized for continuing professional education.

6. Social work faculty and programs need to implement proactive faculty development programs that incorporate technical and pedagogical knowledge and the skills of teaching and learning in online environments. Faculty development needs to include a focus on the professional and pedagogical challenges specific to social work educators. Programs should consider the use of incentives to encourage faculty development focused on e-learning. Programs should encourage faculty development through the linkage of individual faculty development plans and overall program goals for technology integration. Faculty need information on e-learning resources for social work education including relevant conferences, journals, and websites.

7. Programs need to provide strong leadership in order to implement e-learning, including strategic planning. Leadership needs to be provided and supported at several levels: faculty and disciplinary leadership, by program administrators, and by institutional leaders. Programs should consider developing technology integration committees. Programs should create leadership roles for faculty and provide compensation or release time for faculty who are leading and supporting e-learning amongst their colleagues. There is also a need for leadership amongst social work educators at a national level.

8. Programs need to secure and find resources in order to implement e-learning. Resources are needed for the cost of development, release time and compensation, incentives, cost of hardware, technical support, instructional design support, faculty development, maintenance of online courses, and faculty and student support. Resources for the development of interactive e-learning activities are a major barrier to implementing e-learning in social work education.

9. Resource acquisition and planning should be built into program and institutional strategic plans for implementing e-learning.

10. Programs should explore collaboration within their institutions and with other social work programs in order to share in the development of e-learning resources and learning objects. Programs in Canada should consider developing a web portal for social work education. This could take several forms including a collaborative non-profit entity, a portal hosted by the CASSW, a linkage of individual program and regional repositories, and partnerships with the private sector or publishing houses.

11. Social work programs should consider approaching their provincial departments of higher education and jointly approaching the Federal Government to secure funding to support the development of e-learning resources in social work education and the establishment of an e-learning resource centre and learning object repository for social work education.

12. There is a need for social work educators to engage in further research focused on e-learning. Areas for research include further evaluation of the specific professional, pedagogical, faculty and administrative challenges identified in this study.

The Relationship
Between Technology Content
in a Masters of Social Work Curriculum
and Technology Use in Social Work Practice:
A Qualitative Research Study

Eric Youn

SUMMARY. In the past several years, Masters of Social Work (MSW) programs around the nation (USA) have been adding technology courses to their curriculums, suggesting the need for more technology education in MSW programs. Literature reviews of attitudes of social work faculty and social workers indicate a historic trend of resistance to use of technology in the field. In order to better understand the purpose of technology content in MSW curriculums and how it relates to social workers' use of technology in the field, this research project does a qualitative study among faculty and MSW graduates working at local human service agencies to answer the following exploratory research questions: (1) What is the technology content of an MSW Curriculum? (2) What is

Eric Youn, MSW, is a PhD Student, University of Texas at Arlington–School of Social Work, Box 19129, Arlington, TX 76019-0129 (E-mail: eyoun@uta.edu). His research interests include technology in social work, and use of online environments for teaching clinical skills.

[Haworth co-indexing entry note]: "The Relationship Between Technology Content in a Masters of Social Work Curriculum and Technology Use in Social Work Practice: A Qualitative Research Study." Youn, Eric. Co-published simultaneously in *Journal of Technology in Human Services* (The Haworth Press, Inc.) Vol. 25, No. 1/2, 2007, pp. 45-58; and: *HUSITA7–The 7th International Conference of Human Services Information Technology Applications: Digital Inclusion–Building a Digital Inclusive Society* (eds: C. K. Law, Yu Cheung Wong, and John Yat Chu Fung) The Haworth Press, Inc., 2007, pp. 45-58. Single or multiple copies of this article are available for a fee from The Haworth Document Delivery Service [1-800-HAWORTH, 9:00 a.m. - 5:00 p.m. (EST). E-mail address: docdelivery@haworthpress.com].

Available online at http://jths.haworthpress.com
doi:10.1300/J017v25n01_03

the purpose of the technology content in an MSW Curriculum? (3) What is the amount of technology use in human service agencies by MSWs? (4) When MSWs first come to human service agencies, do they have the technological competence needed? (5) What skills are they lacking (if any?) This exploratory study used three series of interviews and a syllabi and job description review in its methodology. The first set of interviews was with human service agency administrators who hire MSWs. The second set of interviews was with human service agency staff members who graduated with an MSW degree. The third set of interviews was with select faculty members in order to find out what the technology content and purpose is for MSWs. Syllabi from technology classes were analyzed. Job application descriptions from human service offices were also analyzed. To ensure the validity of the data, interviews with all sets of interviewees were tape-recorded. doi:10.1300/J017v25n01_03 *[Article copies available for a fee from The Haworth Document Delivery Service: 1-800-HAWORTH. E-mail address: <docdelivery@haworthpress.com> Website: <http://www.HaworthPress.com> © 2007 by The Haworth Press, Inc. All rights reserved.]*

KEYWORDS. Technology, education, curriculum, fieldwork, students

INTRODUCTION

Computer technology has become more and more mainstream in the American business climate during the last two decades. The profession of social work has not been an exception to this transition. Several years ago, The University of Texas at Arlington School of Social Work (UTA SSW) became one of the first schools of social work to add a technology class to its Masters of Social Work (MSW) curriculum. Soon after, the technology course became a requirement for all MSWs (UTA SSW, 2004)

Although the Council on Social Work Education (CSWE) states that MSW programs should be "developing and applying instructional and practice-relevant technology" (CSWE, 2001), the CSWE does not, at this time, require that a technology course be provided in an MSW curriculum. Despite the absence of a requirement, several other MSW programs around the country have followed the example set by UTA SSW and have added technology courses to their curriculum. Many have also made it a required course (University of Arkansas SSW, 2004).

In order to study the links between technology learned in an MSW curriculum and how that relates to how a social worker utilizes technology in practice after he/she graduates, it was determined that a broad range of agency staff must be selected in order to study how the MSWs use technology when employed there. The staff selected for this study were from the following agencies: Tarrant County Health and Human Services, The Arlington Women's Shelter, Tarrant County United Way, City of Fort Worth–Mental Health Mental Retardation Services, and the Arlington Arrow Project (a private adoption/foster care agency).

This purposeful sample of staff were chosen because their agencies seemed to represent popular atypical agencies that employ many UTA SSW MSWs. This was determined by the larger than average number of MSW interns who do their field placements at these offices and information received through personal conversations with the MSWs placed there that attested to the large number of MSWs from the UTA SSW who are employed there.

EXPLORATORY RESEARCH QUESTIONS

"In a research proposal, the function of your research questions is to explain scientifically what your study will attempt to learn or understand" (Maxwell, 1996, p. 51). In this research proposal, the exploratory research questions are as follows: (1) What is the technology content of an MSW Curriculum? (2) What is the purpose of the technology content in an MSW Curriculum? (3) What is the amount of technology use in human service agencies by MSWs? (4) When MSWs first come to human service agencies, do they have the technological competence needed? (5) What skills are they lacking (if any?)

LITERATURE REVIEW

The literature review was focused primarily on past research concerning uses of technology and attitudes towards technology by social work faculty, students and social workers. In 1993, Seabury and Maple conducted research on students' perceptions of an Interactive Video Disk (IVD)-based clinical skills development program. The program was designed to show a series of video clips to the students that depicted client-social worker interactions in a counseling environment. The IVD program required students to know how to turn on a standard personal computer and run a program using a mouse. These videos used in the original IVD study are now available for students to take over the internet from the University of Michigan School of Social Work Website.

Seabury and Maple noted that this utilization of technological methods to teach clinical skills was in spite of a strong sentiment of doubt among their academic colleagues (p. 430). They also found that this sentiment was also present within social workers working in the field (Cooper, 1989; Mandell, 1989). This theme of technological resistance is important to note, as it is present throughout the historical development of teaching clinical skills in online environments.

There have been many distance education studies conducted in recent years focusing on the World Wide Web where students would receive mainly text-based course content over the internet (Faux & Black-Hughes, 2000; Peters, 1999) often using a web-based distance education software program medium such as Web-CT or Blackboard (Hollister & McGee, 2000, p. 419). This type of program would require the student to know how to access the internet using a computer and also know how to navigate through a web page. It could also require the student to know how to utilize communication technology such as e-mail or chat rooms.

It is interesting to note that the resistance to technology theme that was present in faculty perceptions of IVD technology and social workers working in the field was also present in perceptions of distance education. Siegel, Jennings, Conklin, Napoletano, and Shelly (1998) conducted a study concerning perceptions of faculty towards distance education and specifically towards technology mediated distance education techniques. The results found a significant and growing use of distance education programs, but only for more "passive-information" courses such as research, policy, and history and not for classes that involved the teaching of clinical skills. This was attributed to a fear that "If one does not teach 'face-to-face,' as is the norm in our profession, how much is lost in the perceived quality of the classroom interaction, in the potential socialization of students, and in the relationship with the instructor as a mentor and role model?" (p. 76)

This was also attributed to a sentiment that social work faculty may see technology more as a vehicle for research than for education and teaching. This is due to a perception of technology being more of an information storage medium than a dynamic environment for learning.

From a philosophical point of view, some schools of social work may be ill prepared to make a paradigm shift to modify traditional classroom and field teaching with multimedia or technologically assisted education. Adaptation to newer teaching methodologies takes time. For many years even the use of computers was slowly accepted within the educational community. When its potential for research purposes, information storage and retrieval, and communication became clear, though, it was embraced quickly. But because distance education can help effective teaching more than research, it may face a slower acceptance time. (pp. 76-77)

Although the literature review did not specifically reveal literature that spoke of students' use of technology programs such as word processors, spreadsheets, power point presentations, etc. . . , it is implied that students are expected to know or be taught how to use various technologies in order to participate in classes that utilize technology. Common knowledge indicates that MSW students generally use word processors to compose papers, power points presentations to give classroom presentations, spreadsheets to create sample budgets for administrative classes, and e-mail to communicate with professors and other students. The attitudes toward technology are also interesting to note since they may indicate that since school of social work faculty view technology as a method of research purposes, information storage and retrieval, and communication, this viewpoint may be passed on to their students.

METHODOLOGY

As a part of the study of the existing technology content in MSW course curriculums, a review of course syllabi was conducted. Course syllabi usually list the goals and objectives of a class. These syllabi are readily available over the internet. Advertisements for social work and human service job postings were also reviewed. Most job opportunity advertisements have a description of duties and list of qualifications. Course syllabi from classes in the MSW curriculum that contain a high amount of technology content were researched and reviewed. Also reviewed were various job descriptions for MSW positions and focus specifically on technology-oriented duties and skill requirements. These job descriptions were found on agency websites, in local newspaper archives, and on the UTA SSW job listserve.

Finally, a series of three interviews was conducted. The first set of interviews was with human service agency administrators who hire MSWs. The second set of interviews was with human service agency staff members who graduated with an MSW degree. The third set of interviews was with select faculty members in order to find out what the technology content and purpose is for MSWs. With all these sources of data, some significant conclusions were able to be drawn about the link between technology education in the MSW curriculum and how MSWs who work at these agencies use technology in practice.

These methods involved an in-depth exploration of the UTA SSW faculty's desires, purposes, and intentions in determining the content of technology education in the MSW curriculum. At the agencies, the methods focused on how the social workers perceived the use of technology in the agency. Focus was also concentrated on the social workers' perceptions and understanding of technology and how comfortable they are in utilizing it within their processes.

These methods are in line with the purposes of qualitative research.

> The perspective on events and actions held by the people involved in them is not simply their account of these events and actions, to be assessed in terms of its truth or falsity; it is part of the reality that you are trying to understand . . . Understanding the particular context within which the participants act, and the influence this context has on their actions. (Maxwell, 1996, p. 17)

SITE AND SAMPLE

In order to find out the technology content of the UTA SSW MSW curriculum, a population sample of any professors of courses that were reported by the head of the MSW department to have a heavy technology content were included in the study.

A purposeful sampling method using UTA SSW Alumni Contact information and Field Department information was used to get in touch with administrators and MSWs working at agencies. From the ones identified, a "snowball method" was used to contact other MSWs at the agencies in order to find information-rich informants (Patton, 2002).

Data Analysis

The analysis of the technology content included a review of running records, "the ongoing continuing records of a society" (Lee, 2000, p. 63), in this case the course syllabi and job postings. This review looked for trends in the technology education content of the courses and technological requirements for employment.

The interviews with faculty members were analyzed to find themes that pertain to what technology content professors want in the curricula. Themes "refer to any qualitative data reduction and sense making effort that takes a volume of qualitative material and attempts to identify core consistencies and meanings" (Patton, 2002, p. 453). They are a powerful tool in drawing conclusions from qualitative data analysis. A similar method was used in order to analyze the data pertaining to the purpose of the technology content in the MSW curriculum.

In order to analyze the data pertaining to what the amount of technology use is in the agencies by MSWs, what technical skills are required of MSWs coming into the agencies, and what skills they are lacking, the semi-structured interviews focused on getting responses to specific questions. The analysis of the amount of technology use by MSWs at the agencies focused around:

- What they consider "technology use"
- What their attitudes are towards it
- Does it make their lives easier/harder?
- Are they afraid of it? Do they enjoy it?
- Are they comfortable with it? How comfortable?

The analysis of the technology requirements at the agencies focused around:

- Finding out if technology skills were required during the hiring process?
- Did they have them?
- Did they get them from the MSW program? If not, where?
- Did they have to learn any "on the job"?

It was important to see if the MSWs felt "ready" when encountering the technical demands of the job. It was also important to analyze their perspectives on whether the MSW program adequately prepared them for the technical demands of the position.

The analysis of what skills the MSWs were lacking focused around:

- What specific skills were they lacking?
- Were these skills taught to them during the MSW program? In what manner?
- How robust was the material?

It was important to get their perspective on what skills they felt they lacked. The analysis also focused on their perspective on whether the material was not covered in the MSW program, was covered in the MSW program but they had forgotten it, was covered in the MSW program but not in enough detail, or was covered in the MSW program but using a version/method that is now different or obsolete.

LIMITATIONS AND OTHER ISSUES

Limitations

One of the major limitations of the study stemmed from the small, localized sample size. It is understood that the results of this study cannot be projected beyond the sample and it is intended as a pilot study in order to foster other similar research studies.

Validity

Methods of insuring validity were to compare the results of the study to the existing literature (syllabi and job descriptions) and to any other literature found. In future studies another comparison group could be developed from focus groups of faculty and agency workers. Focus groups are "interview[s] with a small group of people on a specific topic . . . to get a variety of perspectives and increase confidence on whatever patterns emerge" (Patton, 2002, p. 385). The focus groups can be comprised of members who are recommended by other faculty members and interview participants. Once that is done, work can be done to triangulate the survey results, themes, literature, and focus group responses, to better insure validity.

There are two main threats to validity involved with this study. One of them is a threat to descriptive understanding, and the other is a threat to interpretation understanding. In the threat related to descriptive understanding, there is the possibility that in the process of gathering data, especially in the interviewing processes, that there was not a complete record of what was said, or something was misheard or misquoted.

The threat related to interpretation understanding could especially be present in the interview data gathering. In the interview process, interpretations could be incorrect or incomplete if details are not clearly communicated or misinterpreted.

The researcher believes the most serious threat to validity stems from another source. This source is the influence (maybe subconscious influence) of personal biases or expected outcomes on how to interpret the data. This threat to validity could change the way the data is interpreted. This could change the final data and thus change the final conclusions of the study.

A few basic safeguards of validity that were utilized in the study include making sure all interviews were recorded (with permission). Also, there was a voicing of the concerns that biases and expected responses would influence conclusions. The researcher sought assurances that themes identified during the interview were drawn objectively.

Ethics and Human Subjects

"Qualitative researchers are guests in the private spaces in the world. Their manners should be good and their code of ethics strict" (Denzin & Lincoln, 1998, p. 154). Keeping this in mind, all responses and identities are to be kept confidential. Nothing was stated that may seem a criticism or hurtful to interviewees during the interviews.

RESULTS

Syllabi and Job Description Review

There are currently two MSW level technology courses being taught at UTA SSW. The beginning course is SOCW 5319–Technology Use in Social Work Practice and the advanced course is SOCW 6355–Advanced Use of IT in Human Services (UTA SSW, 2004). The beginning course is a requirement for all MSWs, while the advanced course is an elective. The course goals and objectives for the beginning class according to the syllabus are:

> . . . to prepare graduate students to enter the work force with the basic computer skills and knowledge needed to function as social work planners, administrators, and direct service practitioners.

> - Students will develop a basic understanding of the role of technology in social work practice.
> - Students will obtain a basic understanding of computer hardware and operations.

- Students will understand and be able to use basic operating system procedures.
- Students will be able to use the Internet, word processing, graphics, data analysis, and presentation software (Jaoko, 2004).

The course goals and objective for the advanced class according to the syllabus are:

To view human services as a data/information/knowledge-based profession and to investigate the computer and telecommunication tools available to work with the data/information/knowledge necessary to support clients and human service practice.

- To view social work as a profession where decision-making can be supported by finding, collecting, manipulating, modeling, and presenting data, information, and knowledge.
- To examine current human services software and telecommunications tools, such as the Internet, that can be used to support clients and human service practice.
- To understand the process of applying computer-based tools to a human service decision or situation.
- To critically examine the potentials and limitations of developing and implementing technology that supports a human service decision/situation of the student's choice.
- To experience use of the Internet as a tool for learning, problem-solving, and supporting practice (Schoech, 2004).

In addition to the technology skills taught in these two classes, it was noticed that many other classes in the MSW program utilize technology. Research classes usually work with SPSS and/or Microsoft Excel to explain and work with statistical data. Also many classes encourage students to make use of presentation programs such as PowerPoint or video technology to enhance their class projects and presentations.

Agency job postings were not very specific about technology skills. The postings usually made general comments and had requirements such as:

- Must have good computer skills.
- Demonstrate and accurately apply computer skills when completing documentation within agency policies and guidelines.
- Assist coworkers with computer documentation functions (TX DFPS, 2004).

In order to compensate for the non-robust nature of the job postings (if further posting examinations come up with the same result), it was assumed that these duties and qualifications could be expanded on during interviews with agency staff members.

Themes Identified in Agency Administrators and MSW Interviews

The themes identified in the agency administrators and MSW interviews were very similar. There were four major themes identified in both sets of interviews.

1. The technology content in the MSW curriculum is adequate for the use of technology in the field by MSWs.
2. Human Service Administrators generally feel that MSWs are technologically competent when they begin work at the agency.
3. MSWs working at human service agencies feel that the technology content in the MSW curriculum adequately prepared them for the technology demands at their agency.
4. Technology demands that MSWs are not prepared for or need additional training to do, generally deal with "agency specific" databases and applications and are not appropriate for content within an MSW curriculum.

Themes Identified in UTA Faculty Interviews

There were some themes that came out of the faculty interviews that were in line with the themes that came out of the interviews with agency staff and MSWs. However, there were some other themes that came out of the interviews that were very different and merit further exploration and study. The themes that came out of the faculty interviews are as follows:

1. The purpose of the technology content in the MSW curriculum is to adequately prepare students for the use of technology in practice, to help students understand the relationship of technology and practice, and to train students to utilize common software and hardware technology for use both in the MSW program and in the field.
2. From the agency administrators' perspective and from the MSWs' perspective, it is expected that they will find the technology education content in the MSW program adequate for the agency's needs.

3. The average agency administrator and the average MSW will not have the technology comprehension necessary to understand the full potential of how technology can facilitate processes in the agency.
4. Technology in agencies is not being used to its maximum capacity.

Although the faculty generally were in agreement that the amount of technology content in the MSW curriculum was adequate from the perspective of the agency administrator and the MSW, there were some opinions that indicated that the technology content was inadequate as far as the potential use of technology in agencies is concerned. Examples were cited that indicated that technology was not nearly being used to its maximum potential in the case of linking agency data together.

It was pointed out that due to the high amount of inter-agency processes that exist in social work and human services today, technology can serve a major role in facilitating these processes, however, it is rarely done. It was also pointed out that human service agency administrators and MSWs may feel that the amount of technology content in an MSW curriculum is adequate since it prepares them to use technology in the manner that the agency dictates. However, agency administrators and MSWs may be unaware of other potential uses for technology.

Implications of Themes for Future Studies, Education, and Practice

The themes identified in the interviews with faculty members strongly imply that there is a need for more technology use in inter-agency processes in social work and human services. This need may begin to be fulfilled by having more robust or focused technology content in social work programs. The reasoning is that if more social workers are aware of the potential uses of technology, this may "push the issue" of establishing more technology enabled processes in agency and inter-agency procedures.

It is therefore important to note some of the resistance to technology themes as noted in the literature review. Although the use of technology to some may seem cold and distant and otherwise out of place in social work environments, it is obvious that technology can also have benefits in terms of ultimately expediting services to clients in a faster and more efficient manner. In response to this, there has been research in developing concepts that will help alleviate the perception of technology use being too impersonal for social work.

Panos et al. (2002) have described the concept of "emotional band-width" within technology-driven communications. This is defined as ". . . a key to quality interactions, hopefully providing the illusion that all the participants [communicating with each other] are in the same room, sharing one space" (p. 428).

MacFadden (2003) states that currently "Online learners have not been considered as 'emotional beings' and web-based education has not addressed this dimension in any significant way" (para.1). MacFadden then presents a new potential model for web-based education that is constructivist and emotionally-oriented in nature in order to compensate for this.

CONCLUSION

As social work enters the new millennium, there is a strong sense of urgency for schools of social work curricula to enhance their technological content. The electronic age allows for social work to be performed at a higher level than before. Although processes should be carefully examined to be sure quality of services to clients is not compromised by the desire for greater efficiency, if the possibility is there, they should be fully explored and taken advantage of; and then, in turn, integrated in school of social work curricula.

REFERENCES

Cooper, R. (1989). The integration of computerized applications in a child welfare oversight agency. In W. LaMendola, B. Glastonbury, & S. Toole (Eds.), *A casebook of computer applications in the social and human services* (pp. 145-147). Binghamton, NY: The Haworth Press, Inc.

Council on Social Work Education (2001). *Educational Policy and Accreditation Standards.* Alexandria, VA. Retrieved March 30, 2004, from http://www.cswe.org.

Denzin, N.K. & Lincoln, Y.S. (Eds.) (1998). *Strategies of qualitative inquiry.* Thousand Oaks, CA: Sage.

Faux, T.L. & Black-Hughes, C. (2000). A comparison of using the internet versus lectures to teach social work history. *Research on Social Work Practice, 10* (4) 454-466.

Hollister, C.D. & McGee, G. (2000) Delivering Substance Abuse and Child Welfare Content through Interactive Television. *Research on Social Work Practice, 10* (4), 417-427.

Jaoko, J. (2004). SOCW 5319-001 *Technology Use in Social Work Practice. Course Syllabus Spring 2004.* Retrieved March 21, 2004, from http://www2.uta.edu/ssw/Documents/Syllabus/Spring04/5319.Jaoko.doc.

Lee, R.M. (2000). *Unobtrusive methods in social research.* Philadelphia, PA: Open University Press.

MacFadden, R. (2003). Abstract: Souls on Ice: Incorporating Emotion in Web-Based Education. *Journal of Technology in Human Services, 23*[Online]. Available at http://www2.uta.edu/cussn/jths/vol23.htm.

Mandell, S. (1989) Resistance and power: The perceived effect that computerization has on a social agency's power relationships. In W. LaMendola, B. Glastonbury, & S. Toole (Eds.), *A casebook of computer applications in the social and human services* (pp. 29-40). Binghamton, NY: The Haworth Press, Inc.

Maxwell, J.A. (1996). *Qualitative research design: An interactive approach.* Thousand Oaks, CA: Sage.

Panos, P., Panos, A., Cox, S.E., Roby, J.L., & Matheson, K.W. (2002). Ethical issues concerning the use of videoconferencing to supervise international social work field practicum students. *Journal of Social Work Education, 38* (3), 421-437.

Patton, M.Q. (2002). *Qualitative research & evaluation methods.* Thousand Oaks, CA: Sage.

Peters, B. (1999). Use of the Internet to deliver continuing education in social work practice skills: An evaluative study (Doctoral dissertation, University of Texas at Arlington, 1999).

Rogers, E.M. (1995). *Diffusion of innovations* (4th Edition). New York: Free Press.

Schoech, D. (2004). SOCW 6355-501 *Advanced Use of IT in Human Services. Syllabus for 2004.* Retrieved March 18, 2004, from http://www2.uta.edu/cussn/courses/6355/syllabus_6355_S2004.htm#goal.

Seabury, B.A. & Maple, F.F., Jr. (1993). Using computers to teach practice skills. *Social Work, 38,* 430-439.

Texas Department of Family and Protective Services (January 5, 2004). *Child Protective Services Specialist II-IV (Protective Services Specialist II-IV) Position.* Retrieved March 22, 2004, from http://www.dfps.state.tx.us/jobs/C03005.htm.

University of Arkansas–School of Social Work. *MSW Program Curriculum Plan.* Retrieved March 18, 2004, from http://www.uark.edu/depts/scwk/msw_curriculum.htm.

University of Texas at Arlington–School of Social Work. *MSW Coursework.* Retrieved March 16, 2004, from http://www2.uta.edu/ssw/mssw/msswcourse.htm.

doi:10.1300/J017v25n01_03

Lessons Learned
in Chat Room Teaching Internationally

Yu Cheung Wong
Dick Schoech

SUMMARY. Web-based teaching opens new opportunities for international collaboration in offering courses to students. It also allows students to attend courses offered by instructors situated outside their own country. This paper presents the lessons learned from one such course offered by instructors located in Texas and Hong Kong to students residing in Shanghai studying in a collaborative Master of Social Service Management Programme (MSSM) between HKU and Fudan University. The course, titled "Information and Communication Technology for Social Service Organizations," was offered twice in the past two years using an Internet-based class chat room supported by a course website and other web based tools. While the offering was successful based on student evaluations, many problems and issues had to be

Yu Cheung Wong, PhD, is Lecturer, Department of Social Work and Social Administration, University of Hong Kong, Pokfulam Road, Hong Kong, China (E-mail: ssycwong@hku.hk). His research interests include internet-based learning environments, measurement and promotion of digital inclusion, and social welfare in China.

Dick Schoech, PhD, is Dulak Professor of Social Work, University of Texas at Arlington School of Social Work (E-mail: schoech@uta.edu). His research interests include virtual learning environments, online social service delivery, performance support systems, knowledge engineering, and high-technology culture.

[Haworth co-indexing entry note]: "Lessons Learned in Chat Room Teaching Internationally." Wong, Yu Cheung, and Dick Schoech. Co-published simultaneously in *Journal of Technology in Human Services* (The Haworth Press, Inc.) Vol. 25, No. 1/2, 2007, pp. 59-83; and: *HUSITA7–The 7th International Conference of Human Services Information Technology Applications: Digital Inclusion–Building a Digital Inclusive Society* (eds: C. K. Law, Yu Cheung Wong, and John Yat Chu Fung) The Haworth Press, Inc., 2007, pp. 59-83. Single or multiple copies of this article are available for a fee from The Haworth Document Delivery Service [1-800-HAWORTH, 9:00 a.m. - 5:00 p.m. (EST). E-mail address: docdelivery@haworthpress.com].

addressed. The course background, learning outcomes, lessons learned, and future recommendations are presented. In addition, an analysis of the Shanghai student IT applications is provided to help understand the current state of human services IT in China. doi:10.1300/J017v25n01_04 *[Article copies available for a fee from The Haworth Document Delivery Service: 1-800-HAWORTH. E-mail address: <docdelivery@ haworthpress.com> Website: <http://www.HaworthPress. com> © 2007 by The Haworth Press, Inc. All rights reserved.]*

KEYWORDS. Online education, chat room teaching, cross-cultural teaching online, multinational teaching

INTRODUCTION

Web-based teaching opens new opportunities for international collaboration in offering courses to students. It also allows students to attend courses offered by teachers situated outside their own country. This is especially beneficial for students residing in developing countries. They can be exposed to teachers in overseas countries without traveling long distances and spending large amounts of money. Part-time students might find web-based courses fitting their tight schedule even better. This paper presents the lessons learned from one such course offered by instructors located in Texas and Hong Kong titled "Information and Communication Technology for Social Service Organizations" to students residing in Shanghai studying in a collaborative Master of Social Service Management Programme (MSSM) between HKU and Fudan U. The course has been offered twice in the past two years (2002-03 and 2003-04) using an Internet-based class chat room supported by tools such as internet phone, web cam, and course website. This paper presents a literature review and a discussion of learning outcomes followed by the experiences of the instructors and students using a lessons learned format. The final section presents an analysis of student papers to help understand the current situation of human services information and communication technology (ICT) in Mainland China. For a more thorough discussion of the course, evaluative data from the first offering, and the cultural issues involved, see Wong and Schoech (Wong & Schoech, 2005).

LITERATURE REVIEW AND BACKGROUND

Effectiveness of web-based teaching for social work courses has been widely demonstrated (Ligon, Markward, & Yegidis, 1999; Stocks & Freddolino, 1998; Stocks & Freddolino, 2000; Wernet, Olliges, & Delicath, 2000; Schoech & Helton, 2002; Macy, Rooney, Hollister, & Freddolino, 2001; Massimo, 2003; Wong, 2003). One web-based teaching format that has been successfully used is the internet chat room (Schoech, 2000; Schoech & Helton, 2002). It has an advantage of being interactive and allowing immediate responses to students' questions and concerns, although it requires fast responses and typing speed from the instructor. The interactivity of chat was seen as a way to avoid the dropout problem often associated with asynchronous web-based courses.

The students in this course studied the collaborative MSSM program offered by the Department of Social Work and Social Administration, The University of Hong Kong (HKU) and the Sociology Department of the Fudan University in Shanghai. It is a three-year, part-time program and the degree is offered by HKU. Because of this, HKU requires that the students should meet the required English proficiency in addition to academic requirements. The program started recruiting students in 2001. The program aims at training experts in social service management. The curriculum covers planning and resource management, research, policy analysis and decision-making, staff management, and leadership. Since ICT is important in managing social services organizations and in providing direct social services, it is offered as a compulsory course for students in the second year of the program.

For the purpose of quality assurance for a HKU degree, 90% of the courses have to be offered by instructors from Hong Kong. Most of the courses were typically offered by instructors sent from Hong Kong on two weekends. The four-days (24-32 hours) teaching covers the whole course content of a typical course. Many students find materials taught in this intensive manner difficult to fully absorb. This course was offered via internet chat over the typical 15-week semester to avoid the problems with intensive offerings.

The course discussed in this paper was offered by two instructors: one based in Texas and another in Hong Kong. The course materials and the textbook were developed and written by the instructor in Texas. The course was offered via the chat room associated with AOL Instant Messenger (IM). This chat room was user friendly, was free and widely available, allowed for individualizing the user's text color and font, provided instant messaging during chat, and allowed the saving of chat transcripts. The Texas course website was enhanced and maintained using FrontPage by both instructors, but primarily by the instructor in Hong Kong. In addition to IM chat, the Macromedia Flash MX web cam tool was used for student presentations. The Skype free internet phone service (www.skype.com) was used for continuous communications between the instructor in the US and Hong Kong.

Students attended 10 class chat sessions within 15 weeks. Internet access was a prerequisite for taking this course. Since Shanghai is the most developed city in China with a per capita GDP of 4904 US dollars in 2002, internet connectivity for the students in this course was not a serious issue, although broad-band connection was not the norm (38.3%) in 2002 in Shanghai (Chu, 2002). China, as a whole, enjoys only one-fifth of that amount in per capita GDP (World Bank, 2003).

Besides the class chat room, the students were required to complete several assignments which included

1. preparation of a personal webpage,
2. reviewing and reporting on several computer applications,
3. conducting a systems analysis about a social or organizational problem or situation, and
4. writing and presenting a term paper outlining the options available to address the system analyzed.

The instructor in Hong Kong went to Shanghai to provide a course introduction to the students and to prepare them for the technical requirement of the course, such as preparing a homepage, installing software, using the class chat room, accessing the course website, etc. At end-of-course, a visit by the Hong Kong instructor was scheduled for students to share their term paper content.

The instructors administered a questionnaire: "Attitudes Towards Technology Based Learning" (23 items) before and after the course. A course evaluation relating to "Course Content" (12 items) "Course Delivery" (24 items), "Overall Experience and Learning" (4 items), and "Basic IT Knowledge and Attitude" (23 items) was administered at the completion of the course.

Chat room discussions were saved and analyzed to generate further information for monitoring students' performance and course evaluative information. Other feedback channels were used, such as online midterm evaluation and an end-of-course evaluation meeting that was face-to-face for the students and Hong Kong instructor with video cam participation by the Texas instructor.

STUDENT LEARNING OUTCOME

Student Background

Table 1 presents the information regarding the background of the two batches of students. Twenty-two students completed the course in the first year while 23 did so in the second. Students both years were quite similar in age, academic background (percentage of students holding human services related degrees), and accessibility to a computer and the internet. However, one striking difference between the two groups was that female students were predominant in the second year (73.9%) while male students predominated in the first year (63.7%). Another difference was that students in the second year had much less experience in paid or voluntary human services (10.7 versus 28.7 months). In fact, more students working in the private enterprises were attracted to this program in the second year. The dropout rate of the program improved. In the first year, 10 out of 32 students dropped out of the program or deferred their studies while only four did so the second year. However, since this course, like most of the others, was compulsory for students studying the program, the dropout rate of this course was actually the dropout rate of the whole program. One reason for the lower dropout rate in the second year was that expectations in terms of the overall content and workload might not have been clear to first-year stu-

TABLE 1. Comparing Students' Backgrounds

	2002	2003
Age (mean)	27.7	26.8
No. of students (beginning)	32	27
No. of students (end)	22	23
Male %	63.7	26.1
Academic background (human services related) %	36	31.3
Months having computer	69.2	78.3
Months on Internet	49.6	51.9
Formal computer training hours	78.4	55.9
Knowledge of software (pieces)	5.4	4.3
Traveling time to campus (round trip)	2.0	1.6
Paid or voluntary experience in human services (months)	28.7	10.7
No computer at work (person)	0	1
No Internet at work (person)	1	2

dents, since they were the first batch of students in the program. Students in the second year might have had a clearer picture of what to expect based on the experience of previous students. Course improvements, which are mentioned throughout this paper, might be additional reasons for the lower dropout rate for year 2 students.

Student Participation and Performance

Table 2 presents and compares the chat room involvement between the two batches of students. In the first year, there were a total of 10 chat room sessions. Four of the chat room sessions took place in weekdays during lunch hours. In the second year, when the same format was proposed to the students, many expressed difficulties in attending chat sessions during lunch hours. As a result, instead of having 10 sessions, seven sessions were conducted. Several of the chat sessions were extended to three hours to cover the curriculum. This improved the average chat room attendance rate from 67.3% in the firstyear to 83.9% in the next. The average number of messages posted by students in each chat session was quite close (33.0 in the first and 31 in the second year). Since several chat sessions were longer in year 2, the overall number of postings slightly declined. However, the distribution of active and less active students (in terms of amount of messages posted in each session) was similar.

In terms of overall performance, of the 22 students who attended and completed the course offered in the first year, six received an "A" grade, ten received a "B" grade, and two received a "C." Four students failed the course. Of the twenty-three students who attended the course in the

TABLE 2. Involvement of Students in Class Chat Sessions: A Comparison

Level of participation in chat room (Average no. of messages in a chat room session)	Average no. of messages in each chat room session		No. of students		% of students		% of chat room sessions attended	
	2002	2003	2002	2003	2002	2003	2002	2003
Low (less than 20 messages)	8.1	10.4	6	5	27.3%	21.7%	40.0%	77.1%
Medium (20-39 messages)	25.1	30.1	9	12	40.9%	52.2%	68.9%	83.3%
High (40+ messages)	64.4	50.0	7	6	31.8%	26.1%	88.6%	90.5%
Overall/Total	33.0	31.0	22	23	100.0%	100.0%	67.3%	83.9%

second year, five received an "A" grade, thirteen received a "B" grade, and four received a "C." Only one failed the course. The data suggest that overall performance improved since more students received grades of "A" and "B" in the second year and only one student failed the course compared to four failures in the first year. The instructors' experience was that English proficiency of the students improved in the second year and more students were able to meet the deadlines in completing their assignments. Also, the improvements implemented in the second year might have helped students overcome difficulties in studying the course and meeting the course requirements.

Overall Satisfaction

Table 3 presents the overall experience and learning of the course in the two years of teaching. The overall level of experience and learning in both years was very positive (4.62 in 2002 and 4.28 in 2003 with 5 being the highest and 1, the lowest). The score of the item "Overall, I am satisfied with how this course was delivered" was the highest among the four items (4.71 in 2002 and 4.44 in 2003). The item with the lowest score was "I would take another internet delivered course if it were offered" (4.41 in 2002 and 3.94) in the second. The scores in all the four items declined in the second year, although the differences were not statistically significant. With various improvements put in place in the second year, the lowered level of scores was unexpected. The reason for the drop might simply reflect that web-based teaching, like other approaches of course delivery, does not fit all students. Another reason is although the improvements implemented enhanced students' learning,

TABLE 3. Course Evaluation–Overall Experience and Learning (Yes = 5, No = 1)

	2002 Mean N = 17	2003 Mean N = 18	t	Sig. (2-tailed)
I would recommend this course to my colleagues	4.71	4.39	1.5685	0.1263
Overall, I am satisfied with the learning that occurred in this course	4.71	4.44	1.5765	0.1245
Overall, I am satisfied with how this course was delivered	4.65	4.33	1.7044	0.0979
I would take another Internet delivered course if it were offered	4.41	3.94	1.7498	0.0905
Overall	4.62	4.28		

they also increased the overall workload. For example, in the second year students had to read and answer questions about the prescribed textbook chapters before each class session. This additional assignment required them to put more effort into the course. Most of the open-end comments written on the questionnaire at course completion reflected that the workload was heavier than the other courses of the program. In addition, website improvements made in the second year enabled the instructors to more easily keep track of the students' performance and involvement in class, thus putting additional pressure on students to complete all assignments.

LESSONS LEARNED

This section presents the lessons learned during the two years of teaching the course. We specifically focused on lessons that have implications for others wanting to duplicate some or all of this format.

Lesson #1: Internet Chat Is a Viable Delivery Medium for International Social Work Courses

The positive feedbacks of the course indicated that web-based teaching using an internet chat room accompanied by the other internet tools mentioned previously was readily acceptable to the students. In fact, the use of internet chat was rated highest among all the items in the "Course Delivery Tools and Techniques" (4.71) in the first year and the score was 4.44 in the second year (see Table 4). The use of the chat room also proved to be particularly useful for the present program in which students and instructors stayed in different places and countries. It also provides students more time to cover and assimilate complex materials than is typically provided by the four-day intensive teaching format of other program courses.

A chat room requires instructors to have both fast responses and typing speed. It is also important that the instructors are resourceful and able to ask stimulating questions to maintain the attention of students. Without stimulating questions and a clear focus, students would send instant messages to each other and attend to the other distractions in their environment due to feeling confused and frustrated. When audio chat was tried, the many distractions of students' homes and offices became obvious, e.g., children, dinner preparations, colleagues, etc. For those teaching via chat for the first time, it is useful to prepare

TABLE 4. Course Evaluation–Course Delivery Tools and Techniques

	2002 Mean Score (N = 17)	2003 Mean Score (N = 18)
I liked the use of email	4.65	4.61
I liked the use of the class listserv	4.47	4.22
I liked the use of Internet chat	4.71	4.44
I liked the ability to send private email to others while in the class chat room	4.29	4.28
I liked breaking away to Internet sites during class discussion	3.29	3.39
I liked the use of guest speakers	4.06	3.94
I liked the grading criteria and checklists for the assignments	3.94	4.22
My instructor was more available in this course than in other courses	4.59	4.33
I know the students in this course better than those in most courses	3.59	3.72
I communicated with students outside of class time in this course more than other courses	4.00	3.39
Working with other students in this course was easier than working with students in most courses	3.53	3.56
I know the instructor in this course better than I know instructors in most courses	4.25	3.94
I am satisfied with how I was able to schedule my time in this course	4.41	4.17
I am satisfied with the amount of time required for the course	3.88	3.89
I felt more comfortable asking questions in this course than in other courses	4.31	4.28
My access to library resources was adequate in this course	3.82	3.94
I participated more in this course than in other courses	4.29	4.22
I felt I was more able to learn at my own pace in this course than in other courses	4.13	4.17
I often felt the need for face-to-face communication in this course	3.47	3.00
Teaching techniques and the technology used enhanced course learning	4.41	4.50
The format of this course encouraged students to learn	4.31	4.56
Overall, the learning environment in this course is better than in most courses	4.35	4.22
I am more satisfied with class discussion in this course than in other courses	4.18	4.39
I had fewer problems getting help in this course than in other courses	3.59	3.56

messages beforehand and paste them during the chat sessions. In fact, one guest speaker used this method effectively. His short, precise sentences helped maintain the attention of the students.

In class chat rooms, it was difficult for the instructor who did not see students at the beginning of the course to associate students' names (which are typically unfamiliar to those outside the culture) with a student's chat name. In other words, it would be easier to personalize the chat room if the instructors and students can "see" each other in the beginning of the course and students use their names rather than handles in the chat room.

A recommendation after teaching the course in the first year to better fit the local students was to improve the feedback of the students about the course. A wed-based mid-term evaluation form was prepared and the students clicked into the form and expressed their opinion. The form included ratings on the course content and course delivery tools as well as open-ended comments. Fifteen students expressed their opinion in the mid-term feedback forms. Though students mostly expressed their satisfaction towards various aspects of the course, it was important for the instructors to know that the course was moving on the right track.

While internet chat has many disadvantages, it also has many advantages, some unexpected. The final presentation session of the first year was rescheduled twice because of the SARS epidemic. While the chat room sessions could still continue over the internet, the presentation session, which required the Hong Kong instructor to travel to Shanghai, did not. Since student presentations could not be conducted in a face-to-face setting, a video-conferencing facility was installed by HKU. Thus, when most of the classes in HKU were cancelled due to SARS, this chat-based course continued on schedule! This experience was common; for example, during the SARS outbreak, over a million Hong Kong students attended classes using the Hong Kong Education City portal for e-learning (Computerworld Honors Case Study, 2004).

Lesson #2: Adapting a Course to a Local Culture While at a Distance Is Difficult

The course content was originally designed for students in North America and has been offered successfully for many years. Since English was the language of information technology worldwide and its applications can easily be understood and transferred technically to all modern cities like Shanghai, the course was the least affected by cultural and linguistic differences compared to other courses of the program. Moreover, the design of the program was to enable students to be exposed to knowledge at the international level. The application of the knowledge to local situations was left to the students. However, unlike taking a program in a foreign country, the students of the present program reside in their local places. Thus, the demand for local knowledge and resources on the subject matter is greater.

The teacher from Hong Kong had many years of experience in supervising social work students from Hong Kong and Shanghai in China. He had formed a bridge to the local culture and context for the course. However, a gap still existed in knowledge of the subject area in the local context. Finding a local partner who was interested in teaching and research in the subject matter would be most desirable. However, if no such person could be found, the students could be enlisted to provide such knowledge and applications. In fact, since many students were actually involved in the work of using information technology applications in human services, they could have been used more effectively as an entry point for collecting knowledge in the local context.

Another limitation was a lack of understanding of the standards to be expected from the students. English proficiency of the students varied greatly as was reflected in the papers they wrote. The instructors found it difficult to know whether students had put enough effort into the course or whether they were simply constrained by their English proficiency. Given this problem, the instructors were often reluctant to push for more work and to insist that deadlines be met. Having a local partner who knew the standards of the students and who was available and willing to be involved in providing and developing local matters on the subject would greatly enhance the content and outcome of teaching. As speculated earlier, this lack of knowledge of local standards could be the reason that students expressed dissatisfaction with the course workload in both years.

Due to the content of the course, it was easy for the instructors to detect in both years that some students either directly downloaded materials from web pages in writing their term paper without acknowledging the source, or submitted papers written for other purposes to this course. In fact, it was easy to detect such behaviors since papers were submitted in Word format. Papers with only a few sections that had exceptionally good English were probably transferred directly from some website. Copying some phrases into any popular search engine could quickly lead to the original sources. Since the students seldom used materials from digital journals, web-based materials were the usual sources on which papers were based. Initially the instructors thought the problem was limited or due to language constraints and that the problem could be eliminated by implementing various recommendations suggested after the first year's teaching experience. However, such phenomena repeated in the second year. In fact, the instructors of other courses in this program also shared the same experience. The reasons for such behavior were complicated. Time constraints, less restrictive plagiarism requirements in the Chinese context, and language proficiency were the likely culprits. Clearly set expectations and standards, demonstrations that copying could easily be identified, and explicit punitive measures should be presented frequently and early in the course. However, this recommendation must be implemented with a clear understanding of local academic culture and norms, both of which were lacking for this course.

Lesson #3: Language Barriers Are Difficult to Overcome When Teaching Internationally

During the first year of teaching, one obvious limitation for the students in studying the present course was that their English proficiency varied greatly. Many students experienced difficulty in reading the textbook as well as other text-based reading assignments. The questions they raised during the chat sessions and the content of the first term paper (analysis of a social or organizational problem using the system perspective) indicated that they might have difficulties in understanding the requirements of the paper as well as the course content. The difficulty of understanding English was discovered by the Texas instructor when he typed questions to students during their web cam (1-way video/audio only) presentations. He could see all the students in the room working as a group to interpret the questions before the presenter answered the question. Other language problems existed. During the chat sessions, the students frequently typed in phrases such as "till good is better and better is best" and "data to summarize the factors through the figures." These phrases were rough translations of certain Chinese slogans. The Texas instructor, and sometimes even the Hong Kong instructor, did not understand these slogans as well as the students did. Getting a thorough explanation of the meaning of these slogans took valuable time from the course content, so often they were ignored. In year two, the instructors had the advantage of discussing the meaning of slogans without disturbing the class using the internet telephone software called Skype. Another example of language constraints involved jumping to websites during class to demonstrate key concepts. While this technique worked well with US students, the Chinese students needed a lot of time to translate the website and grasp the concept well enough for future chat discussion. Students would bookmark the websites and return to study them after class ended.

In order to overcome the language constraints, several measures were introduced in the second year. The students were asked to answer questions for the prescribed textbook chapters. Forms were designed for this purpose. Answering these questions also formed part of the assessment. In addition, the students shared their understanding of the chapters in the class forum. Most students did both. To help with paper organization, web-based forms were introduced through which students could record their ideas and generate a draft of their paper. The forms automatically emailed the contents to the instructors for immediate feedback, thus helping to quickly identify problems before students took the time to write their ideas into a formal paper in English. In addition, sample papers of the previous year were posted on the course webpage for student reference.

Lesson #4: Technical Difficulties Are a Major Concern and Difficult to Handle Remotely

The cooperation of the collaborating institutions was most important for constructing the learning environment for this course. As with any new international program, many problems existed. For various reasons in the first year, students could not use the library facilities of Fudan University and were not able to use the digital library resources in HKU until the end of the course. Hence, the students relied mainly on the course materials provided in the course website and from the internet to write their term papers. In the first year, the publisher of the textbook kindly offered 15 textbooks for the students to share. In the second year, the publisher allowed the course textbook to be available in PDF format on the course website. The free textbooks greatly facilitated students reading the textbook content.

Since Fudan computer labs were not available the first year due to bureaucratic complications, the instructor accompanied the students to a nearby Netbar (*Wang Ba* in Chinese, or cyber café in other places) to get a hand-on session in making homepages, trying the email facilities, and browsing through the course website. In the second year, Fudan University made a computer laboratory available for the introductory session and the final student presentations. They also made internet connected computers available in the laboratory. However, the connection to AOL chat was blocked, and thus students could not use the class chat room during the two events. Fortunately, access to the course website in HKU was still possible. Thus, students could get into the course website and use the alternative chat room and video-conferencing facilities prepared by HKU. To avoid misunderstanding and embarrassing situations, clearer requirements, backup facilities, and final testing of course technologies are necessary with the local partner.

The AOL IM chat room was particularly suited to this course, since it took only a few minutes to set up a totally new chat room and email all class members the login information. This feature was used several times over the two years when systems failed, firewalls prevented access, thunderstorms disrupted connections, or the internet stalled for unknown reasons. AOL IM had other useful features such as color/font customization for each student which aided recognition especially when message volume was high. Another useful feature was that users could save the chat text at any time. Thus students could review all class transcripts, which were also posted on the course website. This was particularly useful as the due dates and class schedules and assignments were frequently renegotiated in chat due to scheduling conflicts and holidays.

The local partner in Fudan University arranged for an instructor to help out in arranging the final presentation session inside an office of the Civil Affairs Bureau of Shanghai. In fact, the same person helped out in the local logistics such as collecting and delivering the free textbooks, booking class rooms, contacting students, etc. Before the final presentation session, the students sent the PowerPoint files to the instructors. They were then uploaded to the course website. During individual presentation, the instructors could actually see and hear the students via the video conferencing facilities while reading the Power-Point files on their own computer. The instructor could also ask questions using a microphone or type questions directly in chat. Fortunately, the video conferencing facility was stable enough to last throughout the sessions, although there were times that the signal was interrupted.

In the two years of teaching, one persisting communication problem with the students was that many email addresses were either no longer in use or mailboxes had exceeded their quota. Whenever a message was sent to the class, several error messages about undeliverable messages bounced back immediately. One reason is that the email addresses were collected from the students at the time they entered into the program. Some students might have shifted to other email addresses without informing the department. Besides, students seldom use the email addresses provided to each student by the department. To overcome this issue, a webpage indicating the most current email addresses was prepared along with a form for students to provide any updates. In addition, copies of important email messages sent by the instructors were also available on a webpage so that email messages would not be missed. Another problem was that the extensive use of email resulted in the threat of virus, such as HTML.Redlof.A. Numerous virus alert messages appeared in the emails coming from the students in China. Constant update of virus definitions and extra-precaution in opening attached files coming from our students was very important.

Since computer proficiency of the students varied, some experienced more problems in dealing with technical aspects of the course, such as installing facilities to get into the chat room, preparing homepages, developing PowerPoint presentations, etc. The students were encouraged to help each other in solving technical problems. Additional marks were given to those who were nominated by their classmates for having provided assistance to their classmates. In the first year, several students were nominated by their classmates. In the second year, the instructors recommended that the nominators be more explicit in describing the assistance they received. Consequently, five students were nominated with explicit descriptions provided by the nominators about the assistance they had offered to their classmates. In summary, attention must be paid to even the smallest technical problem, which can quickly and unexpectedly turn into a major stumbling block for one or all students.

Lesson #5: Students Overlook Technical Problems Because of Course Availability and Convenience

Despite the technical issues just mentioned, students' general rating about the course arrangement was very high. Table 4 presents the students' evaluation of the "Course Delivery Tools and Techniques." As was mentioned above, the use of chat room in teaching was highly rated by the students. In fact, many students also indicated that they were "more satisfied with class discussion in this course than in other courses" (4.18 in 2002 and 4.39 in 2003). Many students found that "the learning environment in this course is better than most courses" (4.35 in 2002, 4.22 in 2003). We were also pleased to learn that many students found that "the format of this course encouraged students to learn" (4.31 in 2002, 4.56 in 2003), that "my instructor was more available in this course than in other courses" (4.59 in 2002, 4.33 in 2003), and that "I felt more comfortable asking questions in this course than in other courses" (4.31 in 2002 and 4.28 in 2003). Many students also appreciated that "teaching techniques and the technology used enhanced course learning" (4.41 in 2002, 4.50 in 2003).

The students liked the homepage assignment and put much effort in preparing their personal websites. Many websites were well-designed and involved features that were beyond the requirement of the course. The personal websites were particularly helpful for the instructors to form personalized impressions of the students in the chat sessions where they could only see the individual user names. Students also actively participated in the class debates during the chat sessions. Though the debates were not graded, students still took them very seriously. Many put much effort in preparing for the debates and could not be stopped in posting their arguments when the debate time was over. The joy of the debate winners, which were decided by class vote, and frustrations of the losers illustrated that competition is one way to encourage participation.

The difficulty of some course assignments may have contributed to the item "I am satisfied with the amount of time required for the course" being scored relatively low by the students (3.88 in 2002, 3.89 in 2003). This low score probably reflected that the workload for this course was heavier than the other courses offered in the program where students typically were required to write only one term paper. However, a trade-off always exists between effort and learning outcomes. Without a better understanding of local academic norms, this issue might repeatedly occur in the future.

The course website was a very convenient tool for providing course materials and communicating about course events. It was always easy for the students to refer to the website for updated events and changes. For example, during the final student presentations, some students' PowerPoint files were uploaded to the website just minutes before the presentation but the whole class could read the presentation materials immediately in the computer laboratory or at home. The course website also saved much time and printing resources. In addition, the course website provided a password protected area accessible only to the class for restricted materials, such as attendance records, the textbook, and links to student homepages. Students showed considerable attention to the information posted. Whenever there was a mistake in any posting, they would immediately inform the instructors. To encourage low chat room participators and curb chat room dominators, the number of messages each student posted during a particular chat session was tallied and sent to the students via email on several occasions during the first year. This was done after every class session in the second year to let the students know that the instructors were concerned about not only the attendance but álso the involvement of each student in class chat sessions.

Lesson #6: Students Gain a More Realistic Understanding of the Strengths and Limitations of Internet Delivered Courses

Table 5 presents and compares changes in the attitude towards technology-based learning between the two groups of students for selected

TABLE 5. Attitude Towards Technology-Based Learning (Selected Items) Where 1 = No and 5 = Yes

Items	2002			2003		
	Pre Test (mean)	Post Test (Mean)	Effect Size (Pooled SD)	Pre Test (mean)	Post Test (Mean)	Effect Size (Pooled SD)
Attitude Towards Technology-Based Learning						
I have a positive attitude towards the use of technology for learning	4.73	4.71	−0.06	4.56	4.78	0.37
I have a positive attitude toward the use of the Internet for learning	4.60	4.76	0.28	4.50	4.78	0.43
Internet-based courses are more flexible in regards to my time than classroom-based courses	4.13	4.00	−0.15	3.44	4.50	0.85**
Students in Internet-based courses learn more than students in classroom-based courses	3.53	3.71	0.20	3.38	3.83	0.49
Students in Internet-based courses learn social work values and ethics better than students in classroom-based courses	3.07	3.00	−0.07	2.69	3.22	0.67#
Students in Internet-based courses will be more satisfied than students in classroom-based courses	3.53	3.59	0.06	2.75	3.50	0.81#
Class discussion in Internet-based courses is of better quality than class discussion in classroom-based courses	3.33	3.59	0.30	3.13	3.56	0.42
Certain social work content should not be taught over the Internet, but reserved for the classroom	3.87	4.41	0.67*	2.94	2.72	−0.17

* Paired t-test of mean difference is significant at the 0.05 level (2-tailed).
** Difference is significant at the 0.01 level (2-tailed).
\# Item with large effect size and with difference close to but not significant.

items of the course evaluation. Pre- and post-scores in most of the other items did not show any significant difference. One reason for a lack of significance was that most of the students hold very positive attitudes towards technology-based learning at the beginning of the course and thus, little room for improvement existed. For example, in the first year, the students rated highly on the item "I have a positive attitude towards the use of technology for learning" (4.73 in the beginning and 4.71 at the end of the course).

There were some significant but inconsistent changes on students' attitudes between the two years. Students in the second year scored much higher on the item "Internet-based courses are more flexible in regards to my time than classroom-based courses" after the course (3.44 before the course, 4.50 after, $t = 3.17$, $p < 0.01$). No such change in attitude existed in first year students. Another inconsistency was that students in the first year scored higher on "Certain social work content should not be taught over the internet, but reserved for the classroom" after the completion of the course (3.87 before the course, 4.41 after, $p < = 0.05$). However, no such change was observed the second year. These inconsistencies suggest that longitudinal research is desirable to determine student attitudes.

Students in the second year also scored more positively on the items "Students in Internet-based courses learn social work values and ethics better than students in classroom-based courses" (2.69 before the course, 3.22 after) and "Students in internet-based courses will be more satisfied than students in classroom-based courses" (2.75 before the course, 3.50 after). Social work values and ethics were discussed during the chat sessions and in class debates. However, without knowing how the other courses dealt with these issues, it was difficult to interpret such changes. In the beginning of the course, the mean score given to the latter item was quite low (2.75), but the change was quite positive after completing the course (3.50). Nevertheless, changes in these two items were only close to statistical significance ($p = 0.07$ and 0.10 respectively). Due to small sample size, the effect size was included in Table 5 to help understand the differences between pre- and post-test scores. The traditional interpretation of effect sizes suggests that $d = .20$ is a small effect, $d = .50$ is a medium effect and $d = .80$ is a large effect (Cohen, 1988). The effect size for these two items was relatively large (0.81 and 0.67 respectively). In the second year, the following items had a medium effect, "I have a positive attitude toward the use of the Internet for learning" (0.43), "Students in Internet-based courses learn more than students in classroom-based courses" (0.49), and "Class discussion in Internet-based courses is of better quality than class discussion in classroom-based courses" (0.42).

LOCAL ICT APPLICATIONS AND AREAS OF CONCERN

This section of the paper examines the IT application students reviewed and the topics of students' papers in order to help understand the current state of human services technology in China. While not specifically related to chat room teaching, these assignments provide a unique view of social services IT in China.

For the application review assignment, students could either choose applications suggested by the instructors or others that they identified. Since many applications are web-based or downloadable from the internet, students could easily find and review local applications that interested them. Table 6 presents the nature and distributions of the 25 applications students reviewed during both years.

The following are examples of the major types of applications reviewed by the students.

Examples of ICT Applications Reviewed

Employment. Job seeking system (http://www.21cnhr.com): Through this application, one can find information about jobs, such as salary, management, and vocation.

Social security. Social security information enquiry (http://www.83666.gov.cn/bszn/index.jsp): This application provides guidance to the social security system in Shanghai. Through the application, the officers or citizens in Shanghai can learn how to solve problems about social security and to understand related policies and legislation.

Health and mental health. Self diagnosis for sleeping disorder (http://www.shimian120.com/jibingzizhen/): This application is an online diagnostic application. If a person encounters sleeping problems and does

TABLE 6. Local Application Reviews (2 Years)

Types of applications reviewed	Number	%
Social/Medical Insurance	4	16.0
Health and Mental Health	4	16.0
Community Services, e.g., Neighborhood-Based Services	4	16.0
Employment	3	12.0
Older People	2	8.0
Housing	2	8.0
Others	6	24.0
Total	25	100.0

not want to disclose it to others, he or she can use this website to seek help without disclosing his/her true identity. However, the application has a great problem: the diagnostic conclusion is too simple and users need to look for help from other sources.

Community services. Community services in Shanghai (information and applications) (www.88547.com): This website provides professional family service. It supplies a large amount of useful information to residents, especially persons who are older or disabled, etc. The website address, 88547, which sounds like *"dial up my community"* in Chinese, is easy to remember.

The term paper required students to identify a social problem or organization problem that they wanted to help solve with information technology. They were required to analyze the problem using the system perspective and to identify major stakeholders along with their information and decision-making needs. The final part of the paper was to develop and evaluate options that enable the stakeholders to better address the problem.

Table 7 presents the topics selected by the students in both years. Nearly one quarter (22.2%) of the students selected topics related to improving services provided by the government. The students selecting these topics were mostly working in various government bureaus in Shanghai and their selected topics usually reflected their work. Term paper topics related to poverty and unemployment, such as income discrepancy between rural and urban areas, were also selected by the same proportion of students (22.2%). The shortage of affordable housing in Shanghai, which is a looming problem, was selected by seven students (15.6%). This topic was followed by education (13.3%) and health and mental health issues (8.9%).

Examples of Term Paper Titles

The titles of students' term papers are listed below because they also provide information about the state of social services and IT in China.

Improvement of Services

- Digitization of the funeral and interment service analysis and recommendations
- Develop a homecare service system to help the elderly of single households

Poverty and Unemployment

- Municipal administration in facing the challenge of beggars and vagrants
- The development of the reemployment system about the jobless workers from the SOEs [State Owned Enterprises].

Shortage of Affordable Housing

- Housing settlement projects and government intervention in Shanghai
- Low-income class affordable housing

Education

- The access of higher education for the people with disabilities
- To improve the education for children from transient populations

Health and Mental Health Issues

- Solutions of the HIV/AIDS situation in China
- Work pressure in big cities–how to relieve people under great work pressure

RECOMMENDATIONS FOR FURTHER IMPROVEMENT OF THE COURSE

Two years of teaching the course resulted in the following recommendations.

TABLE 7. Term Paper Topics

Category	2002-03	2003-04	Total	%
Improving services (community, elderly services, etc.)	5	5	10	22.2
Poverty and unemployment	3	7	10	22.2
Shortage of affordable housing	5	2	7	15.6
Education	1	5	6	13.3
Health and Mental Health Issues	3	1	4	8.9
Crime Control and Prevention	3	0	3	6.7
Digital Divide	1	0	1	2.2
Pollution	0	1	1	2.2
Others	1	2	3	6.7
Total	22	23	45	100.0

Reconsideration of the English Proficiency Requirement

The arrangement of allowing students not meeting the English proficiency to enter into the program on condition that they can meet the requirement upon graduation needs to be reconsidered. Our experience demonstrated that even some of those who had met the minimum entrance requirement could barely manage to speak and write English. It might take them a considerable amount of time to read an article written in English. Some told the Hong Kong instructor that they actually wrote their assignment papers in Chinese first and either translated them afterwards by themselves or with the help of a friend. The online course allowed the instructors to experiment with a number of measures, such as creating forms for students to generate a draft paper, encouraging students to read the required chapters by requiring them to answer questions about the related chapters before the class chat sessions, etc. With this additional support, the number of students who failed was reduced. An alternative arrangement might be to ask students to attend an English improvement course for a few months (or more) before they are accepted into the program. Of course, another option is to have the language requirement for the program reconsidered so that students can learn in their own language, if a teacher knowing the Chinese language is available. In fact, the department in HKU has applied several times to have such a requirement waived but without success. Meeting this request would require HKU to change its policy concerning the use of language and medium of instruction.

Keep Track of New Internet Communication Tools

The instructors have tried out new internet tools as a substitute for the text chat rooms, e.g., voice video cam and voice chat. We felt that voice or video would help communications and personalize the students and instructors. Our experimentation with Yahoo voice chat was not successful. Some students had problems installing Yahoo voice chat and inviting everybody into a chat room was complicated. Some students could not hear the voice messages; connections were unstable, and there were time lags. For one trial session, it took more than 15 minutes to get students into a voice chat room and some students were left behind. New voice chat services, for example, PalTalk (http://www.paltalk.com), are becoming available. PalTalk handles the bandwidth issue by only allowing one person to speak at a time. For the present course, text-based functions are still the most useful tools since text chat is stable and messages can be saved and easily reviewed.

Skype, a free internet phone service used in the second year, was very useful in allowing the instructors to communicate with each other before, during, and after the chat sessions. It helped the instructors to handle various learning and student issues, such as when to start the debate sessions, arrangement of guest speakers, and other division of work. Since progress in technology and connectivity changes rapidly, it is important to keep track of and experiment with new communication tools that might improve course delivery.

Involving Students and Graduates

Since many students have valuable experience in using information and communication technology in human services organizations, they can be very valuable resources in sharing and compiling local knowledge and applications. One option is to invite current and ex-students to present the IT applications they use in their work as well as their experience and comment in using them. PowerPoint files and materials from previous students could be saved with instructor comments and feedbacks for future uses. Previous papers and projects completed by students could also form a pool of valuable resources for the course, provided previous students granted permission.

Limiting Class Duration

In the second year, some chat sessions were combined into three-hour sessions. This was far from satisfactory for the instructor who conducted the chat sessions. This was probably unsatisfactory for the students also, if they read all the chat messages throughout the three hours. It should be noted that the number of student chat messages being posted dropped with the longer classes. It is recommended that chat sessions should not last more than two hours. This recommendation emphasizes another lesson, that the course must balance convenience and availability with learning. Better scheduling is an option, but one which is difficult to implement given local circumstances. Another option is to conduct a few sessions using the asynchronous bulletin board system (BBS) with clear topics of discussion, useful and manageable assignments, prompt responses by the teacher, and a fixed period for posting and responding to messages. However, our experience with the course BBS and listserv suggests that this option may not work well.

Explore Other Class Exercises

Instructors should always be thinking of ways to better use the internet for leaning. New class activities could be considered, for example, putting up some Chinese human service IT problems/situations and let student teams discuss how they would address the problem/situation. Students could vote on which team addressed the situation best. Then the class can discuss the result of voting and have a final vote. This would also prepare students for their term paper. By examining the success of others in web-based teaching and keeping track of new technological developments, instructors can bring in and test out new ways of course delivery. We have just begun to explore the power of the internet in teaching.

CONCLUSION

Teaching this web-based course was very fruitful for the instructors as well as the students. The lessons learned from the two years of teaching this course should be useful for instructors preparing to offer web-based courses for students residing in a country with a different culture. The course content and delivery format has been demonstrated to be relevant and readily accepted by the students of this programme in Shanghai. Online courses can enhance the exposure of students in developing countries to overseas experts in an effective and affordable manner. However, the lessons learned also indicated that difficulties relating to cultural, linguistic, and technical aspects need to be addressed.

REFERENCES

Chu, L. (September 10, 2002). A million users getting online. *Jeifang Daily* (in Chinese).

Cohen, J. (1988). *Statistical power analysis for the behavioral sciences (2nd ed.).* Hillsdale, NJ: Lawrence Erlbaum.

Computerworld Honors Case Study (2004). i-Classroom for the education community of Hong Kong. Retrieved January 5, 2005, from http://secure.cwheroes.org/briefingroom_2004/pdf_frame/index.asp?id=5067.

Ligon, J., Markward, M. J., & Yegidis, B. L. (1999). Comparing student evaluations of distance learning and standard classroom courses in graduate social work education. *Journal of Teaching in Social Work, 19*(1/2), 21-29.

Macy, J. A., Rooney, R. H., Hollister, C. D., & Freddolino, P. P. (2001). Evaluation of distance education programs in social work. *Journal of Technology in Human Services, 18*(3/4), 63-84.

Massimo, V. (2003). Integrating the WebCT discussion feature into social work courses: An assessment focused on pedagogy and practicality. *Journal of Technology in Human Services, 22*(1), 49-65.

Schoech, D. (2000). Teaching over the Internet: Results of one doctoral course. *Research on Social Work Practice, 10*(4), 467-486.

Schoech, D., & Helton, D. (2002). Qualitative and quantitative analysis of a course taught via classroom and Internet chatroom. *Qualitative Social Work, 1*(1), 111-124.

Stocks, J. T., & Freddolino, P. P. (1998). Evaluation of a World Wide Web-based graduate social work research methods course. *Computers in Human Services, 15*(2/3), 51-69.

Stocks, J. T., & Freddolino, P. P. (2000). Enhancing computer-mediated teaching through interactivity: The second iteration of a World Wide Web-based graduate social work course. *Research on Social Work Practice, 10*(4), 505-518.

Wernet, S. P., Olliges, R. H., & Delicath, T. A. (2000). Postcourse evaluations of WebCT (Web Course Tools) classes by social work students. *Research on Social Work Practice, 10*(4), 487-504.

Wong, Y. C. (2003). *Constructivist online learning environment for social work education: An evaluation of students' learning process and outcome.* Unpublished Ph.D. thesis, University of Hong Kong, HK.

Wong, Y. C., & Schoech, D. (2005). A tale of three cities: Teaching online to students in Shanghai from Hong Kong and Texas. *Journal of Technology in Human Services*, 24(1/2), 121-145.

World Bank (2003, July 2003). World development indicators database. Retrieved November 25, 2003, from http://www.worldbank.org/data/databytopic/GNIPC.pdf.

doi:10.1300./J017v25n01_04

The Forgotten Dimension in Learning: Incorporating Emotion into Web-Based Education

Robert J. MacFadden

SUMMARY. This paper explores the neglected role of emotion in education and particularly of emotion in online education. It presents some historical considerations concerning emotion, and some recent findings on brain research, emotion and learning. A CEO model that incorporates consideration of emotion in web-based education is presented along with recent findings from an e-focus group that asked participants, who had just completed a web-based course, about their perceptions of emotions in online education. It concludes with a summary of early findings and suggestions for those developing and conducting web-based courses on how to incorporate emotions into web-based learning. doi:10.1300/J017v25n01_05 *[Article copies available for a fee from The Haworth Document Delivery Service: 1-800-HAWORTH. E-mail address: <docdelivery@haworthpress.com> Website: <http://www.HaworthPress.com> © 2007 by The Haworth Press, Inc. All rights reserved.]*

KEYWORDS. Online learning, web-based education, emotions, affect, learners' perceptions

Robert J. MacFadden, PhD, is Associate Professor, Faculty of Social Work, University of Toronto, 246 Bloor St. West, Toronto, M5S 1A1, Canada.

[Haworth co-indexing entry note]: "The Forgotten Dimension in Learning: Incorporating Emotion into Web-Based Education." MacFadden, Robert J. Co-published simultaneously in *Journal of Technology in Human Services* (The Haworth Press, Inc.) Vol. 25, No. 1/2, 2007, pp. 85-101; and: *HUSITA7–The 7th International Conference of Human Services Information Technology Applications: Digital Inclusion–Building a Digital Inclusive Society* (eds: C. K. Law, Yu Cheung Wong, and John Yat Chu Fung) The Haworth Press, Inc., 2007, pp. 85-101. Single or multiple copies of this article are available for a fee from The Haworth Document Delivery Service [1-800-HAWORTH, 9:00 a.m. - 5:00 p.m. (EST). E-mail address: docdelivery@haworthpress.com].

Available online at http://jths.haworthpress.com
doi:10.1300/J017v25n01_05

Emotion remains a mystery in Western culture and is simultaneously feared and revered. Henri (1865-1929) exhorts us to "Cherish your own emotions and never undervalue them," while Sagan (1980) warns us that "Where we have strong emotions, we're liable to fool ourselves." Carl Jung celebrates the profound nature of emotion when he says that "There can be no transforming of darkness into light and of apathy into movement without emotion" (Jung, 1938, p. 32).

This paper explores the neglected role of emotion in education and particularly of emotion in online education. It briefly presents some historical considerations concerning emotion, and identifies some recent findings on brain research, emotion and learning. A model that incorporates consideration of emotion in web-based education is presented along with recent findings from an e-focus group that asked participants, who had just completed a web-based course, about their perceptions of emotions in online education. While knowledge about this phenomenon is at an exploratory level, it does underscore the importance of considering the affective dimension in understanding and facilitating learners' experiences and in constructing web-based education.

Historically, emotion has been ignored in education in favour of a heavy emphasis on cognition (Astleitner, 2000). As mentioned by the e-focus participants within our study, the expression of emotion has been seen as inappropriate in education (Coles, 1999; Sylwester, 1994). Astleitner (2000) describes an historical progression in education of seeing emotions as intangible factors which are disruptive of cognitive objectives, to becoming consequences of the learning process, to being attitudes towards or against something. Goleman, more recently, views emotions as a type of intelligence (Goleman, 1997) and emotions have become the content of instruction itself. A more current approach has been termed "emotionally sound instruction" and highlights the importance of incorporating emotions in learning and the need to increase positive and decrease negative emotions during instruction (Taylor, 1994; O'Regan, 2003).

Educational theorists and practitioners have more recently identified emotions as a key element in learning. Sylwester (1994) notes that emotion ". . . drives attention, which in turn drives learning and memory." Goleman (1997) remarks that anxious, angry and depressed students don't take in information efficiently and do not learn well. And Vail (2002) describes emotions as the "On-Off Switch" for learning and that faced with frustration, despair, worry, sadness or shame, children lose access to their memory, reasoning, and the capacity to make connections. Pekrun (1992) notes that emotions may initiate, terminate or disrupt information and result in selective information processing.

Brain research has recently provided some knowledge that illuminates the relationship between emotion and learning. Increasingly, emotion is being seen as mediating all learning and cannot be separated from logical, rote learning. Jensen (1998) remarks that emotions drive attention, meaning and memory and are critical to patterning in the brain. Stock (1996, p. 6) notes that ". . . every sensory input we receive is processed through our emotional center first . . . before it is sent on and processed in our rational mind . . ." Emotion is described as central to learning and ". . . making possible all creative thought" (Greenspan, 1997), ". . . a sort of biological thermostat which activates attention. . . which then activates a rich set of problem-solving and response systems and . . . In fact, of driving everything" (Brandt, 2000).

Pekrun and his colleagues (2002) in one study found that university students' emotions measured early in the semester predicted cumulative grades and final course exam scores at the end of semester. These researchers noted that academic self-efficacy, academic control of achievement and subjective values of learning and achievement related significantly to students' academic emotions (Pekrun et al., 2002).

Norman (2002), who has written extensively on the science of design, notes that emotions directly impact cognition. Positive feelings enhance creative, breadth-first thinking whereas negative affect encourages depth-first processing and minimizes distractions. Norman (2002) remarks that ". . . neurochemicals change the parameters of thought, adjusting such things as whether reason is primarily depth first (focused, not easily distracted) or breadth first (creative, out-of-the-box thinking but easily distractible)." Negative affect, to a point, can focus the mind leading to better concentration. Norman remarks that, "Anxiety and fear squirt neural transmitters into the brain that narrow the thought process. In general this is good to focus upon a specific threat or problem." Positive emotion can broaden the thought process and leads to creative thinking with a side effect of easy distractibility. This is noteworthy for online education where the Web presents such opportunities for exploration and losing focus. Positive emotions can improve our performance in tasks and negative emotions can make it harder to do even simple tasks. Fredrickson (2003, p. 333) notes that ". . . 20 years of experiments . . . show that when people feel good, their thinking becomes more creative, integrative, flexible and open to information." Fredrickson terms this "The Broaden and Build Theory" associated with positive emotions. Positive emotions solve problems around personal growth and development and lead to states of mind and modes of behaviour that prepare an individual for difficult situations and help build enduring personal resources, including social supports.

The author has been involved with three colleagues in developing and evaluating a model of web-based education that incorporates a focus on emotions in online learning. This has been described in MacFadden, R. J., Herie, M., Maiter, S., and Dumbrill, G. C. (in press) and in MacFadden, R. J. (in press). The details about this model have been taken directly from these sources.

THE CEO MODEL:
A CONSTRUCTIVISTIC, EMOTIONALLY-ORIENTED MODEL OF WEB-BASED INSTRUCTION

This CEO model utilizes a constructivistic approach that emphasizes the emotional dimensions in online learning. Learning involves participants formulating and reformulating ideas, to order, reorder, test and justify their ideas, all within an emotional context of safety and trust (Gold, 2001).

Rather than encouraging positive emotions and discouraging negative emotions, this model recognizes that sometimes learning involves negative emotions. Piaget (Bybee & Sund, 1982) views learners as changing their perspectives when they are brought to a place of some discomfort, when their existing ideas no longer explain new information. The disequilibrium that is created can result in new understandings and new paradigms in thinking for learners.

The CEO model incorporates three learning stages which reflect the constructivist paradigm, enhanced by a focus on emotions.

A Model for Online Education Focusing on Emotions and Paradigmatic Change

Stage	Purpose	Activity	Potential Feelings of Learners
1: Safety	To create a safe learning environment that facilitates risk taking and examining one's ways of thinking	Construct rules to foster free communication and ensure safety. Monitoring of communication to ensure compliance and safety	Safety, support & acceptance
2: Challenge	To provide the opportunity for participants to critically examine their knowledge and worldviews	Introduce exercises and processes that allow participants to step outside their existing ways of thinking	Disequilibrium, confusion, anxiety, frustration in a context of safety, support & acceptance
3: New thinking	To create opportunities for engaging with new knowledge and gaining new ways of viewing the world	Introduce alternative knowledge and ways of viewing the world	"Ah ha!" moments leading to a new equilibrium, satisfaction, exhilaration

Safety

Creating a safe learning environment is critical for learners to be able to think freely, to express opinions, and to challenge oneself and others. All learners and facilitators are asked to deliberately make the course a place where they and others feel safe to risk themselves through expressing ideas. Rules of netiquette are posted, discussed and monitored, and group discussions are reviewed by facilitators to ensure a safe and supportive environment. Group members are encouraged to use any of the various channels to contact facilitators (i.e., course e-mail, private e-mail, phone) early if they have any concerns in this area. Safety is always a fundamental and primary concern and this is communicated throughout the course.

Challenge

A constructivist approach offers a deepening of the educational experience through challenging participants' thinking (Gold, 2001). In this web-based course on enhancing cultural competency which utilized the CEO model, participants were asked to describe their own cultures by finding and sharing a website with other learners that reflects this. This assignment usually provoked considerable annoyance and frustration because many found this to be impossible. Learners were asked to explore their feeling experience about this and to reflect on how clients might feel about professionals who attempt to understand their cultures based on a single source. With these emotions "switched-on," learners were asked to think about what this means for professionals who rely on a cultural literacy approach which relies more on written content about cultures. Many learners who depended solely on the cultural literacy approach experienced some dissonance and understood both cognitively and experientially the limitations of catalogued definitions of culture.

New Thinking

When dissonance and disequilibrium occur, it is important to encourage new ways of thinking. When information is introduced that promotes this, new models are explored to provide alternatives. Additionally, strengths of existing models are reviewed to acknowledge parts that might still inform the learners' practice. In the previous example, some learners did not experience dissonance since their experience confirmed what they already knew.

In the CEO model, there is recognition that the early stages (e.g., first two weeks) of a course should be devoted to assisting the learner to become comfortable and engaged with the online environment. This includes meeting other learners, test driving the website, understanding the structure and knowing where things are. Social engagement is critical since so much of learning is socially oriented, and co-learners can be an important source of support and confirmation. Some web-based courses give bonus grades to fellow students who assist others with problems (Wong & Schoech, in press). Friendly biography sections where learners can travel to and remind themselves about the background of co-learners and facilitators can be helpful to build connections and ongoing support.

In this early stage, the CEO model focuses the learning objectives on understanding and using the technology to develop a sense of competency, and connecting with fellow learners and facilitators to begin development of a positive working alliance. Assignments are aimed at building technical expertise and experiencing early success, posting the bio information to foster connections and overviewing the content of the course. Course assignments become progressively more challenging as the learner feels increasingly comfortable with the technology, the content and the co-learners.

AN E-FOCUS GROUP ON LEARNER PERCEPTIONS OF EMOTION IN WEB-BASED EDUCATION

Much research exploring emotion in learning is still at an exploratory stage. This is particularly the case for emotion and web-based education. An e-focus group was recently conducted with learners who had just completed a web-based course on Cross-Cultural Social Work Practice. This was a 12 week credit course offered at the M.S.W. level that was completely web-based. A convenience sample of six M.S.W. students volunteered to attend this virtual e-focus group that was held three weeks after the course finished and after grades were submitted. The author, who was not connected with the course, was the moderator and students signed on anonymously, although it might have been possible to identify a few participants given the names that they chose. A complete university ethics review was conducted and students agreed to have their comments shared in a non-identifying manner. This e-focus group was essentially a secure chat session over a two-hour period.

The exact dialogue could be captured easily and subjected to analysis. Participants were asked about their perceptions of emotions, emotions in education and particularly in web-based learning. Some of the preliminary results are reported below. The comments in square brackets are the actual comments of participants without any editing.

Emotion in Society, Science and Social Work

Participants commented on their perceptions of the role of emotion in society, in Social Work and within education. First there was acknowledgement that emotions are a problem for society: "well thats kinda how our society is built i think. any strong emotion, sadness, happy, anger expressed in public makes people uncomfortable"; "i think people in general have difficulty in discussing their emotions and feelings to others"; "emotion makes people uncomfortable." Science, in particular, was seen as being negative towards emotion: "i think science and so on has tried to stifle emotion and take it out of the equation, however i personally dont think thats possible." Social Work, although it is seen as acknowledging emotion ("SW acknowledges the role of emotion which i think is important") is similarly ambivalent: "because the field of social work is still quite insecure about itself and is trying to prove that there is, indeed, a knowledge base to social work–and so academia steers clear of emotions which have been second rate in academia"; "because 'professionalism' is supposed to be 'intellectual', 'objective', not emotional and subjective"; "Emotions are still considered weak, which is completely false"; "western professionalism is science-oriented . . . so, anything that wants credibility, has to be quantified, observable, objective"; "i think mainstream 'western' professionalism and science, doesn't, right now, have space for emotions."

Emotion in the Classroom

Within the classroom there are other issues with emotions: "I don't always feel like emotions are welcomed in the classroom"; "the professor is afraid of his or her own emotional response to a student's emotion." One participant suggested the emotions are compartmentalized, kept out of the classroom but shared outside the classroom: "emotional discussion definitely take place after class." One participant summarized by suggesting there is a message given in classes "sometimes it's like 'suck it up, you're a professional now.'"

Emotion in the Online Class

The author and his colleagues (MacFadden, Herie, Maiter, & Dumbrill, in press) have described a range of emotions experienced in an online class which they termed the "emotional topography" of the course.

In this course, the participants described a wide range of emotions. Examples include: "Excited by the readings, but nervous about how quickly one could be misunderstood"; "i felt frustrated because i felt isolated in my experience"; "i also felt frustrated with the work we were supposed to do collectively as a group"; " i felt disconnected from the group." When these emotions were examined the following pattern was identified. The numbers in round brackets indicate the frequency of the emotion explicitly mentioned: frustration (9), disconnected (3), disappointed (2), overwhelmed (2), uncomfortable (2), fear (1), hurt (1), nervous (1), vulnerable (1), not feeling well (1) and excited (3), free (to speak) (2), happy (1), connected (1) and comfortable (1). The ratio of "negatives" to "positives" is 2:1 . This may or may not reflect the actual subjective feelings of the majority of the class participants since the e-focus group was only six out of 21 participants. Course evaluations are being compiled and will be compared with these findings. It may be easier to remember and to focus on "negative" emotions since these may be viewed as more interesting or more important as "problems" than to acknowledge more "positive" emotions.

Stifling and Stimulating

There was some implication that emotion can make an educational situation unsafe and stifle discussion: "I agree that one needs to be considerate of others, but it seems sometimes we are more hesitant than is necessary and I feel that good discussions about uncomfortable topics are thus avoided"; "even the facilitator (prof) steers the discussion away from emotionally charged discussions."

Yet emotions also seen as stimulating discussion: "I think it could improve the educational experience," "in face-to-face, we might have fed off of the excitement others had for the subject a little more."

Tools for Expressing Emotion

To compensate for the lack of richness in text-based online communication, users have employed a variety of tools to communicate emotion online.

In this two-hour e-discussion on emotions in online education, most emotions were expressed in textual form, e.g., "I was really excited about most of the readings as well" but there was some use of other tools. Emoticons were used twice: "where did p6 go? : ("; and 'evidence-based' :)." Ellipses were employed by many for effect, e.g., "i think i used a lot of smiley faces . . . a lot of '. . . ' to express hesitation or thinking . . . ." Question marks were indicative of hesitation or puzzlement: "lots of ???"; "or in the same ways??"; actually i'm not sure." Exclamation marks indicated excitement, enthusiasm or emphasis and were well-used: "for sure online!!!!"; "i hated that!!!"; "i agree!!"; "plainly discuss it!!!! there have been a couple of times when I have felt various emotions about a client situation/interaction, but would have liked a safe place to say that I was 'feeling' (insert an emotion here. . . . . .)." Capitalization was also well-used to denote agreement or to "shout" out something: "moderator–YES!"; "but i think face to face discussions CAN help"; "since my opinions and views are NOT mainstream"; "MAYBE i might have felt the need to address it right there." Some unique comments were added to imply humour, for instance "hehe" "haha" or amazement "wow, i (as a member of the 'majority') never thought of that"; "oh wow. good question."

Personal Styles

E-focus group participants discussed their perceptions of emotions and the expression of emotions online. It seemed that there was a personal style involved in online expression. Some participants termed emoticons "corny": "I think it doesn't really capture emotions–emotions are too complex–yeah, emoticons are not my style; seem a little corny." Others expressed a preference with putting emotions into words: "I'm more likely to type my emotions as well instead of using the emoticons"; "I think I would describe my behaviour to indicate my feelings." Some viewed emoticons as gender-based: "the smiley faces seem like a girlie thing–I can say that because I'm a woman"; "i do notice women use emoticons and so on more often in instant messaging but i think it's because its more socially acceptable for women to express emotions"; "I notice that in e-mail my women friends use the smiley faces, not the men." One respondent wasn't sure: "i think, in my experience, men and women have used emotion tools in instant messaging pretty equally when chatting with me . . . but maybe in different ways."

Gender

Some participants connected the attitudes towards emotion as being related to gender: "stereotypically–men are supposed to be 'logical', women 'emotional'. . . so it would make sense if 'logic' and 'rational thought' are given credibility in a world controlled by men"; "i think women are supposed to be more emotionally open"; "i think emotion may be more valued in virtual spaces for women"; "yes there is . . . . women tend to demonstrate their emotions more than men"; "the stereotype is that the realm of emotions belongs to women and rational thought to men"; "and 'emotion' is considered frivolous and useless"; "I think there is power in emotion, however, and perhaps there is fear of that power"; "Men perhaps will stick to statistics of racism or proven facts and stay clear of the more invisible acts of racism and the strong emotions attached."

Emotion, Familiarity and Comfort

Online emotional expression for some participants appeared to be a function of how well they know the persons they are communicating with. Respondents stated: "I tend to use emoticons only with people I know really well"; "I think emoticons work best when you know the person you're interacting with"; "I felt much more of a connection to the people in my group that I knew from my other classes–because I could picture them in my mind"; "i think emotion is different from opinion. a safe place to express emotion for me is familiarity with people"; "my best discussions, intellectual and moreso emotional, have been in small groups–2 or 3 people,–but people i KNOW, in that i would know how they would respond, i would know that they are allies."

Group Size

Group factors are also seen as playing a role in emotional expression online. Size seems to be an important factor: "Yes, even though I'm not usually for small groups, I think if we were incorporating emotions, especially speaking personally, small groups would be best"; "yay for small groups"; "for small groups and group composition i think to bring emotion into education would require different formats for example i've always felt more comfortable in small groups of 3 rather than the whole class, in small groups though, you're less likely to find an ally who might understand and relate." However, some participants identified a preference for larger groups in promoting the expression of ideas, but not necessarily emotional expression: "see, i don't connect emotionally to everyone . . . and with my non-mainstream experiences and thoughts and feelings, i am more likely to find someone who understands if i have a greater pool of people . . . not to say that I could express emotion in a large class setting"; "i just don't find small groups to be any more useful to me, in fact i feel more disconnected because it makes me even more aware that i am not understood or related to." One participant wasn't sure about the effect of group size: "i'm wondering if the format (large or small) has both pros and cons, is there another way to make a safer place to express emotions? maybe certain group rules and norms?"

Newness

One interesting issue that was identified is the newness of online communication and knowing how to express oneself emotionally online. Some participants noted: "was difficult to know how to challenge someone online when I disagreed with them"; "to be honest, I don't even know how to do an emoticon if I wanted–it has come onto the scene too recently for me"; "i think online learning is new for all cultures as the tech itself is pretty new." The ability to express oneself online may be related to developing skill and comfort over time: "I did not say as much because I had to type it and I am a slow at typing"; "i think like anything the online env. takes time to get used to as it is markedly diff from face to face, after getting used to it one can decide if it works for them."

Designing Web-Based Education

When asked if they were to design a web-based course whether participants would introduce a consideration of emotion, there was some ambivalence: "yes, but how I'm not sure"; " i'm not sure . . . " "yes"; "it seems that participants may just not be interested"; " i would but i'm not sure how"; "i might try to create an environment where emotion is "ok"; "i think it is important"; "i think a discussion of the issue would be good, sometime into the course–not right at the beginning." Some participants saw the constructive side of focusing on emotions: "– i don't think we use it as much as we could, even in F2F discussions" and the significance of emotion for learning: " one's emotional state can have a huge impact on how he or she may respond to a given issue"; "If I am involved emotionally it enhances my learning, my thinking/intellect."

Face-to-Face versus Online

In some of the literature, online education has been termed as "cold" and dehumanizing. There was one positive comment about FTF, "but i think face to face discussions CAN help, in humanizing the experience" and how this particular online experience, "lacked live interaction, therefore I did not feel any connection of any kind with the other members" and how "i felt frustrated because i felt isolated in my experience."

It is instructive to examine the participants' perceptions of FTF versus online education in terms of emotion. FTF education is generally seen as containing more emotional expression than online: "emotionally though i think class discusssions bring out more emotions"; "in face-to-face, we might have fed off of the excitement others had for the subject a little more"; "but i think face to face discussions CAN help, in humanizing the experience"; "maybe people are more engaged in face-to-face conversations? i think"; "i think it's harder to convey emotion in an online setting which is why when it comes to emotion id rather have a face to face conversation." In response to asking whether online education was "safer" one participant agreed, "yes, but less emotionally satisfying."

Yet some participants felt more free to express themselves online: "that was helpful to me, in that i could express myself without 'seeing' 'judgement' on others' faces"; "actually i felt free to express myself in my own way." It may be that some participants appreciate some of the lack of visual cues: "i am pretty sure that if this were a face-to-face class, i would have felt even LESS comfortable expressing myself– since my opinions and views are NOT mainstream"; "i found the online env. sort of sterile, but in terms of expressing oneself i do think there is less risk"; "i think it is easier to express ones views online given the saensitivity of the subject matter"; "but ultimately, it was helpful for me that it was online, because i am very affected by people's reactions to what i say, and i couldn't see their reactions online, so i was more free to say what i wanted to say."

For some, FTF situations provide more feedback and connection with others and permit more clarification: "In class you can see people's faces and see if they have registered what your point is or totally missed it"; "in class, you can make shrugging gestures, to show that you aren't quite sure about what you're saying"; "clarification and understanding of an issue would be different in a face to face"; "you can automatically address an issue and receive immediate feedback . . . more or less"; "it's also easier to identify allies in a face-to-face course, i think"; "I would have said something (well most likely) in a face-to face right away"; "It's more difficult online because my demeanor says a lot about who I am–and not sure I can show my demeanor online."

Delay in Communication

The delay factor in asynchronous web-based education has a significant impact on the experience of participants. From a positive perspective, it permits an opportunity to think about one's responses and to craft a reply that is well thought out: "but i think the delay also allowed 'thinking time'. . .?"; "i think the time lag does allow people to step back and comment"; "i was able to express a lot online due to the time allowed to think things through as typing, as well as the absence of others reactions"; "yes, it allowed me to phrase things better, rather than just responding at the moment. and allowed me to think out the comment, think out my response"; "yes, it did give that moment to really think through my thinking–writing is slower than speaking and you can see the words you have written, whereas your words are invisible yet present and cannot be erased after looking at them."

From a negative perspective, the significant delay in communication caused problems: "not being live online does not allow for clarification"; "well, for one thing, it was difficult when you didn't get any response to a post that you put a lot of emotional energy into"; "at one point I felt hurt that someone had misunderstood me for a whole week before posting back"; "sometimes if i didnt log on till late in the week, i wouldnt respond to some of the earlier comments because they seemed to already be dealt with in the group"; "It leaves you wondering what the other people are thinking for that whole time–especially when your posting was not understood the way you meant it." The disappointment involved in taking the time to create a detailed response and then having it ignored was mentioned by several: "well, for one thing, it was difficult when you didn't get any response to a post that you put a lot of emotional energy into"; "because there were times that I thought a really important comment (well, important in my opinion) would be discussed in more depth, but then it was dropped as though it really meant nothing"; "–it might sound silly–but there were a couple of times that I was excited to go back and read what people in my group thought about a comment–but no one else thought it needed to be commented on . . . "

There is a whole world of learner experience that many facilitators may not perceive in a web-based environment. Hara and Kling (2001), in their qualitative study of a web-based course, discovered that much early learner communication was negative and reflected considerable learner discontent. When some of this discontent seemed relieved, the facilitator believed the early problems had been remedied. Additional analysis indicated that many learners had given up expressing concerns and essentially decided to tolerate the problems until the course was over. Even after the finish of the course, the facilitator was not aware of the deep level of discontent within the course.

CONCLUSION

This paper has drawn from a range of sources, including recent qualitative research, to identify some findings, attitudes and perceptions regarding emotion in learning and in online learning. Given that our knowledge of the impact of emotion on learning is at such a beginning level, the following statements are offered as hypotheses that can be considered and explored in further studies:

1. The role of emotion is poorly understood in society and in learning.
2. Educators and learners may have ambivalent attitudes towards emotion.
3. Science and professionalism may de-value emotion.
4. New research in brain functioning is supporting a major role for emotion in memory, cognition and learning.
5. Emotion can enhance focus, motivation and reasoning. Under certain situations it can also impair memory, motivation and reasoning.
6. Positive emotions may stimulate more creative, integrative, flexible thinking and an openness to information.
7. Emotion has been associated with academic performance.
8. Emotions are too complex to be categorized as strictly positive and negative. Lower levels of anxiety, for instance, may enhance focus, motivation and performance.

9. Learning involves a wide range of emotions.
10. The emotional experience within a course may be an important factor in valuing the course.
11. The expression of emotion may be seen as a danger in creating a "safe" classroom for discussion.
12. Facilitators may deliberately discourage the expression of emotion.
13. Learners may compartmentalize emotion, "saving" it for outside the classroom.
14. Learners may have a "personal style" in communicating emotion online.
15. Some of the features of online education and communication may limit the expression of emotion.
16. Various tools can be used to enrich online communication with emotion.
17. Online emotional expression may be related to gender, personal style, comfort with others, size of the group, and skill and knowledge with computers and the internet.
18. Facilitators may be missing important emotional experiences of learners such as feeling ignored or unappreciated in an asynchronous communication environment.
19. Course experiences can be described as having an "emotional topography" with common feelings and experiences among users at different points.
20. Web-course developers should consider the emotional experiences of learners in designing courses.
21. Web-course facilitators should be aware of the variety of emotions experienced by learners throughout the course and be prepared to respond to them.

REFERENCES

Astleitner, H. (2000a). Designing emotionally sound instruction: The FEASP approach. *Instructional Science, 28*, 169-198.

Astleitner, H., & Leutner, D. (2000b). Designing instructional technology from an emotional perspective. *Journal of Research on Computing in Education, 32*(4), 497-510.

Brandt, R. (April, 2000). On teaching brains to think: A conversation with Robert Sylwester. *Educational Leadership.*

Bybee, R. W., & Sund, R. B. (1982). *Piaget for educators* (2nd Ed). Columbus, OH: Charles Merrill.

Campbell-Gibson, C. (2000). The ultimate disorienting dilemma: The online learning community. In Evans, T., & Nation, D. (Eds.), *Changing university teaching: Reflections on creating educational technologies*. London: Kogan Page.

Coles, G. (1999). Literacy, emotions and the brain. Retrieved May 24, 2004 from http://www.readingonline.org/critical/coles.html.

Collie, K. R., Mitchell, D., & Murphy, L. (2000). Skills for online counseling: Maximum impact at minimum bandwidth. In Bloom, J. W. & Walz, G. R. (Eds.), *Cybercounseling and cyberlearning: Strategies and resources for the millennium*. Alexandria, VA: American Counseling Association.

Currin, L. (2003). Feelin' groovy. *Elearn Magazine*. Retrieved May 2, 2004, from http://www.elearnmag.org/subpage/sub_page.cfm?article_pk=10221&page_number_nb=1&title=FEATURE%20STORY.

Fredrickson. B. (July/August, 2003). The value of positive emotions. *American Scientist*, 91, 330-335.

Glazer, C. (2002). Play nice with others: The communication of emotion in an online environment. Retrieved May 2, 2004, from http://www.scholarlypursuits.com/dec_comm.pdf.

Gold, S. (June, 2001). A constructivist approach to online training for online teachers. *JALN*, 5(1), Retrieved May 23, 2004, from the World Wide Web: http://www.sloan-c.org/publications/jaln/v5n1/v5n1_gold.asp .

Goleman, D. (1997). *Emotional intelligence*. New York: Bantam.

Greenspan, S. (1997). *The growth of the mind and the endangered origins of intelligence*. Reading, MA: Addison-Wesley.

Hara, N., & Kling, R. (2001). Student distress in web-based distance education. *Educause Quarterly*, 3, 68-69.

Hiltz, S., & Turoff, M. (2002). What makes learning effective? *Communications of the ACM*, 45(4), 56-59.

Jerry, P., & Collins, S. (2005). Web-based education in the human services: Use of web-based video clips in counselling skills training. In MacFadden, R., Moore, B., Schoech, D., & Herie, M. *Web-based education in human services: Models, methods and best practices*. New York: The Haworth Press, Inc.

Jung, C. G. (1938). Psychological reflections: A Jung anthology. *Psychological Aspects of the Modern Archetype*, 9.

LeDoux, J. (1996). *The emotional brain: The mysterious underpinnings of emotional life*. New York: Simon & Schuster.

MacFadden, R. J., Herie, M., Maiter, S., & Dumbrill, G. C. (in press). Achieving high touch in high tech: A constructivist, emotionally-oriented model of web-based instruction. In Beaulaurier, R., & Haffey, M. (Eds.) *Technology and social work education*. New York: The Haworth Press, Inc.

MacFadden, R.J. (in press). Soul on ice: Incorporating emotion in web-based education. In MacFadden, R., Moore, B., Schoech, & D., Herie, M. *Web-based education in the Human Services: Models, methods and best practices*. New York: The Haworth Press, Inc.

MacFadden, R. J., Maiter, S., & Dumbrill, G. (2002). High tech and high touch: The human face on online education. In Resnick H. & Anderson, P. (Eds.). *Innovations in technology and human services: Practice and education*. New York: The Haworth Press, Inc.

Murphy, L., & Mitchell, D. (1998). When writing helps to heal: E-mail as therapy. *British Journal of Guidance and Counselling*, 26, 21-31.

Myerson, D., Weick, K. E., & Kramer, R. (1996). Swift trust and temporary systems. In Kramer, R. M. & Tyler, T. R. (Eds.), *Trust in organizations* (pp. 166-195). Thousand Oaks, CA: Sage.

Norman, D. A. (2002). Emotion and design: Attractive things work better. *Interactions Magazine*, ix (4), 36-42. Retrieved May 24, 2004, from http://www.jnd.org/dn.mss/Emotion-and-design.html.

O'Regan, K. (2003). Emotion and e-learning. *Journal of Asynchronous Learning Networks*. Volume 7, Issue 3, September, 78-92.

Pekrun, R., Molfenter, S., Titz, W., & Perry, R. (2000). Emotion, learning and achievement in university students: Longitudinal studies. Paper presented at the annual meeting of the American Educational Research Association, New Orleans, LA, April.

Pekrun, R., Goetz, T., & Titz, W. (2002). Academic emotions in students' self-regulated learning and achievement: A program of qualitative and quantitative research. *Educational Psychologist*, *37*(2), 91-105.

Redden, C. (2003). Emotions in the cyber classroom. *Educator's Voice*. Retrieved May 24, 2004, from http://www.ecollege.com/news/EdVoice_arch_0611.learn.

Rice, R., & Love, G. (1987). Electronic emotion. *Communication Research*, *14*(1), 85-108.

Sagan, C. (1980). Cosmos. New York: Random House.

Stock, B. (1996). Getting to the heart of performance. *Performance Improvement*, *35*(8). Retrieved May 24, 2004, from http://www.byronstock.com/pdfs/heart.pdf.

Sylwester, R. (1994). How emotions affect learning. *Educational Leadership*, Vol. 52, Number 2.

Thissen, F. (2000). The medium and the message. Interface design for online learning environments and cooperative learning in virtual worlds. Retrieved May 24, 2004, from http://www.frank-thissen.de/mediumandmessage.pdf.

Vail, P. (2002). Emotion: The on/off switch for learning. Retrieved May 23, 2004, from http://www.schwablearning.org/pdfs/expert_vail.pdf.

Witmer, D., & Katzman, S. (1997). On-line smiles: Does gender make a difference in the use of graphic accents? *Journal of Computer Mediated Communication*, 2(4). Retrieved May 23, 2004, from http://www.ascusc.org/jcmc/vol2/issue4/witmer1.html.

Wong, Y. C., & Schoech, D. (in press). A tale of three cities: Teaching online to students in Shanghai from Texas and Hong Kong. In MacFadden et al., *Web-based education in human services: Models, methods and best practices*. New York: The Haworth Press, Inc.

Zheng, J., Veinofft, E., Bos, N., Olson, J. S., & Olson, G. M. (2002). Trust without touch: Jumpstarting long-distance trust with social activities. In *Proceedings of Conference on Human Factors in Computing Systems*. Minneapolis, MN: ACM Press, 131-146.

doi:10.1300/J017v25n01_05

Including Indigenous Knowledge
in Web-Based Learning

Gary C. Dumbrill
Jacquie Rice Green

SUMMARY. This paper explores differences between Indigenous knowledge and Western/European ways of knowing, and considers the pedagogical implications for Web-based learning. Moving beyond a simple examination of the nature of Indigenous knowledge, this paper explores ways that "education" has been used by colonizers to subjugate Aboriginal peoples. Outlining ways to avoid colonization, this paper contends that rather than simply being sensitive to the nature of Indigenous knowledge when designing Web-based education, instructors need to be sensitive to ways Western/European knowledge subjugates other forms of knowledge by situating itself as "the" way of knowing rather than "a" way of knowing. doi:10.1300/J017v25n01_06 *[Article copies available for a fee from The Haworth Document Delivery Service: 1-800-HAWORTH. E-mail address: <docdelivery@haworthpress.com> Website: <http://www.HaworthPress.com> © 2007 by The Haworth Press, Inc. All rights reserved.]*

Gary C. Dumbrill, PhD, is Assistant Professor and Chair of Undergraduate Studies, McMaster University, School of Social Work, Kenneth Taylor Hall, Room 319, 1280 Main Street, West Hamilton, Ontario, L8S 4M4, Canada.

Jacquie Rice Green, BSW, MPA, is Assistant Professor, University of Victoria, School of Social Work, P.O. Box 1700, STN CSC, Victoria BC, V8W 2Y2, Canada.

[Haworth co-indexing entry note]: "Including Indigenous Knowledge in Web-Based Learning." Dumbrill, Gary C., and Jacquie Rice Green. Co-published simultaneously in *Journal of Technology in Human Services* (The Haworth Press, Inc.) Vol. 25, No. 1/2, 2007, pp. 103-117; and: *HUSITA7–The 7th International Conference of Human Services Information Technology Applications: Digital Inclusion–Building a Digital Inclusive Society* (eds: C. K. Law, Yu Cheung Wong, and John Yat Chu Fung) The Haworth Press, Inc., 2007, pp. 103-117. Single or multiple copies of this article are available for a fee from The Haworth Document Delivery Service [1-800-HAWORTH, 9:00 a.m. - 5:00 p.m. (EST). E-mail address: docdelivery@haworthpress.com].

Available online at http://jths.haworthpress.com
© 2007 by The Haworth Press, Inc. All rights reserved.
doi:10.1300/J017v25n01_06

KEYWORDS. Web-based learning, colonization, Indigenous knowledge, anti-racism

INTRODUCTION

To include Indigenous knowledge in Web-based learning, course developers need to understand and resolve the conflicts between the nature and form of this knowledge, and the Western/European framework in which formal education is almost universally based. In this paper we outline these conflicts and suggest ways that they can be resolved. Our exploration of this matter is based on lessons we learned while working together to deliver both classroom and Web-based education to Indigenous and non-Indigenous students. Delivering this education required us to not only understand the learning differences between Indigenous and non-indigenous students, but to understand and work across our own differences as instructors; Jacquie Rice Green is an Aboriginal professor from the Haisla Nation, while Gary Dumbrill is a White professor originally from London, England. Our collaboration began in 2001 at the School of Social Work, University of Victoria on the west Coast of Northern Turtle Island (known as Canada to non-Indigenous peoples); and although Gary now teaches on the other side of the Island, at McMaster University in Ontario, we continue to collaborate in examining the ways Indigenous and European knowledge can coexist in an academic environment.

Our primary discovery, and the central theme of this paper, is that successfully incorporating Indigenous knowledge into Web-based or any other learning, does not hinge on understanding the "digital divide" or being "culturally sensitive" to the ways Indigenous knowledge is more holistic than European thinking. Nor does it rest on an understanding that there are different communication patterns in White European and Native traditions. Rather, success hinges on understanding the relationship between power and knowledge and on recognizing that colonization has caused, and continues to cause, a divide between Aboriginal and non-Aboriginal learners. This divide is not digital, it is not a matter of Aboriginal peoples, who tend to be marginalized, gaining access to the World Wide Web; rather it is a matter of Indigenous peoples gaining access to self-determination and sovereignty. Consequently, including Indigenous knowledge into Web-based courses does not simply involve incorporating Indigenous content into the curriculum and ensuring that Aboriginal learners have access to the Internet, but rather incorporation must respect Indigenous people's right to define that which is regarded as knowledge and must also facilitate their gaining the power to specify the ways such knowledge is taught and learned.

Recognizing the interconnection between power, knowledge and colonization is crucial when considering Indigenous knowledge in the academy. One of the ways Aboriginal peoples have been and continue to be subjugated is through situating European ways of knowing as superior to Indigenous ways. The superior position given to European knowledge has been used to justify the systematic destruction of Indigenous knowledge and Aboriginal ways of life. The residential school system, for instance, interned Aboriginal children in schools where they were separated from families and indoctrinated into European ways of knowing. Educators perpetuate aspects of this history every time a course is taught in a way that unquestioningly situates European language and thought as the framework in which education is conceived and delivered (Battiste, Bell & Findlay, 2002; Graveline, 2002; Rice Green & Dumbrill, in press; Vickers, 2002).

In this paper we outline ways to avoid repeating this history. Using Web-based learning as an example, we show how education processes can rely less on European thought and more on Indigenous ways of knowing. We begin by Jacquie describing the nature and characteristics of Indigenous knowledge and Gary follows by exploring his understanding of Indigenous knowledge. From the juxtaposition of Jacquie's Indigenous perspective and Gary's non-Indigenous perspective, we raise ontological and epistemological questions about the nature of knowledge and knowing, and we examine the connections between power and knowledge, and the "knower" and the "known." We move on to show how the relationship between power and knowledge has been exploited by colonizers to subjugate Indigenous peoples. Finally, we present ways for Web-based educators to incorporate Indigenous knowledge into education in a decolonizing manner.

JACQUIE SPEAKS ABOUT INDIGENOUS KNOWLEDGE

The word indigenous comes from the Latin term "indigena" and means "born of the land." Describing an "Indigenous perspective," Cardinal (2001) interprets "land" as "context" and contends that an Indigenous perspective is "born of context," which means that "Indigenous peoples with their traditions and customs are shaped by the environment, by the land. They have a spiritual, emotional, and physical relationship to the land" (p. 180).

Context for Indigenous peoples involves engaging with and relating to all living things. From an Indigenous perspective, relationship to all living things is the key to survival because this enriches economic sustainability, facilitates migration, and enables interconnection and cooperation between many groups of people. Context, however, also includes a spiritual dimension as Indigenous knowledge is rooted within an understanding of spirituality as seen in ceremonies, which are known to many in Turtle Island as potlaching, feasting, sweat lodge and smudging (to name a few). Indigenous peoples see within these ceremonies the expertise of elders, medicine men and women who teach the history of naming (people, territory, mountains, rivers); the teachings of life (birth and dying); interpersonal relationships (how to teach others); and how to respect and honor all other forms of knowledge. Indigenous peoples at one time understood that listening and observing the "other" people only enriches their lives. Consequently, there has never been a system of imposing Indigenous knowledge on other peoples.

The interconnection of Indigenous knowledge to the land, to respect for others, and to spirituality, can be seen through the teaching of The Medicine Wheel (see Figure 1). The circularity of the wheel is found throughout nature, and in relationship to all living things: the turning of the seasons, the shape and direction of the sun and moon, and even the path of the stages of life. There are many teachings within the philosophies of the wheel. The teachings that we share in this paper stem from the teachings of our friend and mentor, Gale Cyr, who is Anishnabe from the East of Turtle Island.

It is important to emphasize, for non-Aboriginal thinkers and learners, that to understand the lessons of The Medicine Wheel one needs to think holistically. A trait found among many European thinkers is to compartmentalize and categorize the things that they are considering. The origins of this trait among Europeans are unknown; but it probably evolved from a primitive survival mechanism that was reinforced in the "Enlightenment" period in which Europeans began to believe that the isolation and microscopic examination of a subject's small parts would lead them to an understanding of the subject, and ultimately to the control of the entire subject, and the entire world. The Medicine Wheel, however, must be read through a different lens. For instance, the situating of four races on the wheel is not a categorization of society into four peoples, but a demonstration that for society to be whole all peoples must belong. Furthermore, the races shown on the wheel are to be re-

FIGURE 1. The Medicine Wheel Showing Interrelated Connections to Context

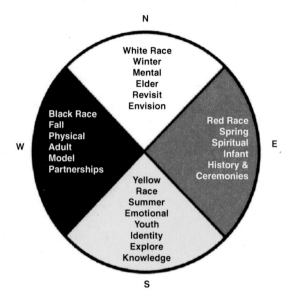

garded as inclusive beyond the limits suggested by their names or as learnt through a white European framework. The boundaries of these constructs are fluid, permeable, and inclusive; and entities are organised as though existing on a circular continuum. Consequently, "mixed-race" peoples and "races" that are not found in the categorisation of "red, yellow, black and white" belong and are present in this representation. Additionally, segments, the quadrants of the Wheel, are not to be regarded as the dichotomous opposite of each other, but must be seen in relation to the other and to the whole. Moreover, particular constructs, such as seasons, life stages, and so on, are not to be regarded as essentially and exclusively associated with those constructs contained in the same quadrant on the wheel. For example, the Black race is not exclusively in the Adult stage of life, nor is it excluded from relationship to the Elder/Infant/Youth stages of life. Therefore, not only is each construct itself fluid, permeable, and inclusive; so too are the relationships between constructs and between quadrants. Ultimately, each construct is to be understood in equal and respectful relationship to all other constructs on the wheel, and most importantly, in relationship to the whole.

To engage with the wheel, start in the East, where the day begins and the sun rises, and move clockwise until arriving at the North. The start of the wheel, the East, is a place of new beginnings, the direction of Spirituality and the life stage of the infant. This is a good place to examine the history of Indigenous peoples within education and also to see the connections between life and all living things. This is also a good place to assert the importance of our relationship to spirituality, ceremony, and direction; it is here that we understand that which comes from Creator and Ancestors. It is here that Indigenous peoples learn knowledge that is linked to all living things: the animals, the plants, the ocean and the sky. It is here where Indigenous peoples understand the importance of respecting nature/environment because without learning this knowledge, and gifts from Creator, we do not know how to respect the land and we destroy the environment.

The South, the direction of Emotionality and the life stage of youth, is a place where we recognize and honour teachings of our Elders and spiritual leaders. This is where we identify different components that encompass our knowledge base. This is where we recognize the many forms of knowledge that are key to our being. One should not think of this segment of the wheel as just representing the life-cycle of a person, but also the life-cycle of an idea, an initiative, a community and so on–remember that the Medicine Wheel is a holistic way of thinking and engaging with all life tasks. Consequently, applying the Wheel to the development of Web-based learning in Indigenous communities, the idea would be conceived in the East, but here in the South, before implementation, we would explore this new knowledge and ask how to include it into our existing frameworks. We would ask how it fits within our culture and teachings. We ask what our spiritual leaders have to say about this way of learning and teaching. When we imagine youth, we remember and recognize that identities, ideas, and concepts are being developed and refined. In this quadrant we enrich our knowledge by exploring ideas that have been developed and have begun to grow.

The West, the direction of Physical and the life stage of adult, is where we implement those things that emerge from the previous stage. For instance, in relation to Web-based learning, it is here that we implement the decisions and ideas formulated in the previous stages. It is here, after considering history and and traditional teachings, where we begin to present and teach new knowledge. Remembering that the Medicine Wheel is based in a holistic worldview and that it emphasises relationship, here we develop and model partnerships and inclusion, emphasising the importance of all races and all stages of life. Here we recognise that the relationship to all living things must be present to teach and must be taught.

The North, the direction of Mental and the life stage of an Elder, is where we revisit our work, our collaboration. After implementation and analysis, we reflect and refer back to our teachers: for my sake as an Indigenous woman, I refer to my Elders; and for Gary as a White European, he will refer to colleagues in the academy and trusted academic friends. It is here that we reflect and examine our knowledge to be sure that it encapsulates sacred teachings in a manner that is respectful to all living things, to those who are in our institutes of where we work; and we make necessary changes as needed–and the cycle of the wheel begins again.

GARY CONTEMPLATES INDIGENOUS KNOWLEDGE

The information Jacquie shares about Indigenous knowledge appears to be a collection of facts that can be taught and known. Yet knowing cannot be separated from the way power and knowledge interact in shaping the known and the knower. For instance, at the University of Victoria we each taught about the nature of Indigenous knowledge in separate sections of a social work class on anti-oppressive practice. The purpose of this class was to review Indigenous ways of knowing and to also de-centre European thought as a way of understanding and engaging with the world. Yet how does one de-centre European thought in relation to Indigenous knowledge when the word "Indigenous" has a Latin root? How do I teach Indigenous knowledge when my teaching context and I are European? To illustrate this point, I utilized the following table.

This table (Table 1) teaches in two ways. First, it provides a comparison between European and Indigenous ways of thinking. Although the table oversimplifies both Indigenous and European knowledge, as well as the comparison between them, it provides a useful entry point to contemplate some of the more dichotomous aspects of each knowledge form. Once these dichotomies are understood, one can then explore some of the more complex similarities and differences between each form of knowledge, especially the ways some of the more recent developments in European qualitative research come close to some Indigenous ways of knowing. The real lesson, however, is not in the table's content, but in its structure–it is Eurocentric. The table's square shape is as culturally bound as the Latin term "Indigenous." If the material had

TABLE 1. Comparing Indigenous Knowledge and Eurocentric Knowledge

Indigenous Knowledge	Eurocentric Knowledge
Belief in unseen powers of the ecosystem	Belief in the power of science to control the ecosystem
Belief that all things in the ecosystem are dependent on each other	Belief that isolating variables leads to understanding and controlling them
Belief that reality is structured according to most of the linguistic concepts by which Indigenous describes it	Belief that an empirical reality exists in its own right and that language describes that reality
Belief that personal relationships reinforce the bond between persons, communities and ecosystems	Belief that personal relationships must be kept separate from the work of science and that the environment is a resource to be exploited
Belief that sacred traditions and persons who know these are responsible for teaching "morals" and "ethics" to practitioners who are then given the responsibility for the specialized knowledge and its dissemination	Belief that scientific methods and the scholars that know them are responsible for teaching "truth" to practitioners who then have the responsibility to use this truth in accordance with ethical codes the practitioners develop for themselves
Belief that an extended kinship passes on teachings and social practices from generation to generation	Belief that disseminating scientific knowledge through conferences and journals passes on "truth" from generation to generation

Based in part on Battiste & Youngblood (2000)

been developed from an Aboriginal perspective, it would have more likely made use of circles and conceptualized issues in the same way as The Medicine Wheel or another holistic and cyclical paradigm. Additionally, the idea of reducing knowledge into manageable bites, ignoring context, and setting knowledge into a tabular format for easy separation, comparison and manipulation, is also distinctly European. Of course, it stands to reason that the table I draw will be distinctly European because *I am* distinctly European, and there is nothing wrong with this. What would be wrong is my European way of thinking and knowing being presented as "the" way of knowing and becoming the frame in and from which all other ways of knowing are understood and presented.

Situating European knowledge as the educational frame in which Indigenous knowledge is presented and understood subjugates Indigenous knowledge and perpetuates colonization (Battiste, Bell & Findlay, 2002; Graveline, 2002; Vickers, 2002). The table above, therefore, demonstrates how colonization operates in education–similar to the Latin term "indigena" it situates and communicates what is understood about "Indigenous" peoples within a European construct. Consequently, to appropriately include Indigenous knowledge in Web-based, or any other form of instruction, requires disrupting the dominant nature of this European frame. To fully appreciate why this Eurocentric framing is problematic requires us to briefly review the ways colonization began and how it crept into education processes.

THE ROOTS OF COLONIZATION THROUGH EDUCATION

Europe used brute force to initiate colonization. With advanced weapons and vast armies, Europe fed the imperial appetite of its industrial machine by systematically wresting nations from Indigenous people and Indigenous people from their lands. Military tactics included biological warfare (Alcabes, 2004). British General Sir Jeffrey Amherst ordered the 1763 Pontiac uprising put down by infecting Natives with the smallpox virus in an action that he suggested might not only end the rebellion but may also "serve to extirpate this exorable race" (Baron, 2003, p. 261). Captain Simeon Ecuyer followed Amherst's orders and replied, "We gave them [Indian Chiefs] two blankets and a handkerchief out of the Smallpox hospital. I hope it will have the required effect" (Baron, 2003, p. 261). More often, however, conventional military force was employed with probably the most infamous North American incident occurring on December 29, 1890 when the US Seventh Cavalry massacred Lakota men, women and children who were surrendering their weapons at Wounded Knee Creek in South Dakota. Congressional Medals of Honor were given to 23 of the soldiers who participated in the massacre (Beasley, 1995; Giago, 2003).

Brute force is an effective means to launch an empire, but an ineffective way to maintain it. Overt coercion triggers guilt in the oppressor and resistance among the oppressed. Consequently, wherever possible, military force operates in the background while more subtle technologies are used to manage the day-to-day business of subjugation. One of the most effective weapons in this mass subjugation has been "education." Targeting the hearts and minds of Indigenous children, schooling was first offered to Indigenous communities on a voluntary basis, but in Canada during the early 20th century when communities did not give up their children, a coercive model started being used and Aboriginal children were forcibly interned in reeducation camps known as "residential schools." Similar practices occurred around the world.

Aboriginal children were taught that European ways were superior to Native ways and were forbidden to speak their native languages or practice their traditions. The objective of these institutions was to remove all trace of Indigenous culture and to indoctrinate Aboriginal peoples in European customs and ways of thinking. The idea of using education to subjugate was an easy choice of Europeans who regarded themselves as morally, racially, and culturally superior to those they were colonizing–they had convinced themselves that indoctrinating Native children in White ways of being and eradicating all trace of Native culture was a benevolent act. Today the residential school system has been recognized by the courts as an attempt at cultural genocide (Downey, 1999; Dumbrill, 2003; Rice, Green & Dumbrill, in press).

Formal "education," therefore, did not bring Indigenous peoples enlightenment, it brought subjugation. Education was designed to rob Indigenous peoples of their distinct ways of sustaining the environment, their economic standing, and their languages. Indigenous peoples resisted, yet Western/European education was successful in almost eradicating Indigenous ways of life and knowing in Canada and around the world. The traditional education of Aboriginal peoples, such as ceremonies, teachings from elders, and the diverse languages, were almost lost and for some peoples have been completely lost.

The processes referred to above have created a divide within society between the colonized and the colonizer, between the oppressed and the oppressor. Even though Aboriginal peoples are reclaiming Indigenous knowledge and such knowledge is surfacing in academic institutes as legitimate education, in most instances Indigenous knowledge is at best framed in a Eurocentric context, or at worst absorbed and appropriated by Eurocentric learning institutes. Of course, unlike the residential school system, the modern academy is not attempting to eradicate Indigenous ways of knowing. Yet perpetuating colonization no longer requires eradicating Indigenous knowledge, it only requires the academy to limit acceptance of Indigenous knowledge to ways that ensure the dominance of European thought–in ways that cause it to be dissected, understood, and taught from a European stance rather than taught and understood in its own right. Enabling Indigenous knowledge to stand in the academy in its own right and in terms defined by Aboriginal peoples is crucial, because incorporating Indigenous knowledge into Western thought and including it in the academy in ways defined by non-Aboriginal peoples will perpetuate its subjugation. Consequently, to include Indigenous knowledge in Web-based or any other form of education requires educators to disrupt the dominance of European thought and the ongoing subjugation and colonization of Indigenous knowledge. The key, therefore, to including Indigenous knowledge in web-based education does not lie in simply being "culturally sensitive" or addressing the digital divide, but in being sensitive to the ways colonization operates and addressing the divide caused by and maintained by such subjugation.

DECOLONISING WEB-BASED EDUCATION

Even seemingly neutral academic conventions, such as capitalization and punctuation, can be markers of a European framework. Refusing to be confined by such regulations, Peter Cole, an Aboriginal scholar, identifies the problems residing in such text division:

> the idea of chapter   is anathema to who I am as an indigenous person
> it implies a western order and format as "the" legitimate shapers of discourse
> the universe being ordered into rationally constructed geometrics
> precluding enthalpy to be the prescribed means of navigating
> rather than   say   entropy   devalidating our own symbolic sense of ourselves
> perceptions of our perceptions   making us take up the tools of the settlers
> hoo hoe hoe   rake shovel   ratiocination   for the nation

> (Cole, 2002, p. 448)

Although Cole writes in English, his personal writing style and spacing of text disrupts Eurocentric dominance by refusing to conform to conventional syntax and grammar established by the colonizers. Cole's message, in both form and content, has relevance to the Web-based educator. Web-based, as well as other education, must similarly identify and disrupt Eurocentric dominance in the ways knowledge is constructed and delivered. There is no simple formula for the ways to undertake this disruption, not least because to devise such a "formula" would be a characteristically Eurocentric approach. Although there is no formula for including Indigenous knowledge in Web-based education, there is a categorical rule that must be followed: Indigenous education needs to be placed back in the hands of Indigenous peoples, because as long as such education is controlled by non-Aboriginal educators and taught from a non-Aboriginal perspective, this knowledge will remain subjugated and colonized (Battiste, Bell & Findlay, 2002; Graveline, 2002; Rice Green & Dumbrill, in press; Vickers, 2002).

This handing back, however, is easier said than done, because in almost all educational institutions European ways of knowing are situated as "the" way of knowing. Dismantling this dominance requires time, dialogue, and cooperation between all peoples represented in The Medicine Wheel. This paper is an example of such dialogue: we have constructed this paper together with neither one dominating, and authorship was decided by where this paper fell in the sequence of papers we are writing together–a principle of alternating first authorship. Such work can only emerge in the context of professional relationships built on trust, respect, and honesty. Such work begins with the colonizer refusing to exercise the power to determine what is regarded as legitimate knowledge and developing dialogue with Aboriginal peoples. The colonizer, not the colonized, has the responsibility to initiate this dialogue because control over education remains in the hands of the colonizer. The process of educational reform needs to be initiated by the colonizer with a real, genuine, and authentic readiness to relinquish power and control.

An example of how this dialogue can operate in relation to Web-based education occurred when we developed a child welfare WebCT course together. The pedagogical technology we considered for this course was a system composed of "learning objects," which are instructional units built around specific teaching objectives that can be reused in several courses (Recker, Walker & Wiley, 2000; Wiley, 2000). A learning object can be any virtual learning activity that has, embedded within it, a self-contained bite of knowledge. Self-containment is the defining characteristic of learning objects because each object must be completely portable and able to stand alone as a bite of knowledge. The self-containment and portability of learning objects make them the building blocks of much Web-based education; and indeed, learning objects are quickly becoming a central part of the pedagogy of Web-based instruction (Hodgins, 2000).

Learning object technology appealed to us because we wanted to reuse and construct more than one course with the virtual educational units we were developing. Yet, by acknowledging and understanding the differing characteristics of Western/European knowledge and Indigenous knowledge, we recognized that although these objects fit well within the way Western/European knowledge compartmentalizes knowing, they are the antithesis of the context-specific and interconnected ways Indigenous knowledge operates. If we were to use learning objects, they needed to be modified and stripped of their propensity to eradicate context. We overcame the limitations of learning objects by constructing them as "way-points" on a learning journey rather than as discrete items of knowledge. These way-points remained portable and reusable; however, rather than being comprised of consumable knowledge items, they were constituted as points at which students could engage and consider various bodies of knowledge.

Because the way-points represented a journey, their sequencing was crucial. For instance, one of the first way-points was a child welfare quiz (http://web2.uvcs.uvic.ca/courses/sw475/) that was not only designed to communicate factual information, but also to disrupt dominant discourse found in much child welfare education that situates Eurocentric notions of childhood as epitomizing civilization. The full details of how we constructed this course are reported elsewhere (Rice, Green & Dumbrill, in press). The issue in this paper, however, is that to decolonize Web-based education we had to find ways to work together and to dialogue about our differing ways of knowing. Dialogue and collaboration did not simply hinge on our being "culturally sensitive" to our differences but more importantly, on our developing a similar vision of decolonizing the academy. In relation to the Web-based course we developed, these efforts seemed to meet with success (Rice, Green & Dumbrill, in press).

As mentioned above, we have no formulaic means to incorporate Indigenous knowledge into Web-based education. The key to success, however, is clear–one must not rely simply on gaining an understanding of the way the digital divide separates those who have and do not have access to the World Wide Web; rather success hinges on an understanding of colonization and the ways this creates a divide in the world between the subjugated and subjugators, the colonized and the colonizers.

CONCLUSION

Web-based educators keen to include Indigenous knowledge in their courses must understand that if education is constructed and framed within a Eurocentric perspective, this will reinforce and perpetuate the colonization of Aboriginal knowledge and peoples. To appropriately include Indigenous knowledge in Web-based or any other form of education, ways must be found to disrupt the propensity of European knowledge to be framed as "the" way of knowing and reconstitute it as "a" way of knowing. There is no formulaic way to undertake this disruption, other than to say that we *must* rise to this challenge and we *must* give back to Aboriginal peoples control over that which was taken by the colonizer–including control over educational processes. Giving back does not mean that those with control of the academy wash their hands of these issues, but that a dialogue is developed about the ways to proceed. Our example above about learning-objects in Web-based education and the need to modify them to fit an Aboriginal perspective shows how a dialogue within an academic institution can take us a step closer to ensuring that Web-based learning is a place that includes knowledge and processes inclusive to Aboriginal peoples–a dialogue that must take place in a context where the ways education has been used, and continues to be used, to colonize Aboriginal peoples are understood and acknowledged, and where there is a commitment to disrupt that colonization.

REFERENCES

Alcabes, P. (2004). The bioterrorism scare. *The American Scholar, 73*(2), 35.

Baron, J. H. (2003). British biological warfare. *British Medical Journal, 327*(7409), 261.

Batisste, M. & Youngblood, H. (2000). *Protecting Indigenous knowledge and heritage: A global challenge.* Saskatoon: Purich Publishing.

Battiste, M., Bell, L., & Findlay, L. M. (2002). Decolonizing education in Canadian universities: An interdisciplinary, international, Indigenous research project. *Canadian Journal of Native Education, 26*(2), 82-95.

Beasley, C. (1995). *We are a people in this world: The Lakota Sioux and the massacre at Wounded Knee.* Fayetteville: University of Arkansas Press.

Cardinal, L. (2001). What is an indigenous perspective? *Canadian Journal of Native Education, 25*(2), 180-182.

Cole, P. (2002). Aboriginalizing methodology: Considering the canoe. *Qualitative Studies in Education, 15*(4), 448-459.

Downey, M. (1999, April 26). Canada's 'genocide'. *Maclean's, 112*, 56-58.

Dumbrill, G. C. (2003). Child welfare: AOP's nemesis? In W. Shera (Ed.), *Emerging perspectives on anti-oppressive practice* (pp. 101-119). Canadian Scholars' Press.

Giago, T. (2003, Dec. 28). Wounded Knee: A day of infamy remembered. *Wisconsin State Journal*, B.2.

Graveline, J. (2002). Teaching tradition teaches us. *Canadian Journal of Native Education, 26*(1), 11-29.

Hodgins, H. W. (2000). The future of learning objects. In D. A. Wiley (Ed.), *The Instructional use of learning objects.* Retrieved on October 14, 2001, from http://reusability.org/read/chapters/hodgins.doc.

Recker, M. M., Walker, A., & Wiley, D. A. (2000). Collaboratively filtering learning objects. In D. A. Wiley (Ed.), *The instructional use of learning objects.* Retrieved on October 14, 2001, from http://reusability.org/read/chapters/recker.doc.

Rice Green, J., & Dumbrill, G. C. (2005). A child welfare course for Aboriginal and non-Aboriginal students: Pedagogical and technical challenges. In R.J. MacFadden, B. Moore, M. Herie & D. Schoech (Eds.), *Web-based education in the human services: Models, methods, and best practices* (pp. 167-181). New York: The Haworth Press, Inc.

Vickers, P. J. (2002). The colonial mind in post-secondary education. *McGill Journal of Education, 37*(2), 241-254.

Wiley, D. A. (2000). Connecting learning objects to instructional design theory: A definition, a metaphor, and a taxonomy. In D. A. Wiley (Ed.), *The instructional use of learning objects.* Retrieved on October 14, 2001, from http://reusability.org/read/chapters/wiley.doc.

doi:10.1300/J017v25n01_06

Web CT–
An Administrative Tool

Bruce D. Friedman

SUMMARY. Web CT (Web Course Tools) is a leading software of integrated e-learning systems for higher education. It was designed as a tool to enhance classroom teaching and learning but the question is, could it be used for other purposes? When a breakdown of department communications occurred, other interventive strategies were developed that included Web CT to improve communication strategies. Utilizing the same criteria to enhance classroom teaching, Web CT was used to promote intradepartmental communications and cooperation. Results of

Bruce D. Friedman, PhD, ACSW, CSWM, LCSW, is affiliated with University of Texas–Pan American Social Work Department, 1201 West University Drive, Edinburg, TX 78541 (E-mail: friedm52@panam.edu).

[Haworth co-indexing entry note]: "Web CT–An Administrative Tool." Friedman, Bruce D. Co-published simultaneously in *Journal of Technology in Human Services* (The Haworth Press, Inc.) Vol. 25, No. 1/2, 2007, pp. 119-122; and: *HUSITA7–The 7th International Conference of Human Services Information Technology Applications: Digital Inclusion–Building a Digital Inclusive Society* (eds: C. K. Law, Yu Cheung Wong, and John Yat Chu Fung) The Haworth Press, Inc., 2007, pp. 119-122. Single or multiple copies of this article are available for a fee from The Haworth Document Delivery Service [1-800-HAWORTH, 9:00 a.m. - 5:00 p.m. (EST). E-mail address: docdelivery@haworthpress.com].

this experiment were mixed but this was not a reflection from the use of the software as a tool, rather from resistance to its use. Web CT proved to be a good tool for improved management and communications. In addition, other management applications for the software also emerged. doi:10.1300/J017v25n01_07 *[Article copies available for a fee from The Haworth Document Delivery Service: 1-800-HAWORTH. E-mail address: <docdelivery@haworthpress.com> Website: <http://www.HaworthPress.com> © 2007 by The Haworth Press, Inc. All rights reserved.]*

KEYWORDS. Web CT, course delivery system, online course management system

Web CT is a leading software package of integrated e-learning systems for higher education that is used to enhance classroom teaching and learning but has not been used as a tool for performing administrative activities in higher education. As an educational tool, Web CT provides students with access to information on demand and mechanisms for communication between groups of students who have difficulty in meeting together in person. These tools are needed because the nature of the educational environment is changing. Students are coming from more non-traditional backgrounds where there is the need to balance school with work and family. Thus, more students prefer to supplement their classroom time through electronic means that utilize a combination of computer-mediated learning and constructivist instructional design (Winfield, Mealy, & Scheibel, 1998). The use of technology provides students with easy access to information at a time that is convenient to them in a variety of formats. It also enables the student to learn at his or her own pace and not have to learn within the structure of a classroom learning environment (Cognition and Technology Group at Vanderbilt, 1993; Winograd & Flores, 1986). Can these same benefits of the software be utilized as an administrative tool to improve department functioning?

The demands on faculty members have changed over the years. Many faculty members are doing more of their work off campus or are coming to campus after business hours to meet the needs of non-traditional students. Thus, there is less opportunity for in-person communication. This led to a breakdown in communication and administrative functions in a social work department. Alternative mechanisms were explored to try to resolve the problem.

There are basic resources that people need to be able to perform administrative duties. These include an easy access to information that will lead to informed decision-making, a mechanism for communicating with other persons to make the decision, and an ability to record the decisions that are made for future reference. The changing nature of faculty being on campus less often meant that it was becoming more difficult for them to acquire the resources needed to perform their administrative tasks. Web CT already existed on campus and it was thought that its benefits as a classroom teaching tool could be applied to faculty to enhance their ability to perform their administrative duties. A residual benefit was also seen as a way to introduce faculty to the tool in order that they may consider it for use to enhance their own classes.

Permission was granted by the University Center for Distance Learning to create an administrative page using Web CT and all faculty were granted access to the page. In addition to mail and discussion functions already existing on Web CT, the page design included sections for all course syllabi, all faculty committees to post their agenda and minutes, the strategic plan, and any other documentation that was necessary for comprehensive decision-making.

Although results have been mixed, there have been some positive results. First, all Department information is now easily accessible asynchronously. Faculty can access information whenever they want and do not have to do so during business hours when the office may be open. In addition, faculty do not have to be on campus to access the information or to participate in Department decision-making. Committees can meet online rather than in person utilizing the chat room feature. This means that although faculty may be traveling, they still have the ability to participate in decision-making processes. Web CT also provides a log of the interaction so all elements of the discussion are recorded for future reference. These features are important as the Department works on its reaffirmation for accreditation. In addition, guest access was granted to adjunct faculty in order that they may participate in Departmental functions. Another positive has been that faculty are beginning to use Web CT to enhance their courses as a result of being exposed to the tool for administrative reasons.

The downside of the experiment has been the faculty, themselves. Whereas, some faculty embraced the experiment, there were others, about 40%, who chose not to log on at all. They continued to want information given to them and would only access the information while on campus. This delayed the process of getting work done in a timely and effective manner. Pressures to obtain information in a timely manner for reaffirmation of the Department's accreditation standards are beginning to change the attitude of those who have been most resistant.

The application of the tool has begun discussion on using this for field education where field instructors rarely have a chance to meet with one another. Given the experience of this experiment, it has been demonstrated that Web CT and other e-learning software packages have other benefits in addition to classroom enhancement and distance learning. By thinking outside the box, many of the aspects of distance education are the same components needed to enhance administrative functioning. Thus, these software packages can provide organizations with an important tool that will enhance their internal communication needs.

REFERENCES

Cognition and Technology Group at Vanderbilt (1993). Designing learning environments that support thinking: The Jasper series as a case study. In Duffy, T.M., Lowyck, J., Jonassen, D.H., & Welsh, T. (Eds.), *Designing environments for constructive learning* (pp. 9-36). Berlin: Springer-Verlag.

Friedman, B.D., Ward, D., & Biagianti, A. (1998). Using technology to forge new allegiances in Social Work Education. *New Technology in the Human Services, 11* (2), 13-18.

Winfield, W., Mealy, M., & Scheibel, P. (1998). Design consideration for enhancing confidence and participation in web-based courses. In *Distance Learning '98*. Proceedings of the Annual Conference on Distance Learning and Teaching, Madison, WI.

Winograd, T., & Flores, F. (1986). *Understanding computers and cognition: A new foundation for design*. Norwood, NJ: Ablex.

doi:10.1300/J017v25n01_07

The Use of Information Technology to Enhance the Quality of Teaching and Learning in Social Work Practicum: An Example from the City University of Hong Kong

Tak-yan Lee

SUMMARY. One of the thorny issues in social work practicum training is how to maintain fairness in assessment. To address this issue, a grade moderation system was set up. Digital practicum portfolios and on-line · assessment were used through the Web CT platform. Two amendments were made: (1) password control to protect access rights and privacy; (2) assessment data transfer through *Common Gateway Interface* (CGI) to conduct automatic descriptive statistical analysis for monitoring possible deviations from the grading standard. A feedback system was built to enhance the quality of teaching using students' survey data. To promote the quality of learning in this individualized teaching mode, the

Tak-yan Lee, MSW, PhD, is Associate Professor and Program Leader, Department of Applied Social Studies, City University of Hong Kong, 83 Tat Chee Avenue, Kowloon, Hong Kong S.A.R., China (E-mail: sstakyan@cityu.edu.hk).

[Haworth co-indexing entry note]: "The Use of Information Technology to Enhance the Quality of Teaching and Learning in Social Work Practicum: An Example from the City University of Hong Kong." Lee, Tak-yan. Co-published simultaneously in *Journal of Technology in Human Services* (The Haworth Press, Inc.) Vol. 25, No. 1/2, 2007, pp. 123-126; and: *HUSITA7–The 7th International Conference of Human Services Information Technology Applications: Digital Inclusion–Building a Digital Inclusive Society* (eds: C. K. Law, Yu Cheung Wong, and John Yat Chu Fung) The Haworth Press, Inc., 2007, pp. 123-126. Single or multiple copies of this article are available for a fee from The Haworth Document Delivery Service [1-800-HAWORTH, 9:00 a.m. - 5:00 p.m. (EST). E-mail address: docdelivery@haworthpress.com].

Social Work Practice Teaching, Learning, and Research site was constructed. doi:10.1300/J017v25n01_08 *[Article copies available for a fee from The Haworth Document Delivery Service: 1-800-HAWORTH. E-mail address: <docdelivery@haworthpress.com> Website: <http://www.HaworthPress.com> © 2007 by The Haworth Press, Inc. All rights reserved.]*

KEYWORDS. Practicum, assessment, practice teaching and learning, Web CT

THE ISSUE:
FAIRNESS OF ASSESSMENT AMONG INSTRUCTORS

This example involved tailor-making the *Web CT* (Mclean & Murrell, 2002) and using the Internet to enhance the quality of teaching and learning of social work practicum which comprises ideological, conceptual, emotional, and behavioral components (Schneck, 1991). Students undertaking practicum had to be closely supervised by qualified and experienced practitioners or university-based instructors on a one-to-one basis. The instructor served as the liaison person, mentor, teacher, coach, quality controller, and the assessor. This individualized teaching mode raised a serious concern over the fairness of assessment.

DIGITAL PORTFOLIO

To minimize the discrepancy in grading standards among individual instructors, a Practice Board was set up to handle the issue of fairness by monitoring the quality of learning and moderating individual instructors' grading profile which might show deviations from the communal norm. To facilitate the process, students were required to submit a digital practicum portfolio comprising reflections and recordings of all practice assignments and incidental learning. Instructors would grade their students on each criterion in four assessment areas, namely (1) Integration of Knowledge with Practice; (2) Professional Practice and Service Delivery; (3) Performance in the Staff/Professional Roles in the Placement Agency; and (4) Fieldwork Learning and Professional Development. Both students and instructors would perform summative and qualitative evaluations through the Web CT.

MONITORING THE GRADING PATTERN

The Web CT was originally designed for many learning activities to be participated in by teachers and students in a specific class. In order to protect access rights and confidentiality for the individual teaching mode of practicum, levels of password control were added on to the Web CT. By using the *Common Gateway Interface* (CGI), assessment data prepared by instructors were stored immediately for review. The function of automatic descriptive statistical analysis of each of the four assessment areas and the overall grades was also added to show the grading profiles of all instructors. A specially formed Practice Board could go through these data to identify cases that might suggest certain instructors' grading patterns deviated from the communal norm and deserved a review. The review was then facilitated by allowing specific reviewers to have access to specific digital practicum portfolios and evaluation reports. Adjustments in grading on specific areas would be made possible through peer review. A board member would serve as the second marker. In case the second marker did not agree with the grades given by the instructor on a student, a third marker would be involved.

MONITORING THE TEACHING AND LEARNING PROCESS

Students were required to fill in an on-line feedback questionnaire on their learning experiences before mid- and end-of-practicum. Survey data were transferred through the *Common Gateway Interface* (CGI) and could be accessed by the secretary of the Practice Board to monitor the teaching and learning process. Reports based on the survey data were generated for individual instructors after the practicum.

SAMPLES OF PORTFOLIOS

Samples of portfolios could be found in a web site entitled "*Social Work Practice Teaching, Learning, and Research.*" This site was developed by the author to support teaching and learning by providing orientation, resources, self-understanding test, feedback in personal scores against the communal norm in specific sub-scales in various measures, and case examples in different contexts.

REFERENCES

Mclean, M., & Murrell, K. (2002). WebCT: Integrating computer-mediated communication and resource delivery into a new problem-based curriculum. *Journal of Audiovisual Media in Medicine*, 25, 8-15.

Schneck, D. (1991). Integration of learning in field education: Elusive goal and educational imperative. In Schneck, D., Grossman, B., & Glassman, U. (Eds.). *Field education in social work: Contemporary issues and trends*. Dubuque, IA: Kendall/Hunt.

WEB SITES

Common Gateway Interface: http://www.w3.org/CGI/
Practice Learning, Teaching and Research: http://www7.cityu.edu.hk/sspltr/
WebCT: http://www.webct.com/

doi:10.1300/J017v25n01_08

SOCIAL INCLUSION

The Reality of Social Inclusion Through Digital Government

Mehdi Asgarkhani

SUMMARY. Over the past few years, there has been much debate over the effectiveness of digital government. This paper addresses the strategic value and the effectiveness of digital government where it concerns enhancing citizen participation and social inclusion. It involves examining four specific facets of "effectiveness"–including: the view of management and ICT strategists; social and cultural implications; the implications of digital inclusion/exclusion and e-readiness upon social inclusion; and

Mehdi Asgarkhani is currently Principal Lecturer in Strategic Management of Information and Communications Technologies, Faculty of Commerce, CPIT, P.O. Box 540, Christchurch 8015, New Zealand (E-mail: AsgarkhaniM@CPIT.ac.nz). The author's previous experience (prior to joining the CPIT) includes taking on various roles in the corporate sector–such as Business Support Services Manager, Business Strategy Analyst/Advisor, Project Director, and ICT Solutions Consultant.

[Haworth co-indexing entry note]: "The Reality of Social Inclusion Through Digital Government." Asgarkhani, Mehdi. Co-published simultaneously in *Journal of Technology in Human Services* (The Haworth Press, Inc.) Vol. 25, No. 1/2, 2007, pp. 127-146; and: *HUSITA7–The 7th International Conference of Human Services Information Technology Applications: Digital Inclusion–Building a Digital Inclusive Society* (eds: C. K. Law, Yu Cheung Wong, and John Yat Chu Fung) The Haworth Press, Inc., 2007, pp. 127-146. Single or multiple copies of this article are available for a fee from The Haworth Document Delivery Service [1-800-HAWORTH, 9:00 a.m. - 5:00 p.m. (EST). E-mail address: docdelivery@haworthpress.com].

Available online at http://jths.haworthpress.com
doi:10.1300/J017v25n01_09

127

the citizens' view of the success of digital government in enhancing public access to information and transparency–based on a pilot study of digital government initiatives by local government in New Zealand. doi:10.1300/J017v25n01_09 *[Article copies available for a fee from The Haworth Document Delivery Service: 1-800-HAWORTH. E-mail address: <docdelivery@haworthpress.com> Website: <http://www.HaworthPress.com>* © *2007 by The Haworth Press, Inc. All rights reserved.]*

KEYWORDS. Electronic government, social inclusion, digital inclusion, digital divide, digital service delivery, effectiveness

INTRODUCTION

Over the past decade, we have witnessed rapid developments in Information and Communications Technology (ICT), which has contributed to the staggering growth in global computer networking. The most prominent of these recent ICT developments has been the emergence of the Internet and Web-based technologies. Today, Web-based technologies play an increasingly significant role in our day-to-day lives and have fundamentally transformed the technological, economic, political and social landscapes.

The competitive imperative of the private sector has driven businesses into the digital world. As a result, the private sector has steadily set higher standards of service (through the application of electronic platforms) both domestically and internationally. However, as public interest in the Internet and Web-based solutions continues to grow, there is an expectation that they will also be utilised in national and local governments. Communities and citizens increasingly expect the same level of service from the agencies in the public sector as they do from private and corporate sectors. Consequently, many innovative public sector agencies world-wide have had to create new ways in which to use Web-based solutions in order to provide digital governance/government facilities and services. Local, regional and national governments throughout the world are attempting to broaden service delivery and citizens' inclusion by providing effective digital government (Heeks 1999). Today, most governments acknowledge that access to ICT solutions is critical for economic and social development.

The introduction of digital government (networked-government) solutions has primarily been concerned with moving away from traditional information monopolies and hierarchies. Governments have traditionally operated on a hierarchical model of information flow and interaction. Generally, the opportunity for providing feedback has been limited to elections for local or national governments. The introduction of digital government within the public sector can potentially reduce these traditional hierarchies and fosters an environment of public inclusion. However, digital government is a challenge to both individuals and organisations alike. Governments must not only maximize the benefits that are offered (through the application of ICT solutions) but must also avoid the many pitfalls (economic, social and cultural) associated with rapid technological change. What's more, difference in access to ICTs and global networks (known as the *digital divide*) can potentially hinder the introduction of digital government initiatives that are aimed at fostering socially inclusive governments.

Overall, it appears that ICT-enabled government has become a catalyst for enabling social inclusion. However, the challenges to effective government within today's knowledge society are profound. There has been much debate (e.g., Asgarkhani 2005, Asgarkhani 2003a, Asgarkhani 2002b, Heeks 1999, Nath 2003, and Reschenthaler 1996) over the role, value and effectiveness of digital government.

This paper elaborates on the value and effectiveness of digital government as a strategic tool for enabling social inclusion. Four specific facets of effectiveness have been examined:

a. Effectiveness from the point of view of management and ICT strategists (concerning the implications of digital government).
b. Effectiveness as it concerns social, cultural and ethical implications.
c. Effectiveness with reference to differences in access to ICTs, digital divide or digital inclusion/exclusion.
d. Effectiveness from the point of view of citizens–a case study of the citizens' view of the usefulness and success of digital government in enabling improved service delivery and social inclusion.

Part one (sections 2-5) of this paper, based on a review of previous studies (and analysis of digital government cases–e.g., Lin et al. 2001, Orrego et al. 2000, Radics 2001, Bhatnagar et al. 2001, and Asgarkhani 2003b), reviews the fundamental concepts of digital government and social inclusion and discusses the effectiveness as outlined in (a), (b) and (c).

Part two of the paper (section 6) is based on a pilot study of the value and usefulness of digital government as it concerns public access and social inclusion. It involves a case study of a digital government project within the Canterbury region of New Zealand and addresses effectiveness as outlined in (d). The methodology for gathering information included interviews with project sponsors and a number of stakeholders and a combination of formal interviews and surveys of several focus groups of users (selected randomly).

DIGITAL GOVERNMENT AND SOCIAL INCLUSION: AN OVERVIEW

In this paper, *Digital or Electronic Governance (e-Governance)* is a term that is used to emphasise the application of ICT in governance systems and processes. Digital governance can be viewed as a tool for providing citizens with the ability to choose the manner in which they interact with governments. It is a mechanism for ensuring that ICTs are used effectively to improve the flow of information between citizen and government.

Digital or Electronic Government (e-Government) is the use of ICT in general and Web-based technologies in particular so as to promote and motivate a more operationally efficient and cost-effective government. Some of the benefits of digital government can include: facilitating more convenient government services to citizens and businesses; enhancing economic development; reshaping and redefining community and government processes; allowing for greater public access to information and making governments more accountable to their citizens. In general, digital government involves electronic service delivery, electronic democracy, and e-governance (digital support for policy-making and the policy process).

Social inclusion (in this paper) is viewed as "striving for reduced inequality, a balance between individuals' rights and duties and increased social cohesion" (Centre for Economic and Social Inclusion 2002). Digital government has become a catalyst in enabling social inclusion through enhanced access to services and the democratic process. However, it is essential to ensure that those who lack access, skills and/or desire to make use of technology are not excluded from access to information and/or the democratic process.

Extensive research has been conducted (and is still being carried out) by various practitioners and advisory/interest groups (such as the International Centre for e-Governance–www.icegov.org) in an attempt not only to examine the role and impact of digital government but also to identify the key parameters that need to be taken into consideration in order to benefit from it (e.g., Asgarkhani 2002b, Asgarkhani 2003c, Asgarkhani 2003a, Samaranayke 2003, Radics 2001, Tapscott 1997, and Wiener 1984). Sections of this paper (where relevant) address some of the findings of previous research that were mentioned previously.

Digital government is dependent upon a sound technology infrastructure. However, it is not primarily a technical exercise, but rather an attempt to improve the political and social environment. The essence of governance and/or government centers on relationships. Hence, an effective model for developing digital government needs to consider the connectivity between different views and domains of government. The introduction of ICTs in order to automate public sector functions will not automatically create a better or more open government–unless it is based on policies to promote the effective utilization of technology. The adoption of digital government solutions needs to take into consideration numerous factors including (but not limited to):

- new models of policy formulation, alternative forms of citizenship and alternative approaches for connecting people to the political process (the relationship governments have with their citizens)
- the ways in which governments can act effectively in this new environment–in the interests of their citizens
- different patterns and trends of relationship and power
- new solutions for economic development
- the boundaries of community and therefore of representation and citizenship that go to the heart of democratic theory
- the role and capacity of government

As the application of ICT and Web-based solutions within the public sector becomes widespread, we begin to observe a progression through the various stages of digital government (Asgarkhani 2003c and Asgarkhani 2005):

- Stage 1–Improving internal functional efficiency through the application of ICT.
- Stage 2–Improving internal communications (through the application of electronic mail) and introducing workflow management systems for increased process efficiency.
- Stage 3–Providing access to information with regards to services and the democratic process (initial stages of enabling public/social inclusion).

- Stage 4–Putting in place applications that would not only enable citizen participation through feedback, but would also allow for transactions between citizens to government (C2G), businesses to government (B2G) and government-to-government (G2G).
- Stage 5–Introducing digital democracy–technological solutions that would enable participatory action and democratic processes.
- Stage 6–Introducing integrated electronic or digital governance.

A review of various cases (e.g., Webster 2001, Radics 2001, NIC 2002, Asgarkhani 2003b, and Asgarkhani 2003c) suggests that government objectives in introducing digital government are likely to concentrate on:

- *Prompt, accurate service*–Local governments can potentially receive millions of calls per year. Setting a target to resolve a high percentage of these calls the first time they occur (through establishing a customer contact centre) can result in significant efficiency gains and cost savings.
- *Improved quality of service*–One client of a local government can potentially generate up to dozens of files in different locations. Local governments are seeking to convert these to one secure and accessible file–helping to provide continuity and coordination of local government support.
- *Removing barriers and tackling social exclusion*–Local governments are aware that many clients do not have the skills to use electronic services. Local government agencies seem to be keen on setting up networks of learning centres in libraries and community centres that teach people relevant Internet and Web technology skills.
- *Local access points*–It has been shown (Webster 2001) that up to 20% of customer queries cannot be addressed immediately. Clients often need to meet with a "professional." Local governments can benefit from setting up community access points to let clients meet "professionals" through online video links.

Today, digital government solutions appear in various shapes and forms. Typical applications (within both local and national governments) are outlined in Figure 1.

There has been much debate over what should drive digital government initiatives in both local and national governments. A survey of the

FIGURE 1. Typical Applications of Digital Government

Type of Digital Government Service	Typical Application(s)	Stage
Providing Access Making information accessible to citizens (public kiosk, Internet, CDs, and so on)	• Citizen access to general information • Directory and directions to parks and community centres • Calendar of city-sponsored events and activities • Manual of policies and procedures • Phone directories	Stage 3
Connection to a Process or Service Provide information and/or access to government ICT-based systems, information management solutions and true web-based services.	• Property information • License renewal and payment • Payment of parking tickets, court fines • Registration for class and sports activities • Online permits, business licenses, court documents • Online auctions • Electronic posting of commodity products with purchase order and invoice transactions • Sales tax collection • Job postings; online application forms • Self-service benefits administration	Stages 3 and 4
Raising Awareness Provide information about the political process, services, and options that are available for the decision-making process.	• Government functions and services • Citizen services • Business services (information) • Employee services • Employee newsletter • Legislative agenda and pending legislation	Stages 2 and 3
Facilitating Consultation and/or Communication Initiate and develop means of capacity building, exchanging prior gained experiences, access to experts, and any other information/knowledge of mutual interest.	• Posting of RFPs and bid documents • Distance learning resources • Web casting of City/County Council Meetings	Stages 3, 4 and 5
Active Citizen Involvement and Participation Involve citizens in government decision-making, problem solving and election processes.	• Digital democracy • Communications with Council Members	Stages 4, 5 and 6

importance of potential driving factors (Webster 2001) indicated that improving service is rated as being the most important reason (Figure 2). As you can observe, there is no direct reference to *social inclusion* as being a reason for initiating digital government solutions.

THE IMPACT OF DIGITAL GOVERNMENT–
MANAGEMENT AND ICT STRATEGISTS' VIEW

A review of viewpoints concerning the implications of digital government (e.g., Asgarkhani 2005, Perri 2000, and Asgarkhani 2002b) indicates that there exist at least four schools of thought (models): *pure optimism*; *optimism with some concerns*; *pessimism*; and finally *technology being viewed as a tool only*–but not a driving factor on its own.

The optimists argue uncompromisingly that the use of technology in governance represents a major once-and-for-all improvement in the capabilities of governance through a more effective management of all domains (Tapscott 1997). The only cost is considered to be the investment and the day-to-day operational running costs, and that the initial investment costs would be compensated through the cost savings and efficiency gains that are likely to be achieved over the lifetime of digital government systems (Reschenthaler et al., 1996). This optimistic view appears to be based on the classical cybernetic theory (Wiener 1984).

FIGURE 2. Perceived Driving Forces of Digital Government

Driving Force	Average Score 5: Essential 0: Not important
Perceived benefit to local people	4.3
Authority's strategy	4.1
Influence of officers	4.05
The need to modernise services	4
Influence of members	3.7
Best value	3.5
Central government initiatives	3.5
Potential cost savings	3.3
Influence of suppliers	2.9

The second group (optimists who have some concerns) accept at least the possibility of greater control, quality and rationality in decision-making. However, they argue that the efficiency gains achieved through digital government come at a price–e.g., threatening the rights to individual liberty and privacy; compromising the right to influence governmental decision-making (Perri 2000 and Raab 1997); and losing control over politicians' decision-making agendas (Zuurmond 1988).

The pessimists argue that digital government will actually compromise the quality of decision-making. They are concerned that excessive demand for policy analysis based on many categories of information will cause delays in action–"paralysis by over-analysis."

The last group view technology as a tool only and argue that the impact of ICT solutions (technical or political rationality of decision-making) cannot be viewed in isolation. They view both continuities and changes in governance as being driven socially and politically, not by technology itself. Technology is seen as a tool for either changing or preserving the style of governance–e.g., *conservative* and *radical* styles of governance (Mackenzie et al., 1985 and Bijker 1997).

Each theory that has been mentioned above has some empirical support–although most empirical studies have been of a rather limited scope and are not in general designed to test, let alone falsify, these rival theories (Perri 2000).

The study of these models raises numerous questions, such as:

- How are these schools of thought to be appraised?
- Is it possible to favour one that is correct or at least not yet falsified?
- Is it perhaps possible to allocate them to different domains?
- Is there more than one valid view?

Providing answers to these questions in a unified manner that applies to every situation across the board would be unrealistic. Potential answers can depend on numerous factors such as: social and cultural aspects; the technological infrastructure; past experience with the application of ICT; the level of education and interest in the political process–to name but a few.

SOCIAL, CULTURAL AND ETHICAL CONSIDERATIONS
OF DIGITAL GOVERNMENT

Some of the perceived social implications of digital government can include:

- *Information Security*–Technological advancements allow government agencies to collect, store and make available to others online data on individuals and organizations. Furthermore, citizens and businesses expect to be allowed to access data in a flexible manner (access to data at any time and from any location). Meeting these expectations comes at a price to government agencies–where it concerns managing information. Information management challenges include: ease of access; data integrity and accuracy; capacity planning to ensure the timely delivery of data to remote (possibly mobile) sites; and managing the security of corporate and public information (Asgarkhani 2001).
- *Impact on Jobs and Workplaces*–In the early days of computers, management scientists anticipated that computers would replace human decision-makers. However, despite significant technological advances, this prediction is no longer a mainstream concern. At the current time, one of the concerns associated with computer usage in any organization (including governments) is the health risk–such as injuries related to working continuously on a computer keyboard. Government agencies are expected to work with regulatory groups in order to avoid these problems.
- *Impacts on Individuals' Rights and Privacy*–As more and more companies and government agencies use technology to collect, store, and make accessible data on individuals, privacy concerns have grown. Some of these concerns are related to maintaining the individual privacy of employees as well as citizens. Some companies choose to monitor their employees' computer usage patterns in order to assess individual or work-group performance (Asgarkhani 2002a). Technological advancements are also making it much easier for businesses, government and other individuals to obtain a great deal of information about an individual without the individual's personal knowledge. There is a growing concern that access to a wide range of information can be dangerous within politically corrupt government agencies.
- *Potential Impacts on Society*–Despite some economic benefits of ICTs to individuals, there is evidence that the computer literacy

and access gap between the haves and have-nots may be increasing. Education and information access are more than ever the keys to economic prosperity, yet access by individuals in different countries is not equal–this social inequity has become known as the digital divide (Accenture 2001a and Asgarkhani 2003a).

- *Impact on Social Interaction*–Advancements in ICT and web-based technology solutions have enabled many government functions to become automated and information to be made available online. This is a concern to those who place a high value on social interaction.

Overall, perceived negative cultural and social implications can compromise the successful introduction and the effectiveness of digital government initiatives for social inclusion.

THE IMPACT OF DIGITAL DIVIDE AND DIGITAL EXCLUSION

Within the information society, access to ICTs is critical for economic and social development. There is much optimism that we are facing myriad digital opportunities where the means exist to broaden participation in the network-based economy and to share its benefits. At the same time, differences in diffusion and the use of ICTs and electronic networks appear to be deepening–which in turn intensifies the socioeconomic divisions amongst people, businesses and nations. Differences in access to and the use of ICTs (known as the *digital divide*) can lead to: *divides between countries*; *divides between the regions of countries*; *social divides within the regions* related to income, education, age, family type, and location.

Developing effective socially inclusive digital government solutions depends on the state of the ICT industry and electronic readiness (e-readiness) within countries, organisations, and societies.

Some of the causes of digital divide that can limit the successful introduction of a socially inclusive digital government can include:

- lack of telecommunications and network infrastructure and limited PC access
- lack of financial resources for developing an infrastructure
- lack of ICT literacy and cultural resistance

- limited Internet access and/or high access costs to global networks and the Internet
- high cost of business investment and strategic business impediments–applicability; the need to reorganise; the need for skills, security and privacy considerations

A review of some of the studies on the digital divide and e-readiness (e.g., Asgarkhani 2005, IDC 2002, OECD Workshop 2000, META Group 2000, Asgarkhani 2002b, UN E-Government Report 2001, Accenture 2001a, COMNET-IT 2002, Meta Group 2000 and UNESCO/COMNET-IT 2000) indicates that there are significant differences in the level of ICT adoption (digital inclusion) and network economy worldwide. A small sample of these studies (mentioned earlier) were reviewed in order to determine which countries are more likely to benefit from digital government for social inclusion. It has to be acknowledged that access to ICTs and digital inclusion is not sufficient in developing and introducing socially inclusive digital government. However, the availability of ICTs and networking infrastructure plays a significant role in the success of socially inclusive digital government.

In 2000, the META Group (Meta Group 2000) examined the electronic readiness of 47 countries in an attempt to establish a digital economy index. The research by the META Group ranked 47 countries in five different categories in order to establish an overall "information age technological competitiveness." These categories included knowledge jobs; globalisation; economic dynamism and competition; transformation to digital economy; and technological innovation capacity. The overall ranking (information age technological competitiveness) for some of the countries that were featured in this study included: Japan (2nd); Australia (8th); Taiwan (10th); New Zealand (11th); Hong Kong SAR (15th); Singapore (17th); Philippines (25th); Malaysia (33rd); India (34th); China (37th); Korea (38th); Thailand (46th); and Indonesia (47th). Countries with a higher ranking in this study (e.g., Japan, Australia, Taiwan, New Zealand, Hong Kong and Singapore) are more likely to be able to put in place effective socially inclusive digital government solutions.

Next, we look at the IDC's Information Society Index (2002). This project considered 23 parameters to compile a ranking list of 55 countries. The countries that were featured in the ISI index were classified under four categories. These four categories (and examples of countries that were featured in the 2002 ISI index) are as follows:

- Countries in a strong position to take full advantage of the information revolution, as they appear to have advanced ICT and social infrastructures–including: Australia (ranked 9th); Taiwan (ranked 10th); Hong Kong SAR (ranked 11th); Japan (ranked 12th); and Singapore (ranked 13th).
- Countries that appear to be moving purposefully into the information age, with much of the necessary infrastructure in place. This category included New Zealand (ranked 17th) and Korea (ranked 18th).
- Countries that are moving forward in spurts before needing to catch their breath and shift priorities due to economic, social and political pressures–e.g., Malaysia (ranked 30th).
- Countries that are moving ahead but inconsistently–due to limited financial resources in relation to their vast populations. Countries that were considered under this category were: the Philippines (ranked 45th); Thailand (ranked 46th); China (ranked 52nd); India (ranked 53rd); Indonesia (ranked 54th); and Pakistan (ranked 55th).

The first eight countries in the 2002 ISI index were: Sweden, Norway, Switzerland, the United States, Denmark, the Netherlands, the United Kingdom, and Finland.

It is fair to say that countries in the first two groups are in a more favourable position so as to benefit from digital government–in order to enhance social inclusion.

A relatively small sample of research outcomes cannot be applied to all countries. However, it appears that numerous countries (including countries within the Asia Pacific, South America, Africa and Middle East) are still at the early or halfway stage of adopting ICT solutions.

THE ROLE AND EFFECTIVENESS
OF DIGITAL GOVERNMENT:
A NEW ZEALAND CASE STUDY

This part of the paper is based on a pilot study of the value and usefulness of digital government in enabling public access and social inclusion. It has to be noted that these results are not final and are based on the information that has been gathered to date.

The digital government project studied was initiated within one of the local governments of the Canterbury region of New Zealand (referred to as the Council hereafter). This project reflects the trends in public sector reform within local government organizations worldwide. This particular local government utilizes ICTs through the implementation of its digital governance initiatives in an attempt to facilitate improved two-way exchange of information and to enhance its public image as a professional customer service oriented organization.

The Council acknowledges that the successful implementation of electronic governance does not result in merely automating the collection and distribution of information, but results in the flow of useful information between the government organization and its citizens–which reflects the 4th model of digital government as discussed in section 3.

The Council seems to be conscious of distinguishing between political rhetoric and the reality of digital government–as demonstrated through measuring the success of the project on an ongoing basis. The performance measures that have been considered include:

- Website Hits: These are monitored to determine the utilization of services. In May 2003 the Council's main service website scored 350,000 hits. The 30 other websites maintained by the Council scored between 150,000 and 180,000 hits.
- Customer Feedback: The Council monitors customer feedback from facilities on the service websites. Feedback is assessed to measure customer satisfaction and service level impact. Suggestions may also result in changes to the services provided.
- Quantifiable Efficiency Benefit: Services provided by this particular digital government initiative are intended to contribute to a reduction in operating costs. Services must continue to meet the desired levels of efficiency–which include cost savings, time saving, and service level impact.

Overall, *Website hits* are not an effective measure of usefulness and usability of a website–unless it is combined with statistics concerning the number of users who actually proceed to access services past the *home page*. *Customer feedback* through service websites can be a more effective measure of user satisfaction. However, it would be beneficial to include feedback from other sources (e.g., phone calls). *Quantifiable efficiency benefits,* as a measure of success, does not directly address public access and social inclusion.

Those who participated in this preliminary study were randomly chosen from various age groups. Sixty-one percent of the respondents were 18-34 years, 26% were aged between 35 and 49 and the rest were over

50 years. It appeared that 76% of the respondents were aware of the digital governance services that are provided by the Council online.

Eighty-seven percent of those who were already aware of the Council's online services viewed the electronic delivery of services as being useful. From those who were previously unaware of the Council's website, 81% considered online local government services desirable.

Results indicated that from those who knew of the Council's online services, the majority (49%) became aware of the Council's website through word of mouth. Web surfing or search engines were second (32%) whilst 19% of them knew of electronic service delivery solutions through advertising.

Those respondents who provided additional information seemed to have used the following services:

- Library information/catalogue (42%)
- Services and hours of operation (38%)
- Events in the city (32%)
- Maps (31%)
- Community services and events (30%)
- Utility rates and local taxes information (25%)
- Bus timetable (23%)
- Permits (13%)
- Art gallery (12%)
- Job advertisements/applications (11%)
- Water resources (10%)
- Population statistics (7%)

Most respondents (who had used the website services) rated the Council's online service as being effective. Those who provided additional information stated the following reasons:

- Immediate access to information anytime/anywhere (77%)
- Saving time–no need for time-consuming phone calls and/or visiting the Council (55%)
- Access to information with reasonable details, simple to follow (40%)
- High level of usability (27%)
- Links to relevant and useful pages and sites (25%)
- Easy to navigate (20%)

Two percent of respondents mentioned that the website did not work correctly. Other difficulties mentioned by those who had used the Council's website included:

- Could not find the required information (9.5%)
- Download time slow (26.2%)
- Access time slow (32.1%)
- Navigation was difficult (8.3%)

Overall, participants did not have any major problems in locating the information they needed–which could be due to (a) participants' familiarity with the basic requirements of using a computer and launching and navigating Web-based applications; and (b) the local government website's usability (ease of use).

Participants suggested that the following services should be considered for online availability:

- Utility rates and local tax payments (37%)
- Other council fee payments (27%)
- Additional general and contact information for the Council's service departments (25%)
- Online submission of applications–e.g., building permits (30%)
- Interactive services: online forums and discussion groups (23%)
- Multimedia: streaming video and audio of local events (30%)
- Online voting facilities (23%)

Participants were asked to state their concerns about using online services. It appeared that data security is the greatest concern for customers (71%). Concerns about confidentiality of data came second (66%). Six percent of the respondents had concerns about document compatibility and 26% were unhappy about the technical infrastructure and speed of access. However, 19% of participants had no concerns over using the Council's online services.

On a scale of 1 to 10 (10 being the greatest), the rating for the website contents was 7.18. Overall, on the scale of 1 to 10 (10 being highly desirable), results showed the average rating of the Council's online services was 7.52. Furthermore, respondents gave the importance of access to online services (in general, not just the Council's services) a score of 7.5 (10 being highly desirable).

The results of this study are not yet final. However, it appears that this particular digital government initiative is rated as being effective. The results of this study to date appear to be consistent with New Zealand's state of access to ICTs and its e-readiness–as outlined in Section 5. However, we cannot assume that the preliminary outcome of this study is applicable to every digital government solution across the board–a perceived successful digital government initiative may not necessarily reach *social inclusion*.

In brief, even though the results of this study are not yet final, it appears that the Council's digital government initiative is rated as being generally effective and workable.

CONCLUSIONS

Within the past few years, much has been argued about the use of ICT and its effectiveness in the reform within the public sector so as to enhance public access to information and enable social inclusion.

Some of the key issues concerning digital government (as discussed in this paper) can be summarized as follows:

- Digital government is to encompass the reform in public management through the improvement of service delivery to the citizen, the creation of economic activity and the safeguarding of democracy.
- Digital government must be oriented towards the citizen. That is to say, digital government requires digital citizens (e-citizens). The benefits of a digital government project can only materialize if the project can be made digitally and socially inclusive. In other words, it must be available to all citizens.
- Digital government can potentially provide an opportunity for service delivery process reengineering. Merely automating existing services is inadequate and does not necessarily produce results.

We examined the success and usefulness of digital government as a tool for enabling social inclusion by considering the different aspects of effectiveness.

There are four schools of thought about the implications of digital government–ranging from the optimists who view digital government as being an effective tool (without concerns) to those who view technology as a tool only (arguing that technology on its own cannot be a driving force for effectiveness). What's more, there are some concerns about social, privacy, cultural and ethical aspects of introducing ICTs within the public sector. We discussed how the *digital divide* and digital exclusion forces can limit the success of digital government initiatives. Finally, a case study of a local government's online services in New

Zealand indicated that citizens rate digital government solutions that were being offered as being workable and socially inclusive. We can observe links between the preliminary results of this study and other facets of effectiveness as discussed previously (sections 2-5)–for instance:

> New Zealand is rated favorably in the adoption of ICT solutions and e-readiness–as outlined in Section 5. Any ICT-enabled solution (such as digital government) in New Zealand is likely to prove more effective compared with countries at the lower end of the e-readiness scale.

There is evidence of support for the *optimism with some concern* school of thought in this case study. The participants in focus groups rate online services as being effective. However, they are concerned with confidentiality and privacy issues. What's more, participants viewed digital government as a tool only–which can be of little value if it is not accompanied with process re-engineering and the resolution of cultural, privacy and educational issues.

Overall, ICTs in the public sector can be considered as a catalyst for reform towards social inclusion. However, there is also a risk. Technology on its own is not enough to drive effective digital government–digital government as a tool has limited value and relevance on its own. Access to ICTs for enabling social inclusion is essential but insufficient. Technology by itself does not necessarily result in better, more efficient and socially inclusive governance in the public sector. Technological advancements are only effective if they are considered alongside other key parameters such as social structure; cultural values and attitudes; governance process reengineering within governments; and ethical issues. That is to say, there are cases where best technology solutions have been made available but results have been less than satisfactory–mainly due to lack of citizens' access, lack of citizens' awareness and training, lack of confidence in public sector agencies, the continuation of complex traditional processes and corruption in the public sector, to name but a few.

REFERENCES

Accenture. (2001a). *e-Government Leadership–Realizing the Vision*, from http://www.digitalopportunity.org.

Accenture. (2001b). *Governments Closing Gap Between Political Rhetoric and e-Government Reality*, from http://www.accenture.com/xd/xd.asp?it=enWeb&xd=industries/government/gove_study.xml.

Asgarkhani, M. (2001). Managing information security: A holistic business process. *Proceedings of the 20th IT Conference.* Sri Lanka, July, 93-100.

Asgarkhani, M. (2002a). Strategic management of information systems and technology in an e-world. *Proceedings of the 21st IT Conference.* Sri Lanka, 103-111.

Asgarkhani, M. (2002b). e-Governance in Asia Pacific. *Proceedings of the International Conference on Governance in Asia.* Hong Kong.

Asgarkhani, M. (2003a). A strategic framework for electronic government. *Proceedings of the 22nd National IT Conference.* Sri Lanka, 57-65.

Asgarkhani, M. (2003b). The effectiveness of digital government as a tool for improved service delivery. *Proceedings of the International Information Technology Conference.* Sri Lanka.

Asgarkhani, M. (2003c). Electronic service delivery in local governments–A strategic tool for service quality improvement in the information age. *Proceedings of the International Symposium on Service Charters and Customer Satisfaction in Public Services.* City University of Hong Kong.

Asgarkhani, M. (2005). The reality of e-service within the public sector: A local government perspective. *Proceedings of the 2005 IEEE International Conference on e-Technology, e-Commerce and e-Service.* Hong Kong, 612-617.

Bhatnagar, S., & Dewan, A. (2001). *Gyandoot Project: ICT Initiative in the District of Dhar, Madhya Pradesh,* from http://poverty.worldbank.org/files/14649_Gyandoot-web.pdf

Bijker, W.E. (1997). Of bicycles, bakelites and bulbs: Toward a theory of socio-technical change. In *Technology, Massachusetts Institute of Technology Press.* Cambridge, MA.

COMNET-IT (2002). *Country Profiles of E-Governance,* from http://www.digitalopportunity.org.

Heeks, R. (1999). *Reinventing Government in the Information Age: International Practice in IT-enabled Public Sector Reform.* London: Routledge.

IDC (2002). *Information Society Index, 2002,* from www.marketresearch.com/product/display.asp?productid=100686&xs=r.

Lin, M., Zhu, R., & Hachigian, N. (2001). *Beijing's Business E-park,* from http://www1.worldbank.org/publicsector/egov/zhongguancun_cs.htm.

Mackenzie, D., & Wajcman, J. (1985). *The Social Shaping of Technology: How the Refrigerator Got Its Hum.* Buckingham: Open University Press.

Massetti, B. (1998). An empirical examination of the value of creativity support systems on idea generation. *Management Information Systems Quarterly, 20* (1), 83-98.

META Group (2000). *The Global E-Economy Index,* from http://www.ecommercetimes.com.

Nath, V. (2003). *Digital Governance,* from www.cddc.vt.edu/digitalgov/gov-cases.html.

NIC (2002). *E- Government: A Strategic Planning Guide for Local Officials,* from www.nicusa.com.

Orrego, C., Osorio, C., & Mardones, R. (2000). *Chile's Government Procurement E-System,* from http://www1.worldbank.org/publicsector/egov/eprocurement_chile.htm.

Perri, 6. (April, 2000). E-governance: Weber's revenge? *Proceedings of the UK 50th Annual Conference for the Political Studies Association.* London, from http:// www.psa.ac.uk/cps/2000/Perri%206.pdf

Raab, C. (1997). Privacy, information and democracy. In Loader, B.D. (ed.) *The Governance of Cyberspace: Politics, Technology and Global Restructuring.* London: Routledge, 155-174.

Radics, G.A. (2001). *Cristal: A Tool for Transparent Government in Argentina,* from http://www1.worldbank.org/publicsector/egov/cristal_cs.htm.

Reschenthaler, G.B., & Thompson, F. (1996). The information revolution and the new public management. *Journal of Public Administration Research and Theory, 6* (1), 125-143.

Samaranayke, V.K. (2003). The reality of digital government. *Proceedings of the 22nd National IT Conference.* Sri Lanka, 1-9.

Stevens, J.M., & McGowan, R.P. (1985). *Information Systems for Public Management.* New York: Praeger.

Tapscott, D. (1997). The digital media and the reinvention of government. *Canadian Public Administration, 40* (2), 328-345.

The Commonwealth Centre for Electronic Governance (2001a). *Electronic Governance in Context,* from http://www.electronicgov.net/pubs/research_papers/eged/chapter1.shtml

The Commonwealth Centre for Electronic Governance (2001b). *Current Issues in Relation to Developments in Privacy and Data Protection,* from http://www.electronicgov.net/pubs/research_papers/eged/chapter5.shtml

UN E-Government Report. (2001). Benchmarking e-government: A global perspective–assessing the UN memberstates. *UN Publication,* from http://www.upan1.org/egovernment2.asp.

UNESCO/COMNET-IT. (2000). *Global Survey of Online Governance,* from http:// www.digitalopportunity.org.

Webster, A. (2001). *Message Beyond the Medium,* from www2.audit-commission. gov.uk/publications/ e-government2.shtml.

Wescott, C.G. (2001). E-government in the Asia-Pacific region. *UNPAN Asia Pacific,* from http://www.unpan.org.

Wiener, N. (1984). *Cybernetics: The Emerging Science at the Edge of Order and Chaos.* New York: Simon and Schuster.

Workshop–Digital Divide–OECD (2000). *The Digital Divide: Enhancing Access to ICTs,* from www.oecd.org/dataoecd/22/11/2428340.pdf.

Zuurmond, A. (1988). From bureaucracy to infocracy: Are democratic institutions lagging behind? *Public Administration in an Information Age: A Handbook.* Amsterdam: IOS Press, 259-272.

doi:10.1300/J017v25n01_09

Redefining Assistive Technology, Accessibility and Disability Based on Recent Technical Advances

Gregg C. Vanderheiden

SUMMARY. Recent advances in information technology, networking and interface research have provided new tools which will allow us to completely redefine the concept of interface. Rather than just being able to use the interface that comes with a product, we can now predict interfaces that adapt themselves to the user, and the ability to use alternate interfaces and devices in lieu of the interface that ships with the product. Also, since accessibility is essentially a human interface issue, the entire area of disability access, including the definition of accessibility and of assistive technology, will need to be rethought as will the strategies that have been used in the past to create access.

Gregg C. Vanderheiden, PhD, is Professor, Department of Industrial and Systems Engineering (Human Factors), and Department of Biomedical Engineering. He is Director, Trace R & D Center, University of Wisconsin-Madison, 1550 Engineering Drive, Room ECB 2107, Madison, WI 53706 (E-mail: gv@trace.wisc.edu).

This work was partially funded by the National Institute on Disability and Rehabilitation Research, US Dept of Education under Grants H133E030012 and H133E040013. The opinions herein are those of the author and not necessarily those of the funding agencies.

This paper is based on a Keynote speech delivered at the HUSITA7 Conference which was held in Hong Kong, August 2004.

[Haworth co-indexing entry note]: "Redefining Assistive Technology, Accessibility and Disability Based on Recent Technical Advances." Vanderheiden, Gregg C. Co-published simultaneously in *Journal of Technology in Human Services* (The Haworth Press, Inc.) Vol. 25, No. 1/2, 2007, pp. 147-158; and: *HUSITA7–The 7th International Conference of Human Services Information Technology Applications: Digital Inclusion–Building a Digital Inclusive Society* (eds: C. K. Law, Yu Cheung Wong, and John Yat Chu Fung) The Haworth Press, Inc., 2007, pp. 147-158. Single or multiple copies of this article are available for a fee from The Haworth Document Delivery Service [1-800-HAWORTH, 9:00 a.m. - 5:00 p.m. (EST). E-mail address: docdelivery@ haworthpress.com].

These concepts will not go away, but their character will change substantially as well as their potential. doi:10.1300/J017v25n01_10 *[Article copies available for a fee from The Haworth Document Delivery Service: 1-800-HAWORTH. E-mail address: <docdelivery@haworthpress.com> Website: <http://www.HaworthPress.com> © 2007 by The Haworth Press, Inc. All rights reserved.]*

KEYWORDS. Accessibility, future, interface, assistive technology, disability

INTRODUCTION

We have entered a new century and there are new technologies and advances both in electronics and biology that will change technology and disability substantially. Some will create new barriers. Others will pose completely new opportunities. In order to overcome the barriers, however, and capitalize on many of these opportunities, it will be necessary to expand our definitions and alter the way we think about disability and accessibility.

In the past, most accessibility has been achieved either by creating specially designed products or by creating special assistive technologies to enable people to access standard products. The concept of "universal design" or "design for all" is often discussed, but has rarely been practiced in mainstream product design to date. With new technical advances and with a growing elderly population, there is an opportunity both to address accessibility in new ways and to do so in a way that creates products that are more flexible for all users. It will also allow alternate interfaces to be used by anyone–as needed. This will result in better interfaces for consumers of all types, but will have the unique advantage of allowing products to be accessible and usable by individuals with functional limitations without having to buy "special" products or "special" adaptations. This is particularly important to elders who often do not realize, do not admit, or do not want to publicly acknowledge their limitations or their need for a different interface than their younger or more able peers. It also has direct implications on the future potential of people with a wide range of disabilities and therefore must be considered in their training and preparation today.

REVIEW OF TECHNICAL ADVANCES
THAT IMPACT THE DESIGN OF PRODUCTS

In order to understand some of these possibilities it is useful to review some of the areas in which technology is advancing and some of the resulting implications for more flexible and accessible product design.

Portability and miniaturization are both advancing rapidly. We have touch screen PDAs the size of a credit card[1] and cell phones not much larger than a brooch. In many cases, this is causing products to be so small that they are hard to see, handle and operate. On the other hand, it has allowed products that were too large to be conveniently carried (e.g., cell phones the size of a brick) to shrink to something that can be conveniently carried in a pocket or purse. Products are also being incorporated directly into clothing, eliminating the need for individuals to find and take out equipment when it needs to be used. It can also allow some devices to be invisible.[2,3,4]

Speech technologies are also continually advancing, and shrinking in size and cost. There is already a single chip that does both speech digitization and speech recognition and costs less than three dollars.[5] There are also chips for less than ten dollars[6] that do the text-to-speech function that used to cost $1000.

Advances in microphones and headsets are also allowing these technologies to be used in environments where they were previously unusable. Noise canceling microphones and earphones allow for clear presentation of audio information and clear pick-up of speech. This is leading to better speech recognition performance in the real world. Bluetooth and other wireless technologies are also allowing users to eliminate the need for audio cables to the headsets. These cables have ranged from inconvenient to impossible to cope with for individuals who have arthritis. And the use of phase-array microphones[7] is allowing individuals to be able to control devices in noisy environments without having to wear any microphone.

For individuals who can hear but not always understand what is said on a phone, we now have captioned telephones[8] that allow them to hear the conversation and simultaneously see the conversation in text on the telephone display.

A key factor in all of this is cost. But the cost of products continues to drop as well. Calculators that used to cost hundreds of dollars can now be purchased for less than two dollars. And disposable cell phones are now being printed on paper that folds into a cell phone–and is tossed when you are done.[9]

FROM THE RESEARCH LAB

Additional glimpses of the potential future can be seen from the research labs. And the time between laboratory demonstration and commercial realization is also decreasing.

For example, five years ago the University of Massachusetts at Amherst demonstrated that complete web servers could be designed that were "about the size of a match-head and cost less than $1 to construct."[10] This was followed, not many years later, with complete web servers built directly into an Ethernet connector. You essentially put a connector on a circuit board and plug in an Ethernet cable connected to the Internet, and the board is on the World Wide Web.

Taking miniaturization to the extreme, the University of California-Berkeley proposed "Smart Dust."[11] The idea was to create devices that were extremely small, that could derive their power from the environment, and that would work together to create sensor and processing networks. One application calls for the "Smart Dust" to be spread out on battlefields to monitor and detect movement of troops and equipment. But it could also be incorporated into coatings, fabric or through other means to provide small unobtrusive sensor nets for tracking that could be used to monitor, track movements, enable gesture recognition, communication, etc., without clumsy wires or batteries that need to be replaced.

To address the issue of obtrusiveness, researchers at IBM's Almaden lab, University of Washington's HIT lab and others have created electronics that masquerade as jewelry and projection systems that can be built into glasses.[12,13,14] The result is the ability for individuals to have large, easy-to-read displays which can appear in front of them as they need them, without requiring that the individuals carry any large displays with them. In addition, the displays are invisible to everyone except to those using them.

Coupling these with text recognition and virtual projection, it is actually possible to have signs in the environment (which would otherwise be unreadable to a person with a disability for some reason) translated into another language, translated into sign language, or translated into audio and played into someone's ear.[12,15]

The ability to be connected anywhere and at any time also opens up the potential for personal services on demand.[16] Essentially, an individual would be able to move about on their own, yet instantly call up any needed services at any time. This could include the ability for individuals who are deaf or hard of hearing to have any speech they encounter instantly translated into text (or sign language) which would then appear instantly floating before them.

Individuals who are blind could have signs or scenes described to them on demand when they encountered a problem, but otherwise operate on their own. Sort of like an instantly available sighted companion who disappeared 15 seconds later when they were no longer needed.

Individuals at all cognitive levels could call up an assistant whenever they encountered a device or system that they did not know how to operate. The on-demand assistant would be able to see and hear what the device they had encountered was and instruct them on how to operate it.

The greatest potential of these and other on-demand services is their ability to allow users to call up assistance for only those minutes or even seconds that they need them. This provides maximum independence with minimum cost, yet allows the assistance to be invoked as needed to address the situations that arise.

In addition to the ability to take services with you into the environment, it's also possible to create very flexible personal environments that adapt to individual needs. Phillips Center for Industrial Design has even considered environments where all of the walls are essentially active displays. The décor, lighting, art, pictures, documents and anything else desired can be projected from the walls, thus making it possible to have very simple environments where displays, graphics, etc., are only present when they are needed. In addition, when they are invoked, the displayed pictures, documents, video or virtual device can be any size that is appropriate for the user. Thus the thermostat can be very large and easy to operate when it is needed and invisible the rest of the time. It can also be large for one user in the house while other users, who do not need a large thermostat, can have a more modest size thermostat projected for them. Someone in a wheelchair could have theirs projected (and operated) low on the wall while a tall person could have it appear at a convenient height for them.

Research on universal remote controls and pluggable user interfaces has also made major advances including the development of a new international draft standard and prototypes for allowing users to control anything, from software to devices around their home (TV, VCR, thermostat, alarm clocks, etc.), from any other device (cell phone, PDA, etc.).[17] This, coupled with advances in natural language research, opens the possibility for users to be able to control things in their house by simply asking for things to be done.[18] For example, user could pull out a V2 enabled cell phone running a natural language program and simply ask "Please record the John Wayne movie tomorrow and turn on Masterpiece Theater,"–and have both of them done without any need to wrestle with the individual devices or their menus. They can also ask, "Please turn the temperature up two degrees and tell me when the mini-series 'Thorns of Spring' is going to be on." Because the devices have pluggable user interfaces, a single natural language-enabled cell phone can act as an alternate interface to all of these devices without the devices themselves having to be special, expensive, or have any capabilities other than the feature allowing alternate interfaces.

Finally, research on direct brain control[19,20] is demonstrating that even individuals who have no physical movement may soon be able to use thought to control devices in their environment directly. The potential to have things done by simply thinking what we want to have done would have tremendous impact on individuals with disabilities, and perhaps for all of us.

IMPLICATIONS FOR PEOPLE WITH DISABILITIES

The implications of these various advances can be seen for individuals with all disabilities.

Hard of Hearing and Deafness. For individuals who are hard of hearing or deaf, we can talk about systems which automatically zero in on a single person talking at a cocktail party and have his/her speech translated into either text or sign language. This could then be projected in a manner that is always in focus and floating in front of the individual no matter where they are looking. This would allow individuals who are deaf to understand spoken speech wherever they encountered it. But it would also be just as important for individuals who are hard of hearing and cannot understand speech except when in quiet environments. In both cases, individuals would be able to communicate in public, regular environments with typical noise level, in a face-to-face manner and without having to invoke physically visible and awkward technologies.

For individuals who are deaf, the systems could also be tuned to listen omni-directionally for particular voices (their children) or particular phrases (warnings) and to project warnings to them. This would allow the individuals to discover emergencies, sirens, alerts or requests for attention that come from locations outside of their visual field.

Low Vision and Blindness. For individuals who are blind, we could have a device that might be called a Text Access Anywhere Device (TAAD). This TAAD could be in a pen or attached to their glasses. It would scan the environment and read all of the text around an individual who is blind, store it instantly and allow the person to access it in whatever manner was most helpful at the time. They could ask it to present (read to them) the largest text first, or to search for particular words. For example, at the mall, it could read large, high items first when the individual is looking to see what stores are there or are near. Later, when they are looking at a menu, it could read the largest text first to give them an idea of what the different categories were. They could then ask it to read just the text in particular categories. Pitch location and volume could also be used to help an individual to spatially sort out the information in their environment or on a page or display. Finally, if they know exactly what they are looking for, they could simply ask the TAAD, if and where the following words appear in their environment.

Interestingly, such a device could actually provide an individual who is blind with capabilities beyond most sighted users. They could walk through a store, for example, and then ask the TAAD for the location of particular items anywhere in the store. They could also read menus in any language and, coupling with online information services, tell you the general ingredients for dishes or how to properly pronounce them to the waiter.

These capabilities and devices could start off as devices that are hand-held and then progress to things that are worn. The control panel for such devices could be something that is held in front of a person–or it could be a keypad that is operated by putting one's hand into one's pocket or purse. Eventually, the devices could even be integrated into a person so that they could be operated with direct brain control.

Cognitive Disabilities. For individuals with cognitive disabilities, these technologies open up the ability for them to have a "companion" with them to provide assistance even when they are alone.[21] Because of GPS (Global Positioning System), it would be possible for such a companion device to know exactly where they are. It could detect if they were outside their regular pattern and alert them (e.g., "You have gone beyond the stop you usually get off each day. Is this intentional or did you miss your stop? If you need help, you could ask the bus driver"). It can also help them secure assistance on demand if they run into a situation and they could use a coach. As the companion gets more intelligent, it could also provide some problem-solving ability locally itself as well as cuing for appointments, holidays ("Don't go to work today"), medications, etc.

Again, the ability to have such a device be very portable can give way to having it built into clothing (so it cannot be left behind) or even someday, built in internally which would allow a person to consult the device quickly and privately, without having to remember to bring the device with them, or being seen using it.

Physical Disabilities. These advances have profound implications for individuals with physical control problems of all types. The ability to more accurately control things in their environment is the first advantage. This is somewhat available today, but usually only for individuals who can afford the cost for special equipment and the cost to configure their house and maintain the electronic remote capabilities. Even then, the control is spotty and easy for some things (like lights) and harder for others (entertainment and security systems). The ability to have remote control capability be a part of standard mass-market products could have tremendous impact on the availability, affordability and supportability of remote control of the devices in their environment. The ability to control things with either special assistive technology or voice would further increase the accessibility.

DEFINITIONS OF UNIVERSAL DESIGN ACCESSIBILITY AND DISABILITY

As we move to such things as the incorporation of alternate interface capabilities and natural language control of mainstream products, we begin to blur the definitions that we have traditionally used to describe devices, strategies and even people. Those of us who wear glasses are not seen to have a disability (even if we cannot read without them), because they are common and everybody uses them. In fact, the definition of legal blindness is based on one's vision after correction. However, not all types of disability are defined by people's ability "after they have been outfitted with all appropriate assistive technologies."

As we move toward having environments where the products can all be controlled remotely (because it is convenient for everyone), and as we move to the situation where everyone pulls out a natural language enabled cell phone or PDA to have the devices in their environment operated, we begin to have a situation where individuals with disabilities are able to use the same devices, using these same "user friendly" interfaces, as everyone else. Where we used to have individuals who needed special intervention because they were not able to figure out how to operate the devices in their environment, or because they were not physically able to operate the devices in their environment, we now have devices that are very flexible in how you control them and are able to be used directly by these individuals. Individuals who have "disabilities" or inabilities to do things, may find that they are no longer unable to operate the standard products. With anywhere assistance (again used by everyone because it's so convenient when we can't figure out how to do something), we may have people with disabilities also able to get assistance as they need it. As we grow older, we depend on our glasses and more, but we don't become disabled until they are no longer good enough. As individuals age, they may also depend more and more on these "standard" alternate interfaces. But will they be "disabled," if they can get along using these interfaces that can be purchased at the store and are essentially the same devices that everyone else is using?

Whereas remote control of devices by voice would be an assistive technology by someone with a spinal cord injury today, in the future it may just be the way the standard products work. They still are "assistive technologies" in that they allow the individual to do things that they would not be able to do otherwise, but they are not "special" assistive technologies. They would instead be mainstream technologies that are important or essential to an individual's ability to live independently or more independently (or independently for a greater portion of the day).

IMPLICATIONS FOR HUMAN SERVICES

The first implication is one of funding. Can human services funding be used to purchase a standard mainstream device? We have already seen situations where a $4000 special device (purpose-built Assistive Technology) had to be purchased rather than a $1000 mainstream device (that would have achieved the exact same function, but more effectively), because the human services funding could not (in these cases) be used to purchase the mainstream technology. As we move in the directions described above, will this increase? This is an interesting and challenging situation. If someone cannot physically write, so they must buy a computer that their peers do not need to buy, then we have a different situation. It is a mainstream device, so it may not qualify for medical funding since medical funds are not to be used for mainstream computing devices. But for this person it is a necessary device (like a wheelchair or brace). If we say, however, that any mainstream device that helps a person with a disability is coverable, then do we pay for cars for people who can't walk far? Or PDAs for people with poor memories? Or cookbooks for people who can remember? There are always easy cases to both accept and reject. But there is also a large grey area where is it less clear. With assistive technologies it is usually clear that the device meets a special disability need because it is sold only to people with disabilities. But with mainstream devices that are used for AT functions it will be much less clear.

This problem does not come up where we are designing mainstream devices to be usable by all. If everyone can use a mainstream device, then we have eliminated their disability–at least with respect to this single device (according to WHO definition of disability). As this happens, however, we may see some interesting situations. People who get free special devices would have to purchase the standard devices along with everyone else. This may not be appreciated by those who lose the free devices but should be offset by increased options and reduced stigma etc., and should not be viewed as negative. However, care must be taken here. If we solve the visible aspects of disability but not the more subtle ones, it may be harder to get services to people who need them–but not so visibly now.

A positive implication is the ability to integrate individuals with a much wider range of abilities into different employment and living situations without having to reengineer the work or living situation to accommodate them. We will be seeing advanced assistive technologies that can better couple with mainstream technologies as a result of these advances. In addition, we will increasingly see mainstream technologies that are flexible enough to be able to directly accommodate a wider range of abilities. Apple computer, for example, has announced that their next operating system will have a screen reader for individuals who are blind built directly into the operating system. For the first time, individuals who are blind will not have to purchase a screen reader (which usually costs more than a computer), in order to use a computer they purchase or encounter at work, at home or in the community. As natural language capabilities are built into these and other products to make them easier for everyone to use, they will be windfalls for individuals who find navigating menus, dealing with a myriad of onscreen buttons, understanding the hierarchical structure of dialog boxes, etc., beyond their capabilities. They will also be of great benefit to individuals who have low vision or blindness and would benefit from being able to simply state what should be done rather than find the button to do it.

CONCLUSION

Recent technical advances have the potential for rewriting much of the landscape. Moreover, they hold the potential to make interfaces more usable by everyone, greatly increasing the probability that they will actually exist in mainstream products. Some of the technologies being discussed, however, are of the variety that can be classified as "perpetually two years away." So a touch of skepticism and realism needs to be mixed with the optimism.

However, as human services professionals, it is important to recognize the potential that is on the horizon and how this could impact on the capabilities of those we work with. It is very important that we do not make judgments today about what people should or should not train for based upon today's expectations or expectations from the past. Our clients may only get one chance at a college education or career training. It is important that we have an open mind about future potential for independence and types of activity that they may be able to successfully engage in, and train them for the broadest possible range.

We've already seen things that look like dreams in science fiction come true in a fairly short period of time. We've also seen things that look fairly simple that have eluded us. However, the current rate of technical progress is astounding. Although it has taken us a long time to create a computer with the intelligence of a dragonfly, we will soon have computers that cost just $1000 and will have a computing power of a mouse. And, according to Ray Kurzweil and others, by 2024 we should have a $1000 computer with the computing power of a human brain; and by 2045, a $1000 computer that will have the computing power of 10 billion human brains–basically everyone on the planet.[22]

So the future looks very different than today, and we will soon be wearing computers in our wristwatches that are more powerful than the most powerful scientific supercomputers today. We should be careful that our lack of imagination of what is possible does not translate into limitations that we place on the expectations of those we serve, and the preparation we give them for their future.

NOTES

1. Rex PDA Intel. Retrieved May 21, 2002, from http://www.rex.net.

2. Charmed Technologies. Retrieved May 21, 2002, from http://www.charmed.com.

3. Wearable Electronics, Philips. Retrieved August 15, 2005, from http://www.design.philips.com/about/design/section-13480/index.html.

4. Sensatex. Retrieved Aug 15, 2005, from http://www.sensatex.com/.

5. $2-3 Digitized Speech and Speech Recognition Chips–Sensory, Inc. Retrieved August 15, 2005, from http://www.sensoryinc.com.

6. Windbond Inc. Retrieved August 15, 2005, from http://www.winbond.com/e-winbondhtm/team/index.htm.

7. Andrea Electronics. Retrieved August 15, 2005, from http://www.andreaelectronics.com/.

8. CapTel by Ultratec. Retrieved August 15, 2005, from http://www.captionedtelephone.com/index.phtml.

9. STTM Technology. Retrieved August 15, 2005, from http://inventors.about.com/library/weekly/aa022801a.htm.

10. iPic by HariharasubrahmanianShrikumar (August 10, 1999). Retrieved August 15, 2005, from http://www.ipsil.com/news/1.htm.

11. Kahn, J. M., Katz, R. H., & Pister, K. S. J. (August 17-19, 1999). Next century challenges: Mobile networking for smart dust. *ACM/IEEE Intl. Conf. on mobile computing and networking (MobiCom 99)*. Seattle, WA. Retrieved May 17, 2002, from http://robotics.eecs.berkeley.edu/~pister/publications/1999/mobicom_99.pdf and http://robotics.eecs.berkeley.edu/~pister/SmartDust/.

12. Digital Jewelry. Retrieved August 15, 2005, from http://www.almaden.ibm.com/cs/user/designlab.html.

13. University of Washington HIT Lab. Retrieved August 15, 2005, from http://www.hitl.washington.edu/

14. Randal Nelson–display in glasses. Retrieved August 15, 2005, from http://www.cs.rochester.edu/users/faculty/nelson/home.html.

15. Smith Kettlewell Rehabilitation Engineering Program. Retrieved August 15, 2005, from http://www.ski.org/Rehab/ComputerVision/index.html.

16. Zimmermann, G., & Vanderheiden, G. (2002). Internet-based personal services on demand. In: Winters, J., Robinson, C., Simpson, R., & Vanderheiden, G. *Emerging and Accessible Telecommunications, Information and Healthcare Technologies–Engineering Challenges in Enabling Universal Access*. RESNA Press. Retrieved August 15, 2005, from http://trace.wisc.edu/docs/2001RESNAIEEESvcsOnDemand/ index.htm.

17. INCITS V2 working group–Universal Remote Console Standard. Retrieved August 15, 2005, from http://www.incits.org/tc_home/v2.htm.

18. Zimmermann, G., Vanderheiden, G., Gandy, M., Laskowski, S., Ma, M., Trewin, S., & Walker, M. (2004). Universal remote console standard–toward natural user interaction in ambient intelligence. *Extended Abstracts for the 2004 Conference on Human Factors in Computing Systems* (pp. 1608-1609). New York: ACM Press. Retrieved August 15, 2005, from http://trace.wisc.edu/docs/2004-CHI-URC-Natural-User-Interaction-Ambient-Intelligence/index.htm.

19. Taylor, D. M., Tillery, S. I. H. & Schwartz, A. B. (2002). Direct cortical control of 3D neuroprosthetic devices. *Science*, 296(5574), 1829-32.

20. Serruya, M. D., Hatsopoulos, N. G. Paninski, L. Fellows, M. R. & Donoghue, J.P. (2002). Instant neural control of a movement signal. *Nature*, 416(6877), 141-2.

21. Vanderheiden, G. (1992). A brief look at technology and mental retardation in the 21st century. In Rowitz, L. (Ed.), *Mental retardation in the year 2000* (pp. 268-278). New York: Springer-Verlag, Inc.

22. Kurzweil, R. The Human Machine Merger: Are We Headed for the Matrix? Retrieved August 15, 2005, from http://www.kurzweilai.net/meme/frame.html?main=/articles/art0552.html.

doi:10.1300/J017v25n01_10

Investigating the Role
of Internet Self-Efficacy
in the Elderly's Learning of ICT
in Hong Kong, China:
A Two-Part Study

Jolie Lam
Matthew K. O. Lee

SUMMARY. This paper discusses the role of Internet self-efficacy and outcome expectations in the elderly's usage of the Internet through a two-part study. The researchers conducted this study by collaborating with three non-government organizations (NGOs) for which funding

Jolie Lam is a PhD graduate of the Department of Information Systems, City University of Hong Kong. She is currently Senior Research Assistant, Department of Social Work and Social Administration, University of Hong Kong, and Director, Multiple Intelligence Development Society, Ltd. in Hong Kong.

Matthew K. O. Lee is Professor of Information Systems and Associate Dean of the Business School, City University of Hong Kong. He holds a PhD from the University of Manchester, UK and is professionally qualified as a barrister-at-law and a Chartered Information Systems Engineer. Dr. Lee is interested in the management of IT adoption and diffusion, electronic commerce, knowledge management and the legal, ethical and policy aspects of IT. He is Associate Editor of *Electronic Commerce Research and Applications*. His publications have appeared in *the CACM, International Journal of Electronic Commerce, Information & Management, Journal of International Business Studies*, and *Journal of the American Society for Information Science and Technology*, among others.

[Haworth co-indexing entry note]: "Investigating the Role of Internet Self-Efficacy in the Elderly's Learning of ICT in Hong Kong, China: A Two-Part Study." Lam, Jolie, and Matthew K. O. Lee. Co-published simultaneously in *Journal of Technology in Human Services* (The Haworth Press, Inc.) Vol. 25, No. 1/2, 2007, pp. 159-176; and: *HUSITA7–The 7th International Conference of Human Services Information Technology Applications: Digital Inclusion–Building a Digital Inclusive Society* (eds: C. K. Law, Yu Cheung Wong, and John Yat Chu Fung) The Haworth Press, Inc., 2007, pp. 159-176. Single or multiple copies of this article are available for a fee from The Haworth Document Delivery Service [1-800-HAWORTH, 9:00 a.m. - 5:00 p.m. (EST). E-mail address: docdelivery@haworthpress.com].

was received from one government unit and a large local charitable organization. A new theoretical model was developed to examine the influence of Internet self-efficacy and outcome expectations on usage intention and perceived user competence. Behavioral modeling training courses were offered to mature adults aged 50 and above in two separate studies over a year. Questionnaire surveys and cognitive knowledge assessments were conducted. In general, the findings in the two studies validated the impacts of Internet self-efficacy and outcome expectations on usage intention. Limitations and implications of this study are discussed. doi:10.1300/J017v25n01_11 *[Article copies available for a fee from The Haworth Document Delivery Service: 1-800-HAWORTH. E-mail address: <docdelivery@haworthpress.com> Website: <http://www.HaworthPress.com> © 2007 by The Haworth Press, Inc. All rights reserved.]*

KEYWORDS. Digital inclusive society, Digital Divide, digital inclusion, Internet self-efficacy, usage intention

BACKGROUND

What is the Digital Divide? It is broadly defined as the gap between the information communication technologies' (ICTs) "have" and "have-nots." The "have-nots" generally are the sociologically and technologically disadvantaged groups: lower income families, senior citizens, people with disabilities and people with lower education attainment, etc. (Internet Professionals Association, 2002). It is the researchers' interests to narrow down the focus on the elderly group, and to address the challenges and opportunities that the Digital Divide brings forth to them. Many countries nowadays acknowledge that the Digital Divide is a real social problem resulting from a clash between cultural and social systems and the merging information communication technologies. Global initiatives include countries like Japan, Korea, Singapore, Taiwan, United Kingdom and United States. The government, the private sector and the non-profit sector of these countries have joined forces in tackling the Digital Divide issue. It is clear that dealing with the Digital Divide is a long and on-going process.

In the United States, for example, the AgeLab at MIT has been partnering with industry and the aging community since 1999. SeniorNet is a nonprofit organization founded in 1986. It provides adults, age 50 and older, access to computer technologies. In order to close the gap, SeniorNet partners, with the eBay Foundation, IBM and the Charles

Schwab Foundation, have provided education and programs that focus on the needs and interests of older adults. In Hong Kong, China, the Social Welfare Department has launched a three-year "Opportunities for the Elderly" scheme and has provided funds enabling Non-Government Organizations (NGOs), including the multi-service centers and social centers for the elderly, to organize activities in 1999. Starting in 2004, the Hong Kong YMCA opened its first content web portal. The portal encourages life-long learning by offering online college-level programs and discussion forums, etc., for adults aged 50 and over. In May 2004, the Internet Professionals Association chaired the global alliance for bridging the digital divide (GABDD) meeting and formulated plans in narrowing the digital divide with delegates from 24 countries.

We see that the global aging population goes hand-in-hand with the Digital Divide. On the one hand, the aging population amplifies the gap in the Digital Divide. On the other hand, this population segment creates numerous profit creating opportunities for business organizations. In the U.S., for instance, there are an estimated 35 million people aged 65 or older, accounting for almost 13% of the total population. In 2030, it is projected that one in five people will be 65 or older, and the size of the older population will grow to 70 million (Federal Interagency Forum on Aging-Related Statistics, 2000). In Hong Kong, China, it is predicted that the proportion of the population aged 65 or above will grow from 11.2% in 2001 to 24.3% in 2031, which means that one in every four persons in Hong Kong will be 65 years of age or older in 30 years' time (Census and Statistics Department, May 2002). In fact, the Elderly Commission (June 2002) advises the Hong Kong government to be aware of this social issue.

However, we shall not forget that seniors represent a huge consumer market segment in the U.S. and Europe. Research shows that people age 55 and above are using the web in increasing numbers (Nielsen/NetRatings, Nov. 14 and 19, 2003). Site owners have an opportunity to promote their products and services to this growing audience; many are already organizing their finances and booking holidays online. In Europe, finance sites are particularly popular among older Internet users, for example, Barclays in the UK and Postbank in Germany. There are currently 11.5 million people age 55 and above using the Internet in Europe (Nielsen/NetRatings, Nov. 14, 2003). In the U.S. due to popular demand, SeniorNet is offering training courses for seniors, such as buying and selling on eBay. In the U.S., it is estimated that seven baby boomers will turn 50 every minute between now and 2014. They account for 74% of personal financial assets, 50% of discretionary income, 65% of cruise travel, 48% of luxury car sales, and 77% of prescription drug sales (Future Dialogue, Dec. 2000). In Hong Kong, the percentage of households with PCs at home connected to the Internet has increased from 52.5% in 2002 to 60% in 2003. The percentage of persons aged 15 and over who have used one or more types of electronic business services for personal matters has increased from 92.6% in 2002 to 93.6% in 2003 (Census and Statistics Department, May 2002).

RESEARCH MOTIVATION

The Digital Divide exists in both developed and less developed countries. How would these governments build a digital inclusive society and/or enable digital inclusion in societies? In Hong Kong, the HKSAR government and NGOs have been subsidizing activities and making efforts to promote IT awareness and accessibility in the elderly population by providing training courses and establishing computer facilities in various Hong Kong locations. However, the researchers in this respect raise challenging questions–(1) Does that mean the digital divide will close eventually? (2) Do we have the appropriate standards of measurements for the success and/or failure of these social projects? (3) Do the elderly intend to continue the usage of PCs and Internet services after the training that is provided to them? (4) How can we know whether the elderly can master the necessary IT skills in using the PCs and can access the Internet or not? (5) Has learning and adopting IT made a difference in their lives?

RESEARCH OBJECTIVES

As a result, the researchers intend to conduct an applied research in order to get a grip on the Digital Divide phenomenon, and to fulfill the following research objectives:

1. To test the validity and reliability of a proposed research model derived from Compeau and Higgins' (1995b), within a specific context, i.e., elderly use of Internet. The proposed model also incorporates the four major information sources of self-efficacy theory (Bandura, 1986)–enactive mastery, vicarious experience, verbal persuasion and emotional arousal.

2. To examine factors of and relationships to elderly Internet self-efficacy, outcome expectation, usage intention, and perceived user competence (cognitive knowledge).
3. To measure the levels of changes, if any, on elderly computer self-efficacy, outcome expectation, and perceived user competence in two separate studies.

RESEARCH MODEL AND HYPOTHESES

The Theory of Reasoned Action (Fishbein & Ajzen, 1975) is the first theoretical model that has gained widespread acceptance in the IT adoption research area. Other researchers have addressed the demand in looking for additional explanatory variables in computer usage (Thompson et al., 1991; Webster & Martocchio, 1992). For example, Compeau and Higgins (1995b) examine the Social Cognitive Theory (SCT), the work of Albert Bandura (1986). Based on the literature review, interactions and observations of the elderly groups and NGOs, researchers believe that SCT serves as an important theory in explaining IT adoption among the elderly in Hong Kong.

Referring to the works of Compeau et al. (1995a and 1995b), several key constructs are integrated into the proposed model: encouragement by others, outcome expectations, and anxiety. Additionally, three constructs are expanded upon: Internet self-efficacy, facilitating conditions, and usage intention in replacing computer self-efficacy, others' use and usage. The construct of user competence (Marcolin et al., 2000; Munro et al., 1997) is adopted as perceived user competence in the proposed model. It is believed that the adapted research model is applicable for this study on the Hong Kong elderly's IT usage and performance (Figure 1).

This study was carried out in collaboration with the Cyber Senior Network and Development Association, Ltd., the Internet Professional Association and Senior IT Advocates. At the start of the research there were numerous meetings held with the representatives from NGOs and several focus groups held with the elderly and social workers. It is hoped that with certain levels of coaching and encouragement, as well as with the availability of hardware/software supports, the self-confidence, usage intention and cognitive knowledge of the elderly may increase.

FIGURE 1. Proposed Research Model

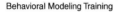

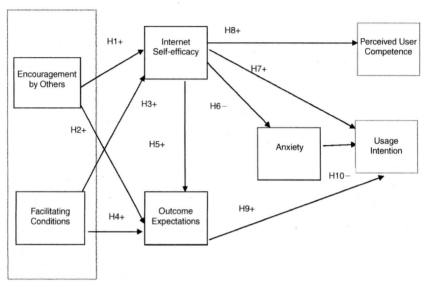

The intention was to capture the changes in elderly computer self-efficacy, their usage intention and competency in three separate studies. This longitudinal study ran from June 2002 to August 2003. Study one was performed from June 2002 to August 2002, and study two was carried out in December 2002 and January 2003. The hypotheses will be applied to these studies, such that the research model for study two is the sub-set of the proposed model in study one.

Behavioral Modeling Training Method

Learning by observation, or behavior modeling, has been shown to be a powerful means of actual user behavior (Latham & Saari, 1979; Manz & Sims, 1986; Schunk, 1981). Behavioral modeling influences behavior in part through its influence on self-efficacy (Bandura & Adams, 1977), and also through its influence on outcome expectations (Bandura, 1971). In this study, the researchers incorporate the behavioral modeling training method into the proposed model, and assume its positive influence on the elderly learning computers.

Encouragement by Others

The encouragement of others within the individual's reference group (i.e., people to whom someone looks to obtain guidance on behavioral expectations) can be expected to influence both self-efficacy and outcome expectations. Encouragement of use represents "verbal persuasion," one of the four major sources of efficacy information (Bandura, 1986). In the current case, the elderly might respond to the opinions of others by forming judgments about their own abilities in using computers. Encouragement of use may also exert an influence on outcome expectations. For example, if people in the elderly reference group (e.g., family, friends, staff at the social centers, and so on) encourage the use of computing technology, the elderly judgments about the probable and favorable outcomes of the behavior will be affected. At the very least, they will expect that their peers will be pleased by the behavior. Thus, the first two hypotheses are as follows:

H1: The higher the encouragement of computer use by members of the elderly reference group, the higher the elderly Internet self-efficacy.
H2: The higher the encouragement of computer use by members of the elderly reference group, the higher the elderly outcome expectations (performance and personal).

Facilitating Conditions

Triandis (1980) defines "facilitating conditions" as external resource constraints. Taylor and Todd (1995) further segregate this construct into two dimensions: one relating to resource factors, such as time and money, and the other relating to technology compatibility issues that may constrain usage. In this research, facilitating conditions, such as organizational and technical supports, are the main focus. The organization will be the learning institution, the community centre and/or the computer laboratory. It is believed that the availability of assistance to the elderly should increase their abilities and, probably, their perceptions of their abilities. Facilitating conditions can also affect outcome expectations because these support systems reflect the expectations of these institutions toward behavior, and therefore may provide clues as to the likely consequences of using the computer. Thus, hypotheses 3 and 4 are as follows:

H3: The better the facilitating conditions provided for the elderly at an institution, the higher their Internet self-efficacy.

H4: The better the facilitating conditions provided for the elderly at an institution, the higher their outcome expectations (performance and personal).

Internet Self-Efficacy

Social cognitive theory provides a prominent role to self-efficacy perceptions. Self-efficacy judgments are seen to influence outcome expectations since "the outcomes one expects derive largely from judgments as to how well one can execute the requisite behavior" (Bandura, 1978, p. 241). Current studies define Internet self-efficacy as the performance of specific tasks such as entering World Wide Web addresses, creating bookmarks and folders, using File Transfer Protocol (FTP) and telnet (Nahl, 1996 & 1997). Ren's (1999) measure of Internet self-efficacy is tailored to searching for government information sources. Eastin and LaRose (2000), however, look at the overall Internet usage and not just performing a specific Internet-related task like emailing. Thus, Internet self-efficacy may be differentiated from computer self-efficacy as the belief that a person can utilize effectively the Internet over and above basic personal computer skills.

These research results are consistent with previous self-efficacy literature in that self-efficacy is found positively related to task performance. Even though the computers at some community centers are often set up by the staff and ready to be used for surfing the Internet, the elderly do need to acquire simple computer skills to go online. Therefore, the researchers would teach the elderly some basic concepts of the computer (e.g., the hardware, software, Windows operating functions, etc.) through our training courses in order to appropriately measure the elderly's Internet usage intention and their competency. The hypothesis is:

H5: The higher the elderly Internet self-efficacy, the higher their outcome expectations (performance and personal).

Self-efficacy judgments are held to have influence on the emotional responses of the individual. Individuals normally prefer and like behaviors that they feel they are good at and avoid those that they are not. Anxiety is measured and not affect in assuming that the elderly have formed a general fondness and genuine interest toward computer learning. It is believed that the elderly will experience a lot of anxiety and then worry that they will cause chaos on the computers. By including the construct, anxiety, at this early stage of the study, a plausible research model for better interpretation and prediction can be obtained. This relationship is predicted by hypothesis 6 as follows:

H6: The higher the elderly Internet self-efficacy, the lower their degree of anxiety.

Usage Intention

Self-efficacy perceptions are predicted to be a significant precursor to computer use. This hypothesis is supported by research regarding computer use (Burkhardt et al., 1990; Hill et al., 1987) and research in a variety of other domains (Bandura & Adams, 1977; Betz & Hackett, 1981; Frayne & Latham, 1987). In this specific context, the elderly are offered computer training for the first time, and then their intention of future computer use is measured.

H7: The higher the elderly Internet self-efficacy, the higher their intention of computer usage.

Perceived User Competence

Marcolin et al. (2000) suggest that user competence by end users is an important measure besides IT adoption and IT usage. Munro et al. (1997) propose a specific research model on user competence and its relationship with certain individual factors–self-efficacy, usage and demographics. No empirical research has been seriously done on this matter, thus in this study the correlation of self-efficacy to the elderly perceived user competence is explored. As at this early stage the elderly are just starting to learn computers, only their perceptions on how much they know about using computers and the Internet can be measured, rather than their actual knowledge. Thus, the researchers add this construct into the model by proposing the following hypothesis:

H8: The higher the elderly Internet self-efficacy, the higher their perceived user competency.

Outcome Expectation

Outcome expectation is also an important predecessor to usage behavior. According to social cognitive theory, individuals are more likely to engage in behavior they expect will result in favorable outcomes. The hypothesis is also supported by previous studies (Davis et al., 1989; Hill et al., 1987; Pavri, 1988; Thompson et al., 1991). Accordingly, the next hypothesis is:

H9: The higher the elderly outcome expectations (performance and personal), the higher their intention of computer usage.

Anxiety

Feelings of anxiety surrounding computers are expected to negatively influence computer use. Not surprisingly, people are expected to avoid behaviors that arouse nervousness. A number of studies have demonstrated a relationship between computer anxiety and the use of computers (Igbaria et al., 1989; Webster et al., 1990). This gives rise to the following hypothesis:

H10: The higher the elderly computer anxiety, the lower their intention of computer usage.

RESEARCH DESIGN

The target population of this research is elderly, aged 65 and above, who reside in Hong Kong, China. However, statistics show that those aged 50 and above have less exposure to computers and Internet usage compared to other age groups (Sin Chung Kai, 2002). Thus, the researchers welcomed interested participants aged 50 and up as well. The target population are novices with no or little previous computer experience, but who want to learn using the computer to access the Internet. Advertisements on free computer training lessons were placed at several local daily newspapers, and were announced over the local radio stations. Potential participants were first screened to ensure that they had little prior experience with computers. The screening took place during a telephone interview, and decisions were based on the judgment of the potential participants. While some had minimal computer use, they all considered themselves to be novices.

Pretest of Questionnaire and Pilot Study

A pretest of the questionnaire (including all construct measures) was conducted with eight people. The eight people included three scholars, two social workers and three administrative staff of NGOs. Since participants of this study could not read English proficiently (most elderly in Hong Kong did not receive formal education), the original script of the questionnaire was translated into Chinese. Each respondent completed the questionnaire and provided feedback regarding the wording of the questions, the process and the measures. A pilot study involving 58 elderly from the sampling frame was also conducted. In this pilot study valuable feedback on the questionnaire instrument was given, and the sample size of this survey was defined.

Training Sessions

In studies one and two, 10 tutors, previously trained by the organizers to teach the elderly basic computer and Internet skills, were hired to conduct the training sessions. Additionally, five student volunteers were recruited from a local high school and a university. The four-hour training course included a one-and-a-half hour lecture/demonstration and practice session. The lecture (45 minutes) provided basic information about the computer equipment, the operating system being used, and the techniques of browsing the Internet. Participants were shown how to operate the keyboard and mouse in order to browse websites and exchange emails on the Internet. The tutors followed a fixed outline but questions related to this course were answered as they arose. Next, participants were given 45 minutes to practice what they had learned. Training notes and pre-registered email logins, passwords, and email addresses were also given to participants. Following the practice session, a questionnaire and a knowledge assessment test (multiple choice and hands-on combined) were then administered. At the end of the session Certificates of Completion were presented to participants.

FINDINGS AND DISCUSSION

In study one, a total of 555 elderly attended the combined beginning and intermediate-levels training classes, thus the response rate was 55.5% (calculated based on an estimation of 1,000 participants). In study two, a total of 338 elderly attended the advanced classes. Respondents were identified and matched in both studies by a unique, preassigned email account and an advanced class voucher. The response rate was 60.9% (calculated based on the sample size of study one).

Data analyses were performed using Partial Least Square (PLS). PLS is a regression-based technique that can analyze structural models with multiple-item constructs and direct and indirect paths. PLS produces loadings between items and constructs (similar to principal components analysis) and standardized regression coefficients between constructs. R^2 values for dependent constructs are also produced. The technique has gained acceptance in marketing and organizational behavior research and was first used in the MIS literature by Rivard and Huff (1988) in an examination of the factors of success for end-user computing. Barclay et al. (1995) provide a comprehensive description of PLS analysis.

PLS analysis involves two stages: (i) assessment of the measurement model, including the reliability and discriminant validity of the structural model, and (ii) assessment of the structural model. For the assessment of the measurement model, individual item loadings and internal consistency reliabilities are examined as a test of reliability. Individual item loadings and internal consistencies greater than 0.70 are considered adequate (Fornell & Larcker, 1981). For discriminant validity, items should load higher on their own construct than on other constructs in the model, and the average variance shared between the constructs and their measures should be greater than the variances shared between the constructs themselves. The structural model and hypotheses are tested by examining the path coefficients (which are standardized betas). In addition to the individual path tests, R^2, the explained variance in the dependent constructs is assessed as an indication of model fit. Finally, it is often useful to assess the indirect effects and common cause effects as in path analysis. The path coefficients and variance explained in the two studies are summarized in Tables 1 and 2. In this research, researchers performed statistical analyses and found the reliability and discriminant validity of the structural model satisfactory.

Overall, the findings gave strong supports to the research models, especially the results in study one and two. Encouragement by others exerted influence on Internet self-efficacy and outcome expectations. Facilitating conditions had no effect on Internet self-efficacy (ISE) in the first study but yield significant impact to ISE in the second study, probably due to these two reasons: (1) the English version of Microsoft Window was used in study one, whereas the Chinese version of Microsoft Window was used in study two; and (2) the elderly were still unfamiliar with typing on a keyboard and maneuvering the mouse in study one. On the other hand, the relationship of facilitating conditions and outcome expectations was significant in the two studies. The elderly were seen to be more likely to perform online tasks after they were exposed to computers and the Internet. The impact of ISE on outcome expectations in study one was weak compared to the strong impact in

TABLE 1. Summary of Hypotheses (Path Coefficients)

Hypothesis	Study 1	Study 2
H1: Encouragement → Internet SE	0.248***	0.240***
H2: Encouragement → Outcome Expects.	0.346***	0.325***
H3: Facilitat. Conds. → Internet SE	0.055	0.353***
H4: Facilitat. Conds. → Outcome Expects.	0.522***	0.461***
H5: Internet SE → Outcome Expects.	0.006	0.091**
H6: Internet SE → Anxiety	−0.289***	---
H7: Internet SE → Usage Intention	0.137**	0.207***
H8: Internet SE → Perceived User Competence	0.698***	---
H9: Outcome Expects. → Usage Intention	0.183**	0.341***
H10: Anxiety → Usage Intention	−0.093	---

* p < 0.10 ** p < 0.05 *** p < 0.01

TABLE 2. Variance in Dependent Constructs Explained by the Models

Construct	Study 1 R^2	Study 2 R^2
Internet Self-efficacy	0.082	0.311
Outcome Expectations	0.621	0.630
Anxiety	0.084	---
Usage Intention	0.074	0.230
Perceived User Competence	0.487	---

study two. As in study one, the elderly were computer novices and were not confident in their capabilities of engaging in various online tasks. However, over time and with adequate training and practice, the elderly's confidence was boosted and they expected that they would have the skill in performing online tasks. ISE was negatively related to anxiety as predicted earlier. The more confidence the elderly had, the less worried they were in using the computer and the Internet.

ISE exerted strong influence on usage intention in both studies one and two. One possible explanation for this occurrence is that in the two studies, participants were novices in using the Internet; hence, they relied on self-efficacy to form judgments on their capabilities. Outcome expectations had significant influence on usage intention, and its path coefficient intensified from study one to study two. When the elderly progress in their skills, they are more likely to engage in online activities. Although anxiety is related to usage intention in the direction hypothesized, its effect was rather weak. Simply lowering the arousal of anxiety of participants did not stimulate elderly continuance of usage. However, Internet self-efficacy and outcome expectations and their antecedents played key roles in generating interest.

Nevertheless, the correlation among ISE, anxiety and usage intention was not measured in study two due to some practical reasons: (i) the elderly were frustrated in answering a lengthy questionnaire; (ii) between study one and two, the elderly gained more hands-on experience using PCs and the Internet. As a result, it was safe to assume that the anxiety level of the participants, in study two, is also negatively related to their confidence and intention in using PCs and the Internet. In addition, ISE exerted a strong influence toward perceived user competence in study one, that is, the more confident the elderly were, the better they perceived their capability in using PCs and the Internet. Yet, the correlation of ISE and perceived user competence was not measured in study two since it was also safe to assume its positive relationship could be carried on from study one.

It is noted that over time it was possible to proceed to measure directly the link between Internet self-efficacy and actual use, and its reciprocal relationship. Previous studies acknowledge that self-efficacy has a direct effect toward computer usage (Compeau et al., 1995b & 1999; Igbaria & Iivari, 1995). Bandura (1986) states the reciprocal relationship of self-efficacy and use–self-efficacy is viewed as an antecedent to use, but successful prior experience with a computer is also viewed as influence on self-efficacy.

In addition, measurement items for constructs such as self-efficacy, outcome expectations, and usage intention, as well as perceived user competence, would need fine-tuning when conducting a longitudinal study. Otherwise, the explanatory power of the structural model could be diminished over time. As the elderly progress, they perceive they have successfully mastered basic computer knowledge, and they thrive for new knowledge as well as expect themselves to perform other complex tasks. The elderly might have advanced in tasks such as emailing, reading online news, etc. In order to keep both their expectations and interest in using the Internet, continuous training and practice are necessary. Perhaps the elderly can move on to other online tasks, like downloading pictures, utilizing search engines, and so on.

LIMITATIONS

There are several limitations to this study. First of all, the differences in sample sizes could be a potential problem, although non-response bias was tested and found insignificant. Also, a convenient sampling approach was used instead of random sampling. Ads were placed through mass media, but participants were not randomly selected from the entire elderly population segment. Thirdly, the assumption of the positive influence of the behavioral modeling training method in this study was made based on similar studies reported in literature. In addition, between trainings and practices, participants gained experience and a construct of "prior experience" was not used in the model to measure its effect. Furthermore, there was a long lapse of time between the three studies. Other exogenous variables may have come into play and affected the results, which could not be foreseen and measured.

CONCLUSIONS

Theoretical Contributions

Compeau et al. (1995a, 1995b & 1999) propose that longitudinal studies and experiment research methods are necessary in confirming the effects of the antecedents of self-efficacy and its influence on outcome expectations and usage, plus the relationship of self-efficacy and user competence. By conducting these three empirical studies, it is believed that the authors' calls have been partially answered, and that the theoretical understanding of the connections of these variables could actually solve a real world phenomenon–the Digital Divide. To a certain extent, a new and critical viewpoint of the causal relationship of Internet self-efficacy and usage intention has been offered. The foundation for future IT research interest has been set, so that scholars may adopt the models and measurement scales in other contexts, in countries that attempt to bridge the digital divide through computer training. This study has focused on studying the impact of self-efficacy on the elderly, a distinct group of computer users compared to the general work force. Currently in the Information Systems discipline, no study has been done in developing a new model to explain causal relationships among the above-mentioned constructs. This study points to a new group for the continuance of ICTs usage–the elderly. This new user group of ICTs could potentially expand to a large (and loyal) virtual community.

Practical Contributions

This study has made an attempt in tackling a real world phenomenon. It is hoped to bridge the Digital Divide by continuously offering computer training to disadvantaged groups, such as the elderly. This is new knowledge for a unique community of stakeholders in world societies–government (policy-making), NGOs (training classes), and business corporations (provide products/services). Through understanding the elderly, new markets have been discovered and services and products can be tailor-made to their special needs, such as online banking, user interface designs, new adaptive software and hardware, etc. Last but not least, the findings indicate that computer training improves the psychological state of mind of the elderly. Their self-confidence is boosted as they gain a developed sense of achievement. They feel better about themselves for they can communicate with other groups in sharing their knowledge about a new subject area, the computer and the Internet.

REFERENCES

Ajzen, I. (1985). From intentions to actions: A theory of planned behavior. In J. Kuhl & J. Beckmann (Eds.), *Action control: From cognition to behavior* (pp. 11-39). New York: Springer Verlag.

Bandura, A. (1971). Influence of model's reinforcement contingencies on the acquisition of imitative responses. In A. Bandura (Ed.), *Psychological modeling: Conflicting theories* (pp. 112-127). Chicago, IL: Aldine/Atherton.

Bandura, A., & Adams, N. E. (1977). Analysis of self-efficacy theory of behavioral change. *Cognitive Therapy and Research*, (1), 287-310.

Bandura, A. (1978). Reflections on self-efficacy. In S. Rachman (Ed.), *Advances in behavioral research and therapy*, (1) (pp. 237-269). Oxford, England: Pergamon Press.

Bandura, A. (1986). *Social foundations of thought and action*. Englewood Cliffs, NJ: Prentice Hall.

Barclay, D., Higgins, C., & Thompson, R. (1995). The partial least squares approach to causal modeling: Personal computer adoption and use as an illustration. *Technology Studies, Special Issue on Research Methodology*, 2(2), 285-324.

Betz, N. E., & Hackett, G. (1981). The relationships of career-related self-efficacy expectations to perceived career options in college women and men. *Journal of Counseling Psychology*, (28), 399-410.

Burkhardt, M. E., & Brass, D. J. (1990). Changing patterns or patterns of change: The effects of a change in technology on social network structure and power. *Administrative Science Quarterly*, (35), 104-127.

Compeau, D. R., Higgins, C. A., & Huff, S. (June, 1999). Social cognitive theory and individual reactions to computing technology: A longitudinal study. *MIS Quarterly*, 23(2), 145-158.

Compeau, D. R., & Higgins, C. A. (1995a). Application of social cognitive theory to training for computer skills. *Information Systems Research, 6*(2), 118-143.

Compeau, D. R., & Higgins, C. A. (June, 1995b). Computer self-efficacy: Development of a measure and initial test. *MIS Quarterly, 19*(2), 189-211.

Davis, F. D., Bagozzi, R. P., & Warshaw, P. R. (1989). User acceptance of computer technology: A comparison of two theoretical models. *Management Science, (35),* 982-1003.

Eastin, M. S., & LaRose, R. (September, 2000). Internet self-efficacy and the psychology of the digital divide. *Journal of Computer-Mediated Communication, 6*(1).

Federal Interagency Forum on Aging-Related Statistics (2000). Older Americans 2000: Key indicators of well-being. Retrieved from http://www.agingstats.gov/chartbook2000/population.html.

Fishbein, M., & Ajzen, I. (1975). *Belief, attitude, intention and behavior: An introduction to theory and research.* Reading, MA: Addison-Wesley.

Fornell, C., & Larcker, D. (1981). Evaluating structural equation models with unobservable variable and measurement error. *Journal of Marketing Research, (18),* 39-50.

Frayne, C. A., & Latham, G. P. (1987). Application of social learning theory to employee self-management of attendance. *Journal of Applied Psychology, 72*(3), 387-392.

Future Dialogue (December, 2000). Ten trends for 2001–Trend #3 undercover aging. *The Intelligence Factory.* Retrieved from http://www.mcvaymedia.com/infopac/01articles/tentrends2001.htm).

Gist, M. E., Rosen, B., & Schwoerer, C. (1988). The influence of training method and trainee age on the acquisition of computer skills. *Personal Psychology, (41),* 255-265.

Hill, T., Smith, N. D., & Mann, M. F. (1987). Role of efficacy expectations in predicting the decision to use advanced technologies: The case of computers. *Journal of Applied Psychology, 72*(2), 307-313.

Hong Kong Census and Statistics Department (7 May, 2002). Hong Kong population projections 2002-2031. Retrieved from http://www.info.gov.hk/censtatd/eng/interest/pop_proj/slide.pdf.

Hong Kong Elderly Commission (8 June, 2002). 2002 symposium cum exhibition on challenges and opportunities of an ageing population. Retrieved from http://www.info.gov.hk/gia/general/200206/08/0608124.htm.

Igbaria, M., & Iivari, J. (1995). The effects of self-efficacy on computer usage. *Omega, 23*(6), 587-605.

Igbaria, M., Pavri, F. N., & Huff, S. L. (1989). Microcomputer applications: An empirical look at usage. *Information and Management, (16),* 187-196.

Internet Professionals Association (October, 2002). Introduction to Internet Professionals Association & The Web Care Campaign. Retrieved from http://www.iproa.org/iproa/iproa_present_20021001.pdf.

Latham, G. P., & Saari, L. M. (1979). Application of Social-learning Theory to training supervisors through behavioral modeling. *Journal of Applied Psychology, 64*(3), 239-246.

Manz, C. C., & Sims, H. P. (1986). Beyond imitation: Complex behavioral and affective linkages resulting from exposure to leadership training models. *Journal of Applied Psychology,* (71), 571-578.

Marcolin, B. L., Compeau, D. R., Munro, M. C., & Huff, S. L. (March, 2000). Assessing user competence: Conceptualization and measurement. *Information Systems Research, 11*(1), 37-60.

Martocchio, J. J. (1994). Effects of conceptions of ability on anxiety, self-efficacy, and learning in training. *Journal of Applied Psychology, 79*(6), 819-825.

Munro, M.C., Huff, S. L., Marcolin, B. L., & Compeau, D. R. (1997). Understanding and measuring user competence. *Information Management,* (33), 46-57.

Nahl, D. (1996). Affective monitoring of Internet learners: Perceived self-efficacy and success. *Journal of American Society for Information Sciences,* (33), 100-109.

Nahl, D. (1997). User-centered assessment of two web browsers: Errors, perceived self-efficacy, and success. *Journal of American Society for Information Sciences,* (34), 89-97.

Pavri, F. (1988). *An empirical investigation of the factors contributing to micro-computer usage,* Dissertation, University of Western Ontario.

Ren, W. (1999). Self-efficacy and the search for government information. *Reference & User Service Quarterly,* (38), 283-291.

Rivard, S., & Huff, S. L. (1988). Factors of success for end user computing. *Communications of the ACM, 29*(5), 486-501.

Schunk, D. H. (1981). Modeling and attributional effects on children's achievement: A self-efficacy analysis. *Journal of Educational Psychology,* (73), 93-105.

Sin Chung Kai Cyber Office (26 February, 2002). Building a digitally inclusive society. *IT in Focus, Digital Divide.* Retrieved from http://www.info.gov.hk/digital21/eng/programme/download/edig_div.doc.

Taylor, S., & Todd, P. A. (June, 1995). Understanding information technology usage: A test of competing models. *Information Systems Research, 6*(2), 144-176.

The Nielsen/NetRatings Press Release (14 November, 2003). Older Internet audience continues to increase in Europe. Retrieved from http://direct.www.nielsen-netratings.com/pr/pr_031114_UK.pdf.

The Nielsen/NetRatings Press Release (19 November, 2003). Senior citizens lead Internet growth. http://www.nielsen-netratings.com/pr/pr_031120.pdf.

Thompson, R. L., Higgins, C. A., & Howell, J. M. (1991). Personal computing: Toward a conceptual model of utilization. *MIS Quarterly,* (15), 125-143.

Triandis, H. C. (1980). Values, attitudes, and interpersonal behavior. In M. M. Page (Ed.), *Nebraska Symposium on Motivation 1979–Beliefs, Attitudes and Values* (pp. 195-260). Lincoln, NE: University of Nebraska Press.

Webster, J., Heian, J. B., & Michelman, J. E. (1990). Mitigating the effects of computer anxiety through training. In J. I. DeGross, M. Alavi, & H. Oppelland (Eds.), *Proceedings of the Eleventh International Conference on Information Systems* (pp. 171-182). Copenhagen, Denmark.

Webster, J., & Martocchio, J. J. (1992). Microcomputer playfulness: Development of a measure with workplace implications. *MIS Quarterly, 16*(2), 201-226.

doi:10.1300/J017v25n01_11

SOCIAL INCLUSION APPLICATIONS

Sanyog:
A Speech Enabled Communication System for the Speech Impaired and People with Multiple Disorders

Samit Bhattacharya
Sudeshna Sarkar
Anupam Basu

Samit Bhattacharya is a research scholar; Sudeshna Sarkar is Associate Professor; and Anupam Basu is Professor; all affiliated with Department of Computer Science and Engineering, Indian Institute of Technology Kharagpur-721302, India.

Address correspondence to: Samit Bhattacharya, Department of Computer Science and Engineering, Indian Institute of Technology Kharagpur-721302, West Bengal, India (E-mail: samit@cse.iitkgp.ernet.in).

The authors thank IICP Kolkata and AADI, New Delhi for the field-testing of and feedbacks on the system.

This work was supported by Media Lab Asia, Mumbai.

[Haworth co-indexing entry note]: "Sanyog: A Speech Enabled Communication System for the Speech Impaired and People with Multiple Disorders." Bhattacharya, Samit, Sudeshna Sarkar, and Anupam Basu. Co-published simultaneously in *Journal of Technology in Human Services* (The Haworth Press, Inc.) Vol. 25, No. 1/2, 2007, pp. 177-180; and: *HUSITA7–The 7th International Conference of Human Services Information Technology Applications: Digital Inclusion–Building a Digital Inclusive Society* (eds: C. K. Law, Yu Cheung Wong, and John Yat Chu Fung) The Haworth Press, Inc., 2007, pp. 177-180. Single or multiple copies of this article are available for a fee from The Haworth Document Delivery Service [1-800-HAWORTH, 9:00 a.m. - 5:00 p.m. (EST). E-mail address: docdelivery@haworthpress.com].

SUMMARY. The paper presents a multilingual communication tool that has been designed for helping in the communication needs of people with severe speech and multiple disorders. The system accepts icons, selected through special access switches, as input and can form natural language sentences, which can be spoken out using in-built text-to-speech synthesizer. The system has been deployed and is being field tested at the schools for the children with cerebral palsy in India. doi:10.1300/J017v25n01_12 *[Article copies available for a fee from The Haworth Document Delivery Service: 1-800-HAWORTH. E-mail address: <docdelivery@haworthpress.com> Website: <http://www.HaworthPress.com> © 2007 by The Haworth Press, Inc. All rights reserved.]*

KEYWORDS. Augmentative communication, iconic communication, natural language generation, Indian languages, text-to-speech

A significant segment of the Indian population is affected with severe speech and motor impairments. Only a very small percent of them have access to assistive devices, which are imported and often very costly to afford. Moreover, these devices are mostly tuned to the western users. For example, for iconic devices–the icons are socially alien to the children in the east. As regards language of communication–these are mostly English. From another perspective, communication systems, such as MinSpeak™, call for special cognitive ability on the part of the users since the composition of icons in MinSpeak™ is complex. Given this perspective, the present paper describes "Sanyog"–a communication tool that can be used by children with cerebral palsy and also by people who are speech impaired due to causes like cancer, stroke or accidents. The salient features of the system are enumerated below.

The system can accept icons as input through an iconic interface. It is possible for an icon to represent a word or a phrase. For the neuro-motor disordered, special access switches are provided for selection of icons. The iconic interface, shown in Figure 1, operates based on a query-response-based interaction mechanism to make the selection of icons easy and intuitive. In this mechanism, the user first selects a verb icon from the interface to initiate communication. For each verb, the system internally stores a set of possible questions that can be asked with that verb. The system poses these questions to the user in a sequential way. With each question, a set of possible answers is then shown to the user. The user can select one/more from this answer set or can ignore and proceed

FIGURE 1. The Iconic Interface

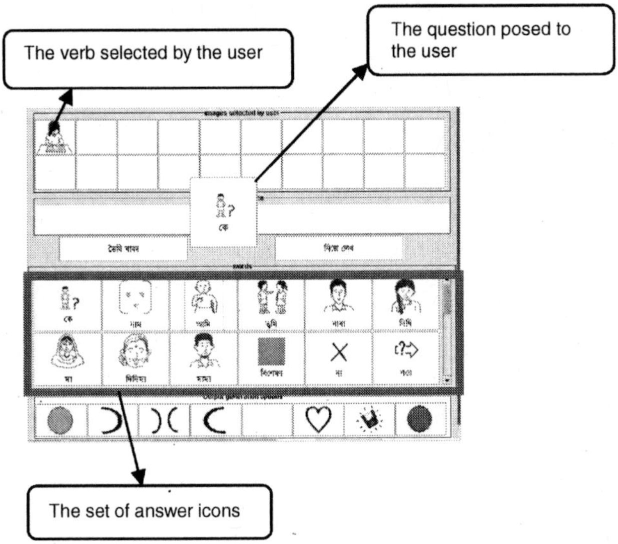

to the next question. The questions and answers are represented in the iconic form. On accepting the icons, the system can automatically form natural language sentences that are syntactically and semantically correct, as shown in Figure 2. Sanyog allows the user to inflect the sentences with respect to tense and mood. The generated sentence can be spoken out using text-to-speech systems that are incorporated with Sanyog.

For those having a better syntactic grasp over communicative language, an on-screen keyboard is available which can also be operated with the special access switches. With this keyboard, the user can compose any text/message. To reduce message composition time, the keyboard is equipped with a word prediction mechanism. Moreover, the composed message can be spoken out using the inbuilt text-to-speech systems.

Apart from the above two methods of communication, the user of Sanyog can also communicate using prestored messages. One very important feature of Sanyog is that the system content can be customized. This implies that the icons or the prestored messages can be changed according to the preferences and needs of the user.

FIGURE 2. The Iconic Interface with Output

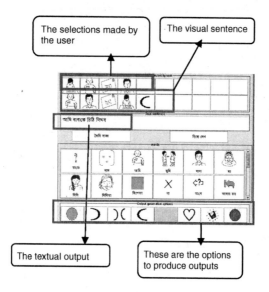

The underlying technology behind the system includes (a) natural language processing such as morphology synthesis, grapheme to phoneme mapping and sentence generation using semantic frames; (b) speech synthesis; (c) human computer interaction principles.

At present, the system works in three languages–Bengali, English and Hindi. The system is currently deployed in a number of institutions around India having students with speech and motor impairments that include IICP, Kolkata, AADI, New Delhi, Monovikash Kendra, Kolkata, and NIMH, Hyderabad.

doi:10.1300/J017v25n01_12

KNOWLEDGE MANAGEMENT IN HUMAN SERVICES

Knowledge Management in Social Work– Towards a Conceptual Framework

Zeno C. S. Leung

SUMMARY. Knowledge management (KM) is receiving increasing attention in the human services such as social work. Social service organizations have started to use information and communication technology for knowledge management purposes with the aim of improving service efficiency and effectiveness. Existing KM studies, particularly in the commercial or industrial sectors, mainly focus on the reductionistic "knowledge-as-object" view, while other perspectives such as "knowl-

Zeno C. S. Leung, BSW, MPhil, is Lecturer, Department of Applied Social Sciences, Hong Kong Polytechnic University, Hung Hom, Kowloon, Hong Kong, China (E-mail: zeno.leung@polyu.edu.hk). He is pursuing his doctoral study on knowledge management in social work at the University of Southampton, UK.

[Haworth co-indexing entry note]: "Knowledge Management in Social Work–Towards a Conceptual Framework." Leung, Zeno C. S. Co-published simultaneously in *Journal of Technology in Human Services* (The Haworth Press, Inc.) Vol. 25, No. 1/2, 2007, pp. 181-198; and: *HUSITA7–The 7th International Conference of Human Services Information Technology Applications: Digital Inclusion–Building a Digital Inclusive Society* (eds: C. K. Law, Yu Cheung Wong, and John Yat Chu Fung) The Haworth Press, Inc., 2007, pp. 181-198. Single or multiple copies of this article are available for a fee from The Haworth Document Delivery Service [1-800-HAWORTH, 9:00 a.m. - 5:00 p.m. (EST). E-mail address: docdelivery@haworthpress.com].

edge-as-process" are less discussed. This paper argues that these mainstream conceptions of knowledge in KM do not fully fit with that of social work knowledge, and that a spectrum view may be more useful for future practice and inquiry in the area. doi:10.1300/J017v25n01_13 *[Article copies available for a fee from The Haworth Document Delivery Service: 1-800-HAWORTH. E-mail address: <docdelivery@haworthpress.com> Website: <http://www.HaworthPress.com> © 2007 by The Haworth Press, Inc. All rights reserved.]*

KEYWORDS. Knowledge management, social work knowledge

When Drucker (1968) proposed, more than 40 years ago, that we were transforming from a post-industrial to a knowledge society, and that knowledge is the critical, if not the only factor that differentiates an organization in terms of success or failure, the "prophecy" may not have been understood by most of us until the explosive development in information and communication technologies (ICT) in the '70s. ICT has changed the world by the computer's capabilities in possessing and transmitting data and information in digitized formats within itself and all over the world, in extremely fast and somehow more accurate ways. Organizations begin to recognize that technologies may help us in better processing, storing, retrieving and disseminating what we know, as well as exploring what we don't know. Knowledge management (KM) has come to our attention, and practices and researches have begun flourishing in the last decade or two.

Although the first discussions on ICT applications in social work and human services can be dated back to the '60s (Hoffer, 1965), more vigorous discussion has not begun until the '80s, mainly around MIS development (Bellerby & Goslin, 1982; Benbenishty & Oyserman, 1995; Caputo, 1988; Hanbery, Sorensen, & Kucic, 1982) and ICT application in social work education (Knowles, 2000; Lynett, 1985; Resnick, 1994). It seems that knowledge management has not come to the attention of social workers until relatively recently (Patterson, 1996; Pawson, Boaz, Grayson, Long, & Barnes, 2003; Rubenstein-Montano, Buchwalter, & Liebowitz, 2001; Schoech, Fitch, MacFadden, & Schkade, 2001). In the new millennium, it has come to be seen as important by many social work organizations in Hong Kong, just like their counterparts in other regions of the world.

However, while KM is undergoing active experimentation in the social work field, respective discussion on what and how social work knowledge can be managed is not yet well-articulated. It should be remembered that while KM discussions and practices are widely studied, mainly in the industrial and business sectors, how or how much of these experiences are transferable to human and social services should be taken into careful consideration.

The following discussion is mainly a review on how the concept "knowledge" has been formulated in the mainstream KM literature. Upon comparison, it is shown that dominant conceptions of "what knowledge is" in KM may not fit perfectly with what has emerged in the social work literature. An alternative view is needed so that the whole spectrum of social work knowledge can be addressed when KM is discussed within the profession. At the end of the discussion, further KM research and practice foci in social work will be suggested.

KNOWLEDGE IN KNOWLEDGE MANAGEMENT

As the word implies, knowledge management refers to the ability to manage "knowledge." It can be generally defined as the collection of mechanisms and processes that govern the creation, collection, storage, retrieval, dissemination and utilization of organization knowledge that help an organization to compete (Krogh, 1998). Contemporary KM strategies rely heavily on ICT-based systems that combine organization information systems, document and multi-media archives with data-mining techniques, and email and other groupwares for communication purposes. Knowledge portals are the common technical infrastructure.

But what is knowledge? How can it be managed in an organizational context?

For centuries, examining what we know and how we come to know were major efforts in academic disciplines such as philosophy and epistemology. Following ancient Greek traditions, knowledge is believed to be something absolute, which exists externally and prior to human perception. Those ultimate truths exist in the world/universe in a priori, whereas to know is regarded as the process of searching it, probably as a never-ending one.[1] Following the convention, when we say someone has knowledge about something, we mean that the person is aware and believes in a certain idea or statement, while that idea or statement accurately describes the truth as far as it is known at the time being. So "truth," "awareness" and "belief" are the three concepts closely linked to the time term "knowledge" in our daily usage.

In KM, however, what knowledge means is somehow different from our general usage. Awareness is still emphasized. In fact, it is often a fundamental objective to manage knowledge in an organizational context; to make people aware what they already know in order to avoid "reinventing the wheel" and to prevent the loss of expertise when people leave their organization. On the other hand, "truth" and "belief" are taken in a more dynamic and contingent account. In KM, knowledge is adopted as a "dynamic human process of justifying personal beliefs as part of an aspiration for the 'truth'" (Nonaka, 1994). For example, when a manager says "I know that when I pay people more, they will work harder for me," we will say the manager has some knowledge in management, though we know there are situations in which his/her claim will fail. Although the "truthfulness" of this claim is also significant (as we will not say s/he has the respective knowledge if s/he claims, "pay less to get people to work harder"), it is not taken in an absolute account. Rather than an existence external and a priori to human perception, knowledge here is viewed as something people choose to believe in, consisting of some explanative/predictive statements about certain phenomena/events and in some context. In an organization these beliefs are usually chosen for the sake of guiding some decisions for actions. In KM, knowledge is generally referred to as "justified belief for action."

It can therefore be said that, under this conception, knowledge, and organizational knowledge in particular, is mainly intersubjectively consented belief chosen by organization members. This organizational knowledge, existing in various formats, tacit or explicit, in organizational artifacts or in people's minds, can somehow be managed as "objects." In fact, this "knowledge-as-object" view is dominant in the mainstream KM discussion. The following illustration on conceptions of the term is a brief account on how this view is reflected in various KM perspectives and conceptions. Examples in social work organizations are also suggested to show their relevance for KM discussion in the profession, though the inadequacy will be elaborated in the next section.

Perspectives in Knowledge Management

KM is now an inter-disciplinary endeavour in the academic world. Despite different categorizations on KM approaches suggested by different theorists and disciplines (Kakabadse, Kakabadse, & Kouzmin, 2003; Shelton, 2002), two tracks together with an "in-between" one can be identified (Maier & Remus, 2003; Sveiby, 1997). The first one is the "management of information" track or technical-oriented perspective, which is concerned mostly about development and construction of intelligent systems so that organization knowledge can be better represented and manipulated. The second track, "management of people" or human-oriented perspective, on the other hand, is concerned more about people-related factors affecting the effectiveness of KM initiatives in organizations.

The technical-oriented perspective is dominant in mainstream KM researches and in practices. The primary aim of KM, following this perspective, is to develop strategies and computer systems that capture, manipulate and disseminate organization information and knowledge in more effective ways (Holtshouse, 1998; Teece, 1998). Externalizing and codification of tacit knowledge are the common strategies adopted, and ICT is often placed at a critical position that leverages the objectives. This perspective, is the main concern of researchers and practitioners in computing sciences, information systems, artificial intelligence, cognitive psychologists, etc.

On the other hand, human-oriented KM such as the community of practice model, is more discussed by management theorists, organization psychologists, etc. They would regard knowledge as something that resides within people's brains and the primary goal of KM is to promote and improve sharing of this knowledge and to develop networks and a community of practice. Sociocultural factors within organizations such as senior management support, commitment and trust, power and group dynamics, etc., are the factors affecting KM success and failure (Krogh, 1998; Yang, 2004), while ICT is usually regarded as complementary mechanisms.

The third approach is suggested as attempts to "bridge the gap" KM (Maier & Remus, 2003). This approach has not ignored the tacit nature of most kinds of knowledge, yet it suggests that the primary goal of KM is to improve knowledge visibility or improve access to knowledge by both codifying tacit knowledge and promoting cultural change, building knowledge portals as well as identifying subject matter specialists (Gaines, 1989; Southon, Todd, & Seneque, 2002). It takes a discursive socio-technical path in KM. Furthermore, this "bridge the gap" approach also emphasizes boundary spanning and puts external knowledge, such as those of business partners and customers, at significant positions.

On the technical-oriented side, knowledge is regarded as some entity that already exists somewhere in the organization. It can be a document, a data set, design blueprints, product prototypes, or any other artifacts that physically exist. It can also be something already existing in people's minds that needed (and was ready) to be externalized and codified. On the human-oriented side, organizational knowledge is largely viewed as tacit and residing in people's brains. Successful KM cannot be achieved solely with technology and without taking human factors into careful consideration. However, as shown below, this tacit view may mean similar or different conceptions of the term when compared to the technical perspective.

Knowledge Vis-à-Vis Data and Information

In this view, knowledge is a continuation of data and information. While data is "streams of raw fact representing events occur(red)," and information is "data shaped into a form that is meaningful and useful to human beings" (Laudon & Laudon, 2002), knowledge is the "authenticated personalized information possessed in the mind of individuals" (Alavi & Leidner, 2001). There exists a hierarchical relationship among the three concepts. Data, usually collected in bulk, is at the lowest part of the hierarchy. Processed data is presented as information of lesser volume, and is located in the middle part, while knowledge is in the uppermost portion, as shown in Figure 1 below.

This data-information-knowledge view is common across different sectors and organizations, usually in discussion areas like management information system design. In social work organizations, discussions take place on clientele information systems, service statistic reporting

FIGURE 1. Hierarchical Relationship Among Data Information and Knowledge

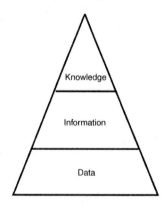

systems and data-mining of these systems, etc. Schoech, Quinn, and Rycraft (2000), in fact, carry this conception about social work knowledge.

Knowledge as a Progression of States

Similar to the above view, knowledge here describes a hierarchical relationship among various states from data to knowledge leading to decision, as shown in Figure 2 below, but its emphasis is on the progression from one state to another within the processor. Advancement of this kind leads to better knowledge quality and thus higher usability. In conventional organizational knowledge archives, this may also refer to expertise stored in experienced practitioners' minds, while retrieval and transfer of it usually take the forms of socialization. In social work organizations, case conferences are often the channels in which these transfers take place. In the author's experience, there are organizations which arrange certain apprenticeship schemes in which novice social workers could be helped to progress by experienced practitioners. In a technology-based system, this view is mainly considered and manifested in the design of decision-support systems.

The above two conceptions on knowledge are in line with the technical-oriented side of KM.

Knowledge as Stock and Flows

This production perspective views knowledge as something similar to other organizational inventories that can be stored and managed in the processors. Industries like automobile engineering in which organization knowledge is extensively stored in knowledge artifacts such as design blueprints and prototypes may probably take this view. In social work organizations, these may correspond to consolidation of practice experience through publication of procedural manuals, case books, or other standard operating procedures (SOPs).

FIGURE 2

Data ⇒ Information ⇒ Structured Information ⇒ Insight ⇒ Judgment ⇒ Decision

gathering   selecting   analyzing   synthesizing   weighing   evaluating

Figure adapted from Holsapple, 2003

Knowledge production and transferral, together with issues like re-plenishment, perishability, tracking, quality assurance, etc., are the ma-jor concerns of this perspective. This knowledge view is also more on the technical side of KM.

Knowledge as Usable Representation

The keywords "usability" and "representation" have highlighted concerns with regard to this view. Representation refers to the cognitive symbols (text, formula, images, mental models, etc.) carried through certain media and through which knowledge is presented. Usability, on the other hand, refers to the extent that a particular piece of knowledge can be used by the people concerned. Whether or not some knowledge is useful will depend a great deal on the match vs. misfit among proces-sors (human users or computer systems) and the representation itself.

In social work organizations, these representations can be therapeutic models adopted by the practicing community, or schemas and jargons used by staff members, etc. Some of these representations are univer-sally held by members of the profession, but there are also many which are of unique use in the individual organizations concerned.

Comprehensibility of the representations (and thus their usability) by processors (people or machine), hence becomes a major concern in KM when this conception is emphasized. On the technical side, it refers to compatibility among component sub-systems so that an integrated sys-tem can be ensured. On the human side, this may refer to human re-source management concerns such as the induction of new recruits, job rotation and cultivating a sharing culture, etc.

Knowledge as Process

Another conception comes from Nonaka's significant knowledge creation theory (Nonaka, 1994). Organizational knowledge is created through four conversion modes according to the theory. The first one is conversion of tacit knowledge among individuals (staff) through "so-cialization," such as mentorship/apprenticeship or informal chats. The second mode is "internalization," in which individuals convert external knowledge (artifacts such as manuals, policies, etc.) into internal tacit knowledge in oneself. Nonaka regards this mode as resembling most our traditional notion of "learning." "Externalization," on the other hand, corresponds to the codification of internal tacit knowledge into organizational artifacts. Finally, the fourth mode, "combination" corresponds to the gaining of new knowledge by combining different pieces of existing explicit knowledge through processes like sorting, adding and reorganizing, etc. The four modes of knowledge creation are summarized in Figure 3.

It should be noted that although Nonaka (1994) uses the term "process," he refers more to moments when knowledge meets, exchanges and combines, i.e., the courses of managing knowledge. For example, when an experienced colleague tells a novice how a difficult customer may be handled, the former is socializing the latter by sharing the tacit knowledge already existing in his/her mind. Knowledge, more or less, is still regarded as something which already exists per se.

When the authors (Nonaka & Konno, 1998; Nonaka & Toyama, 2003) revisited their theory, however , they emphasized the dynamic nature of the process. Knowledge creation is then described as synthesizing and self-transcending processes. Organization actors do not merely receive the knowledge. Rather they compare and contrast the different kinds of knowledge they are exposed to, linking them to other beliefs they may hold, and putting them into the whole context they or the events are in, until some solution or conclusion is reached and some new knowledge is formulated and adopted. The authors suggest that these are the dynamic interactive dialectical processes of knowledge creation. These processes may be in the form of internal dialogues within the individuals' minds or explicit conversations among groups

FIGURE 3

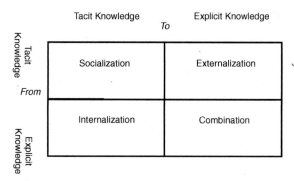

Figure adapted from Nonaka, 1994

of individuals, face-to-face, through paper documents or through digital channels. Nonaka's revised knowledge creation theory is illustrated in Figure 4.

Nonaka's revised view of "knowledge as process" is regarded as significant in the human-oriented KM approach, as it shows not only managing knowledge being a process, but "knowing" being a dialectical process in itself. This view appears to have much relevance in social work knowledge management, in particular when "process knowledge" is concerned, as is discussed in the following section.

SOCIAL WORK KNOWLEDGE

Early discussions of social work practice knowledge[2] usually followed the path and logic of intervention processes and were conceptualized with respect to intervention stages, problem natures, targets and methods of intervention (Gordon, 1981; Pincus & Minahan, 1973; Reid, 1981; Reid & Epstein, 1972). Reid (2002) describes this as the scientific model in social work knowledge development. Together with

FIGURE 4

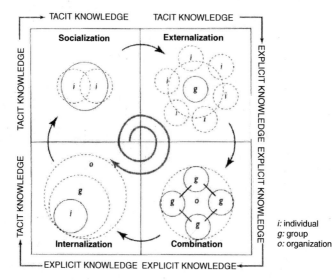

i: individual
g: group
o: organization

Figure adapted from Nonaka & Konno, 1998

other theoretical knowledge borrowed from other social science disciplines, they form the substantive knowledge base for anyone who wants to practice social work nowadays. Discussions along these lines can best be described as the evidence-based school of thought which has emerged in recent decades. Advocating on informed practice supported by knowledge gained through scientific research, it is believed that social work commitment towards the clients' best interest and well-being can be reaffirmed and better actualized (Rosen, 2003).

Another line of discussion focuses on the practitioners' ability to use the know-how of knowledge application, instead of merely the know-what. Gibson and Nurius (1992) use the term "procedural knowledge" to represent the practitioners' know-how of when to apply the substantive knowledge effectively. Sheppard et al. use the term "process knowledge" in contrast to what they call "product knowledge" as discussed above (Sheppard, Newstead, DiCaccavo, & Ryan, 2000; Sheppard & Ryan, 2003). Practitioners' abilities in making sound inferences, reasoning and making judgments during intervention processes are emphasized. Klein and Bloom call this "practice wisdom" and define it as ". . . a personal and value-driven system of knowledge that emerges out of the transaction between the phenomenological experience of the client situation and the use of scientific information" (Klein & Bloom, 1995).

Schon (1991) argues that social work practice, instead of being a process in which practitioners hold a whole set of information and formal knowledge and who offer solutions to the problem situation, is more ". . . a process of reframing through which the practitioner creates meaning (to interpret) and 'meaning for action.' " With exemplary themes developed through his/her past experiences, the practitioner is involved every time in a new "experiment" in which s/he will actively hypothesize by assigning meaning to the situation s/he comes across, and seeks confirmatory evidence to confirm the hypothesis. It is further suggested that such an experiment is, in fact, a dialectical process occurring between the practitioner and the client. That is to say, both parties jointly create the meaning of the client's situation as well as a meaning for what action is to be taken (Cooper, 2001).

The discussions have reflected different epistemological views on social work knowledge. On the one hand lies the positivistic perspective by which knowledge is defined as that gained from logical, scientific, reductionistic researches. Knowledge, under this perspective, once created, exists per se and is independent of the carrier. On the other hand, social constructionists view knowledge as a collection of subjective experiences, a creation of language used to endorse a shared decision made by a certain community to see things in a certain way, in particular time and space (Gergen, 1985). Social workers are also reminded to look into this socially constructed nature of human related knowledge (Imre, 1984). For postmodernists, what is further emphasized is that these discourses of creation and use of language, so-called knowledge, are always power struggle processes instead of some mere "neutral" inter-subjective agreements on the players' common experiences. Minorities and their words are subjugated while majorities and experts will create and own the knowledge in their regime.

As a value-laden profession committed to both care and social justice, Hartman (1992) describes, in particular, the postmodernists' comments as a paradox for social workers. Facing their day-to-day practice, social workers, on the one hand have, to "believe" in their expert position in terms of understanding and analyzing their clients' situations, or knowing of community resource availability and limitations, etc. On the other hand, they are committed to core values of care and social justice and the belief that they should not participate in any oppressive practice. Clients should be facilitated to uncover their own meanings for their situations, their words should be heard or even amplified, and their own knowledge should be established. This should involve a co-constructing, meaning-making process between clients and social workers rather than some application of so-called "expert knowledge" by the latter upon the former. Value-related scenarios may further sharpen this paradox. In other words, knowledge in use during practice should not be, at least not only be, the application of the "product knowledge" mentioned before, but rather a meaning-making process in which product knowledge is "blended in" through the practitioner's improvisation of his/her process knowledge.

Now if the above situation is a paradox for social work practitioners, it will be a conceptual challenge for people discussing knowledge management in social work, as there are different, dichotomized views on what social work knowledge is. To link the discrepancy, Caspi (1992) suggests a continuum approach between the extremities. The continuum approach, according to the author, is a pragmatic perspective that allows no room for the debate between objectivism and relativism. It regards research or scientific inquiry (of human related phenomena) as pragmatic problem-solving activities in which "satisfying heuristics" are used. "(T)hey are aids for learning, discovery or problem solving which generate knowledge without (100%) claims for its (absolute) validity" (p.116). Scientific theories and concepts "relate to some objective reality by responding to a need to solve a problem by their ability to offer some solution, to create some change. They are relative because they can only be proven able to relate to a specific problem in a specific context." Payne (2001: 117) also reminds us to hold a complex and fluid understanding of the structure of social work knowledge. Interpretation and reinterpretation, using and reconstitution are, in fact, a must, and a continuing interacting (and political) process when social work knowledge is learnt and transferred.

This reconstituting and co-constructing of views during the knowledge creation and application process is not unique to social work. In fact, there has been criticism of mainstream KM discussion for its predominant reductionistic perspective and ignorance of the complex nature of human knowing. Styhre (2003) uses the term "logocentric" to describe the situation and comments that such a trend has closely followed the resource- or asset-based view in management theories: that knowledge can be managed more or less the same way as its tangible counterparts within organizations such as financial resources and human capital. We should be reminded that such criticism is not just limited to the technical side of KM. The human-oriented approach has, in fact, often posed a "static" or "per se" view of organization tacit knowledge. This can be shown by some of the conceptions of knowledge discussed above.

So different theorists argue for an alternative way of perceiving knowledge and thus knowledge management, regarding knowledge as an ongoing "social accomplishment," fluid, moving and embedded in social relationships (Orlikowski, 2002; Styhre, 2003), a "residue of thinking" that is always re-created in the present moment (McDermott, 1999). The difference between human knowledge and a piece of data/information/knowledge stored in a computer or an artifact stored in an organization filing system is that, for the latter, knowledge is retrieved by searching, while for the human brain, we engage in an "act of knowing" (McDermott, 1999). The author suggests that most of us, professionals in particular, do not articulate what we know until we come to the moment to answer a question or solve a problem. In this act of knowing, we have to make sense of the present situation and interpret it with related insights acquired from our past experiences, so that some new sensible judgment can be arrived at and action can be taken.

This discussed alternative perspective does not aim at refuting the contribution of the mainstream reductionistic perspective. In fact, it can not. However, it is certainly worth further discussion as it brings the complexity of human knowing processes back to our attention when practicing KM, especially in social work.

TOWARDS A CONCEPTUAL FRAMEWORK

Summing up the discussion, a continuous spectrum in viewing social work knowledge is suggested. At the one end, "knowledge-as-object," is the view that substantive knowledge exists per se. These types of knowledge are clearly articulated and codified, provide descriptive (or prescriptive) and procedural understandings in specific domains in social work practice. These kinds of knowledge are often created through conventional research processes, or as some systematic consolidation of practice experiences. They are explicit and, though originally tacit in nature, are readily being externalized. Application of the knowledge usually involves a recapping process and there is often a time gap between knowledge creation and utilization.

At the other end of the continuum lies "knowledge-as-process," denoting knowledge socially constructed among people involved in social work intervention. As relational knowledge or the worker's self-knowledge, they are tacit in nature and rest within the service users, practitioners and other people as community in organizations. They are processes instead of entities and come to realization when situations arise, instead of having preexistence in people's minds. They are re-created or co-constructed simultaneously when they are applied.

For knowledge in the middle of the spectrum, there are often blended conceptual representations of substantive knowledge and subjective experiences of the practitioners. They may be in explicit forms such as programme manuals and case books, or tacit in the form of mental models or "rules" (Sheppard & Ryan, 2003). However, these conceptual representations, when formulated, have very often trimmed out the contextual details of those previous experiences. Practitioners facing different clients with different situations have to reconstitute their understandings in the here-and-now context.

Concepts and related characteristics of the above continuum with regard to the understanding of social work knowledge can be illustrated as shown in Figure 5.

For a comprehensive understanding of how knowledge management can be applied in the profession, the above different characteristics of social work knowledge along the continuum must be addressed. It can

FIGURE 5

	Knowledge-as-object		Knowledge-as-process
Examples	• guidelines for service eligibility or referral procedures • policy papers guiding service direction • theoretical knowledge internalized to practitioners	• programme kits and manuals • rules of practice	• dialectical intervention processes between practitioner and service user • supervision processes between practitioner and supervisor
Source	Mainly organization, policy and research knowledge	organization and practitioners	practitioners and service users, organization as community
Mode	Explicit	Explicit or tacit	Tacit
When applying	recapping	reconstituting	co-constructing

easily be imagined that if a social work organization focuses only on data-mining or stocks and flows of organizational artifacts in its KM initiatives, then no matter how sophisticated the technology-assisted knowledge systems are and how comprehensive knowledge capturing mechanisms are built in, the complex, emerging, here-and-now re-created process knowledge and act-of-knowing in the practice processes will be missed. A comprehensive framework in KM for social work is needed, whether for research or for practical purposes. At the "knowledge-as-object" end of the spectrum, KM practice and research concerns may have been well-informed by the mainstream perspective, though it is believed that specific understanding on what it can be like in a social work organization is still worth further discussion. The "knowledge-as-process" side, on the other hand, may involve studying discourses on how the process knowledge is being reconstituted and co-constructed. Questions like: how some meanings are constructed to become legitimized organization knowledge (probably the practitioners'), how other uses of language and knowledge (such as the service users') are recognized or marginalized, how may every unique reconstituting or co-constructing process inform organization practice in general, and how much of this process knowledge is transferable, etc., do need further discussion.

CONCLUSION

In this paper, the dominant perspective in knowledge management and its underlying conceptions about the nature of knowledge have been reviewed. These conceptions are compared to those that have been articulated in the social work literature. It is suggested that, when knowledge is dominantly perceived as some objects or assets in the mainstream KM discussion, it may not be fully compatible with how social work knowledge has been discussed. Viewing the latter as a continuum from "knowledge-as-object" to "knowledge-as-process," it is suggested that an alternative non-reductionistic approach is also needed. It is believed that such an understanding is beneficial to the development of both practice and research on knowledge management in social work, as it helps to bring the complex nature of social work knowledge back to our attention.

NOTES

1. Definitely there are still vigorous debates on whether such ultimate truth exists at all, or if human beings really know it. Some philosophers argue that we can only believe in what we perceive to be the truth, rather than prove it so.

2. Practice knowledge is chosen as the scope of discussion here, as it is assumed that all KM initiatives should aim primarily at enhancing the operation of the core processes in the respective businesses and, in this case, social work practice.

REFERENCES

Alavi, M., & Leidner, D. E. (2001). Knowledge management and knowledge management systems: Conceptual foundations and research issues. *MIS Quarterly, 25*(1), 107-136.

Bellerby, L., & Goslin, L. N. (1982). Managing for success: Assessing the balanced MIS environment. *Administration in Social Work, 5*(3/4), 69-82.

Benbenishty, R., & Oyserman, D. (1995). Integrated information systems for human services: A conceptual framework, methodology and technology. *Computers in Human Services, 12*(3/4), 311-325.

Caputo, R. K. (1988). *Management and information systems in human services: Implications for the distribution of authority and decision making.* The Haworth Press, Inc.

Caspi, Y. (1992). A continuum theory for social work knowledge. *Journal of Sociology and Social Welfare, 19*(3), 105-120.

Cooper, B. (2001). Constructivism in social work: Towards a participative practice viability. *British Journal of Social Work, 31*, 721-738.

Drucker, P. F. (1968). *The age of discontinuity: Guidelines to our changing society.* New York: Harper & Row.

Gaines, B. R. (1989). Social and cognitive processes in knowledge acquisition. *Knowledge Acquisition, 1*, 39-58.

Gergen, K. J. (1985). The social constructionist movement in modern psychology. *American Psychologist, 40*, 266-275.

Gibson, J. W., & Nurius, P. S. (1992). Procedural knowledge in education for direct practice: Definitions, baselines, and recommendations. *Journal of Teaching in Social Work, 6*(1), 21-40.

Gordon, W. E. (1981). A natural classification system for social work literature and knowledge. *Social Work, 26*(2), 134-138.

Hanbery, G. W., Sorensen, J. E., & Kucic, A. R. (1982). Management information systems and human service resource management. *Administration in Social Work, 5*(3/4), 27-42.

Hartman, A. (1992). In search of subjugated knowledge. *Social Work, 37*(6), 483-484.

Hoffer, J. R. (1965). *Toward an international social welfare information and document retrieval system.* Paper presented at the National Conference on Social Welfare, Ohio.

Holsapple, C. W. (2003). Knowledge and its attributes. In C. W. Holsapple (Ed.), *Handbook on knowledge management: Knowledge matters* (Vol. 1, pp. 165-188). Berlin: Springer.

Holtshouse, D. (1998). Knowledge research issues. *California Management Review, 40*(3), 277-280.

Imre, R. W. (1984). The nature of knowledge in social work. *Social Work, 29*(1), 41-45.

Kakabadse, N. K., Kakabadse, A., & Kouzmin, A. (2003). Reviewing the knowledge management literature: Towards a taxonomy. *Journal of Knowledge Management, 7*(4), 75-91.

Klein, W. C., & Bloom, M. (1995). Practice wisdom. *Social Work, 40*(6), 799-807.

Knowles, A. (2000). *Implementing web-based learning: Evaluation results from a mental health course.* Paper presented at the 4th Annual Technology Conference Social Work Education & Practice, Charleston, SC.

Krogh, G. V. (1998). Care in knowledge creation. *California Management Review, 40*(3), 133-153.

Laudon, K. C., & Laudon, J. P. (2002). *Management information systems: Managing the digital firm.* Upper Saddle River: Prentice-Hall, Inc.

Lynett, P. (1985). The current and potential uses of Computer Assisted Interactive Videodisc in the education of social workers. *Computers in Human Services, 1*(4), 75-85.

Maier, R., & Remus, U. (2003). Implementing process-oriented knowledge management strategies. *Journal of Knowledge Management, 7*(4), 62-74.

McDermott, R. (1999). Why information technology inspired but cannot deliver knowledge management. *California Management Review, 41*(4), 103-117.

Nonaka, I. (1994). A dynamic theory of organizational knowledge creation. *Organization Science, 5*(1), 14-37.

Nonaka, I., & Konno, N. (1998). The concept of "Ba": Building a foundation for knowledge creation. *California Management Review, 40*(3), 40-54.

Nonaka, I., & Toyama, R. (2003). The knowledge-creating theory revisited: Knowledge creation as a synthesizing process. *Knowledge Management Research & Practice, 1*, 2-10.

Orlikowski, W. J. (2002). Knowing in practice. Enacting a collective capability in distributed organizing. *Organization Science, 13*(2), 249-273.

Patterson, D. A. (1996). An electronic social work knowledge base: A strategy for global information sharing. *International Social Work, 39*(2), 149-161.

Pawson, R., Boaz, A., Grayson, L., Long, A., & Barnes, B. (2003). *Knowledge review 3: Types and quality of knowledge in social care.* Retrieved July 24, 2004, from http://www.scie.org.uk/publications/knowledgereviews/kr03.pdf

Payne, M. (2001). Knowledge bases and knowledge biases in social work. *Journal of Social Work, 1*(2), 133-146.

Pincus, A., & Minahan, A. (1973). *Social work practice: Model and method*. Itasca: F. E. Peacock.

Reid, W. J. (1981). Mapping the knowledge base of social work. *Social Work, 26*(2), 124-132.

Reid, W. J. (2002). Knowledge for direct social work practice: An analysis of trends. *Social Service Review, 76*(1), 6-33.

Reid, W. J., & Epstein, L. (1972). *Task-centred casework*. New York: Columbia University Press.

Resnick, H. (Ed.) (1994). *Electronic tools for social work practice and education*. New York: The Haworth Press, Inc.

Rosen, A. (2003). Evidence-based social work practice: Challenges and promise. *Social Work Research, 27*(4), 197-208.

Rubenstein-Montano, B., Buchwalter, J., & Liebowitz, J. (2001). Knowledge management: A U.S. Social Security Administration case study. *Government Information Quarterly, 18*, 223-253.

Schoech, D., Fitch, D., MacFadden, R., & Schkade, L. L. (2001). From data to intelligence: Introducing the intelligent organization. *Administration in Social Work, 26*(1), 1-21.

Schoech, D., Quinn, A., & Rycraft, J. R. (2000). Data mining in child welfare. *Child Welfare, 79*(5), 633-650.

Schon, D. (1991). *The reflective practitioner* (2nd ed.). Aldershot: Arena.

Shelton, R. E. (2002). *The development of knowledge management in SMEs: A discourse analysis of facilitation*. Unpublished PhD, University of Central England in Birmingham.

Sheppard, M., Newstead, S., DiCaccavo, A., & Ryan, K. (2000). Reflexivity and the development of process knowledge in social work: A classification and empirical study. *British Journal of Social Work, 30*, 465-488.

Sheppard, M., & Ryan, K. (2003). Practitioners as rule using analysts: A further development of process knowledge in social work. *British Journal of Social Work, 33*, 157-176.

Southon, F. C. G., Todd, R. J., & Seneque, M. (2002). Knowledge management in three organizations: An exploratory study. *Journal of the American Society for Information Science and Technology, 53*(12), 1047-1059.

Styhre, A. (2003). Knowledge management beyond codifcation: Knowing as practice / concept. *Journal of Knowledge Management, 7*(5), 32-40.

Sveiby, K. E. (1997). *The new organizational wealth: Managing and measuring knowledge-based assets*. San Francisco: Berrett-Koehler Publishers.

Teece, D. J. (1998). Research directions for knowledge management. *California Management Review, 40*(3), 289-293.

Yang, J. (2004). Job-related knowledge sharing: Comparative case studies. *Journal of Knowledge Management, 8*(3), 118-126.

doi:10.1300/J017v25n01_13

KNOWLEDGE MANAGEMENT IN HUMAN SERVICES APPLICATIONS

Web-Based Disability Information Resource in Japan

Iwao Kobayashi

SUMMARY. In this paper, the author reports information regarding a Japanese website which was named "SenSui." It was established in 1995 and has been managed since then to provide Japanese disability information to Japanese and other global citizens in a bilingual form. Results of the access to the site, e-mail consultation, and collaboration with other web-masters and researchers for about 10 years showed the effectiveness of the site, especially the importance of interactive and worldwide exchange of disability-related information. doi:10.1300/J017v25n01_14 *[Article copies available for a fee from The Haworth Document Delivery Service:*

Iwao Kobayashi, PhD, is Associate Professor, Center for the Research and Support of Educational Practice (CRSEP), Tokyo Gakugei University, 4-1-1 Nukui-Kitamachi, Koganei, Tokyo 184-8501, Japan (E-mail: iwan@u-gakugei.ac.jp).

[Haworth co-indexing entry note]: "Web-Based Disability Information Resource in Japan." Kobayashi, Iwao. Co-published simultaneously in *Journal of Technology in Human Services* (The Haworth Press, Inc.) Vol. 25, No. 1/2, 2007, pp. 199-200; and: *HUSITA7–The 7th International Conference of Human Services Information Technology Applications: Digital Inclusion–Building a Digital Inclusive Society* (eds: C. K. Law, Yu Cheung Wong, and John Yat Chu Fung) The Haworth Press, Inc., 2007, pp. 199-200. Single or multiple copies of this article are available for a fee from The Haworth Document Delivery Service [1-800-HAWORTH, 9:00 a.m. - 5:00 p.m. (EST). E-mail address: docdelivery@haworthpress.com].

KEYWORDS. WWW, Internet, disability

In 1995, the author established and began managing a website dealing with disability information in Japan (http://www.sd.soft.iwate-pu.ac.jp/sensui/). The site was named "SenSui" and was one of the earliest web-based disability resources in Japan. It was constructed in a bilingual form, providing English-language explanations. Thereby, it provided disability information to people throughout the world. People of numerous nationalities have accessed it for about 10 years.

The site's access-log and e-mail requests from users to the manager were analyzed. Results revealed the following four salient points.

1. The number of accesses by month increased through the first 18 months. After that, there were about 10,000 requests per month.
2. Users from 128 countries' domains accessed the site. In the first six months, access instances from foreign countries outnumbered those from Japan. Subsequently, accesses from Japanese domains became about 60%, followed by the US domain.
3. The number of e-mail requests from Japan and foreign countries were almost equal during the first three years. After four years, requests from foreign users exceeded those from Japan. Frequently received requests from foreign countries requested information on travel within Japan by and for people with disabilities, and on books and associations related with disability in Japan.
4. The web-master was able to collaborate with other web-masters and researchers both in Japan and in foreign countries to widely disseminate disability information.

These results demonstrated the site's effectiveness. Notwithstanding, further examination is necessary to advance such services using new technology and to enrich Japanese disability resources written in foreign languages, at least in English, for those who cannot read Japanese.

doi:10.1300/J017v25n01_14

Index